Rising from the Muck

RISING FROM THE MUCK. First published in France as *La nouvelle judeophobie*, copyright © 2002 by Mille et Une Nuits, a division of Librairie Arthème Fayard. English translation and the special contents of this edition copyright © 2004 by Ivan R. Dee, Inc.
For information, address: Ivan R. Dee, Publisher, 1332 North Halsted Street, Chicago 60622. Manufactured in the United States of America and printed on acid-free paper.

The English translation of this book was made possible by a grant from the American Jewish Committee.

Library of Congress Cataloging-in-Publication Data:
Taguieff, Pierre-André.
    [Novelle judéophobie. English]
    Rising from the muck : the new anti-semitism in Europe / Pierre-André Taguieff ; translated from the French by Patrick Camiller ; with an introduction by Radu Ioanid.
        p. cm.
    Includes bibliographical references and index.
    ISBN 1-56663-571-3 (alk. paper)
        1. Antisemitism—France—History—20th century. 2. Antisemitism—Islamic countries—History—20th century. 3. France—Ethnic relations.
    I. Title.

DS146.F8T3413 2004
305.892'404'090511—dc22

                                                            2003067475

RISING
FROM THE MUCK

The New Anti-Semitism in Europe

Pierre-André Taguieff

Translated from the French by Patrick Camiller
With a Foreword by Radu Ioanid

Ivan R. Dee

CHICAGO 2004

To Philippe Gumplowicz,

Alain Seksig,

and Jacques Tarnero,

fraternally

Contents

Foreword by Radu Ioanid   xi

Introduction   3

1   Surveying the Landscape:
Figures of Contemporary Judeophobia   9

2   Israelophobia and Palestinophilia:
The Paths of Hatred   40

3   Construction, Content, Functioning, and
Metamorphoses of the "New Anti-Semitism":
*Toward the Islamization of Absolute
Anti-Zionism*   62

4   Silence in the Face of the New Judeophobia:
Blindness, Complacency, or Design?   88

Notes   122

Index   203

A first version of this text, entitled "Judéophobie post-nazie," formed the basis for a number of lectures I gave in 2001, which were then summarized and published in *Le Figaro*, October 8, 2001, under the title "Les nouvelles vagues de l'antisémitisme."

I wish to express my thanks to Annick Duraffour, Valentine Zuber, Alain Polcar, Philippe Gumplowicz, and Gilles Kepel, who did me the kindness of attentively reading an intermediate version of this book.

Foreword

IN MAY 1968, when students seized the streets of Paris in a massive protest against the French government that ultimately forced the resignation of President Charles de Gaulle, one of their slogans was "*Nous sommes tous des Juifs Allemands*: (We are all German Jews). This rallying cry was in fashion after the French Ministry of the Interior expelled Daniel Cohn-Bendit, a German Jew who was one of the protest leaders. During the spring of 2002, when French youth again took the streets of Paris, they chanted pro-Palestinian slogans and others such as "Death to the Jews" and "Jews to the ovens."

A powerful new strain of anti-Semitism, which combines the old clichés of hatred with new anti-Semitic arguments and anti-Israel feelings, is clearly on the rise in France. But this is not exclusively a French problem. As Ian Buruma has written in the *New York Times Magazine*, "Most mass demonstrations in Europe and elsewhere against the war in Iraq, contained banners in support of the Palestinians, even the religious extremists of *Hamas*, and against global symptoms of capitalism. . . . The Palestinian cause has become the universal litmus of liberal credentials."

On August 4, 2001, Pascal Boniface, director of the Paris-based Institute for International and Strategic Relations, published an article in *Le Monde* under the title *Lettre à un ami israelien.* The letter was indeed open but was not in fact addressed to any Israeli "friend" of Boniface but to the French Jewish community and the French Socialist party. Boniface told the French Jewish community to stop "blindly defending a policy considered by more and more people as not simply unjust, but odious." A direct threat followed the warning: by continuing to defend Israel, the French Jewish community risked isolating itself from the French national community. Boniface, a member of the French Socialist party that was then in power, and an adviser to its leadership, asked his party to abandon its "impartiality" and to side with the Palestinians in the Middle East conflict: "Because they want to maintain an equal balance between the Israeli forces of order and the Palestinian protesters, to compare the attacks authored by desperate people who are ready to commit suicide because they have no other options with the repressive policies put into practice by the Israeli government, the Socialist Party and the [French] government are considered by a more and more important part of the public opinion as 'unjust.'" After emphasizing that "today the main victims are the Palestinians and not the Israelis," Boniface also urged the Socialist party to ally itself with French Muslims, a community eight to ten times larger than that of French Jews.

In some cases Boniface's advice was followed. When François Zimmeray, a Socialist member of the European Parliament, asked for an investigation of European Union funds directed to the Palestinian Authority, which he accused of using the money for anti-Semitic textbooks, the Socialist party organization of Seine-et-Marne talked of officially reprimanding its MP.

On April 22, 2002, an electoral disaster struck France when Jean-Marie Le Pen, a populist, extreme right demagogue, won enough votes to reach the second round of

the presidential elections. Olivier Duhamel, a well-known political scientist and a Socialist member of the European Parliament, declared that France was "joining the degenerate
democracies, such as the U.S., Austria, and Italy." Degenerate
or not, the French democracy had shown that an extreme
right-wing candidate could gain the strong support of a siz-
able portion of the French electorate, including the Communist vote. The 2002 elections also demonstrated what
Jean-François Revel pointed out in his recent book *L'Obsession anti-americaine*—that one-third of the French electorate,
whether extreme left or extreme right, opposes "globalization." It took almost two years, and an interview with Pascal
Boniface published in the Swiss newspaper *Le Temps*, in
which he stated that the United States should have included
Israel in the so-called axis of evil, for the French Socialist
party leadership to disavow Boniface, and for the politicians
of several parties on the board of his institute to resign.

Boniface is only a symptom of a much larger problem. A
Palestinian terrorist who blows himself up in a bus filled with
civilians in Israel is routinely described by the French media
as a "militant" or "activist." When a McDonald's is destroyed in France, the anti-globalist attack is called a "dismantling" by the mainstream media. Anti-Jewish cartoons
are now common in French newspapers. When a French peas-
ant trade-union leader wishes to achieve greater notoriety, he
goes to Ramalah to meet a besieged Yasser Arafat in order to
show where his sympathies lie, and he blames the anti-Semitic
violence in France on Mossad, the Israeli foreign intelligence
service. During the exercise of their official duties, two French
ambassadors were overheard using what one might euphemistically call nondiplomatic language about Israel.

This atmosphere may be found generally throughout
Western Europe. While Eastern Europe still attempts to deal
with a more "classic" or traditional form of anti-Semitism,

xiv   *Foreword*

inherited from the rule of wartime fascism and postwar communism, in Western Europe it has again become fashionable
to express anti-Semitism openly. This new anti-Semitism is no
longer the monopoly of neo-Nazis or extremists from the
fringes of society. It is mainstream. According to the British
press, unreserved anti-Semitism may be found at respectable
London dinner parties while British academics advocate the
boycott of their Israeli counterparts. Alvin Rosenfeld illustrated this trend in his new study *Anti-Americanism and
Anti-Semitism: A New Frontier of Bigotry* by describing the
cover of Britain's *New Statesmen* for January 2002: "a gold
Star of David piercing the British Union Jack over the caption
'A Kosher Conspiracy?'"

In Italy the prime minister declares that Mussolini, whose
regime deported thousands of Jews to the Nazi death camps,
killed no one but only sent people on "vacations." In Italy
and Austria the Green parties oppose circumcision (which
concerns Jews and Muslims equally) on grounds related to
the fight against cruelty. And in Germany it has become fashionable for some prominent intellectuals to talk about the
"arrogance," the "intolerance," and the "maliciousness" of
the Jews.

As the French philosopher Alain Finkielkraut wrote in his
recent book *Au nom de l'autre*, significantly subtitled "Reflections on the Anti-Semitism to Come," "Political, social,
cultural Europe is once more disfigured by this most ancient
and vile prejudice. . . . And the Jews have a heavy heart. For
the first time since the war they are afraid." Indeed, as the
Jewish Telegraphic Agency and the *Wall Street Journal* have
recently reported, "More than 25 percent of France's Jews
have considered leaving." In February 2002, Roger Cukierman, head of CRIF, the most important Jewish umbrella organization in France, stated in an open letter addressed to
President Jacques Chirac and published in *Le Monde*: "The

leaders of the country like to play down the anti-Jewish acts. We are deluged with statistics designed to show that an attack against a synagogue is an act of violence and not anti-Semitism. Some Jews who have lost touch with reality like to buttress their personal status by turning a deaf ear and blind eye to the danger in order to curry favor with the public. . . . Judicial authorities don't like to mete out strong punishment for acts of anti-Jewish violence even when the perpetrators are caught red-handed. . . . Why this laxness? Because this violence perpetrated by only one side is linked to the conflict in the Middle East. Because too often the Jew and the Israeli mean the same thing. . . . Because the Muslim population is all-important. . . . Once again we are a scapegoat. It's a part we are no longer prepared to play."

But why has France, more than any other Western European country, witnessed such an extraordinary number of anti-Semitic incidents during the last few years? The answer may be partly related to the numbers of French citizens of Jewish and Arab origin. With 650,000 Jews, France has the largest Jewish community in Western Europe. France also has close to 6 million residents of Arab descent, most of them with origins in Algeria, Morocco, and Tunisia. The new French anti-Semitism is not confined to the level of intellectual debates or street protests. And it is usually not the intellectuals who act frivolously or in bad faith, as Pascal Boniface did, or who utter death threats, or physically attack Jews, or set fire to synagogues or Jewish schools. Of course, anti-Arab racism and the actions of the extreme right are also characteristics of the French scene. But according to official French statistics for the year 2001, among dozens of anti-Semitic offenders arrested by the police, only two belonged to the "classic" French extreme right. The number of anti-Arab incidents fell dramatically just as the number of anti-Semitic attacks rose sharply.

"In France, anti-Semitism has been particularly acute. . . . Scores of French synagogues and Jewish day schools have been firebombed or desecrated," wrote Mary Robinson, former UN commissioner for human rights, in the June 19, 2003, *International Herald Tribune.* In its July 17, 2003, issue, the *Wall Street Journal Europe* described this situation: "The file grows almost daily: 309 incidents in the past 15 months in the Paris region, according to Jewish council officials, and more than 550 since the second Palestinian *intifada*, or uprising, broke out in the West Bank and Gaza Strip in September 2000. . . . The number of incidents appears to spike depending on events in Israel and the Middle East. . . ." The perpetrators of these acts are overwhelmingly marginal young Frenchmen of Arab origin, whom the French media call euphemistically *jeunes de banlieu*—young people from the suburbs. They are frequently not integrated into French society; their unemployment rate is extremely high. In the year 2000, while the average unemployment rate for French citizens was 11 percent, the unemployment rate for the French of Arab descent was 20 percent. Either through sheer naiveté or deliberately, the governing Socialist party, in power until April 2002, ignored a major problem that became a ticking bomb for French society.

A French researcher who took the pen-name of Emmanuel Brenner describes in his book *Les Territoires perdus de la Republique* (The Lost Territories of the Republic) how in certain French public schools, where French students of Arab descent are dominant, Jewish students and teachers are terrorized because of their ethnic or religious affiliation. Supporting this charge, Alvin Rosenfeld writes that in these schools, "teachers who are prepared to teach about the Holocaust in French classrooms are often intimidated from doing so by angry Muslim students, some of whom act aggressively to prevent knowledge of Jewish victimization during World

War II from being disseminated in the schools. The subject has effectively become taboo, and many of these schools are almost extraterritorial enclaves." Along the same lines, Brenner castigates the "civic and political regression of French society, which creates an educational ghetto where Jewish children will leave for Jewish schools, followed by Jewish teachers often disgusted of working under conditions of permanent tension."

Pierre-André Taguieff's book is a precise x-ray of this Judeophobia and its roots, as it can be found in Western Europe generally and France in particular. Taguieff does not rely on the term "anti-Semitism" simply because the Arabs too are people of Semitic origin. But the reader can easily replace Taguieff's word "Judeophobia" with the word "anti-Semitism" without distorting his argument.

Taguieff alerts the reader in his opening pages: "I advocate a negotiated solution to the Israeli-Palestinian conflict. More precisely, I would support a political solution based upon the principle of two independent states, one Israeli, one Palestinian, existing alongside each other and open to federation at some time in the future." An agnostic and a firm believer in the separation of state and religion, Taguieff respects all religions. But he is firmly against "the political use of religion, which turns social and political conficts into religious or pseudo-religious wars." He cautions the reader not to confuse Islam with Islamism, his term for the radical fundamentalist movement with Islam, and he says "that no weakness or concession should be displayed in combating Islamism. . . . This 'ism,' in which obscurantism merges with terrorism, is today the main vehicle lending fresh fanaticism to Judeophobia."

"The spread of so-called 'anti-Zionist' rhetoric now affects all Western countries, not only France," writes Taguieff. This new Judeophobia, he says, employs a "massive and virulent" anti-racist propaganda for anti-Jewish purposes, and deliberately equates the Western democracies with totalitarian regimes. Taguieff describes in compelling fashion how a faction in European and North American intellectual circles consistently describes the history of Western civilization and of Israel only as a long series of crimes against humanity. As part of this distorted approach, many terrorist acts are viewed by the same observers as the legitimate reactions of the historically "oppressed." Certain human rights organizations have become the fellow travelers of a new Islamic totalitarianism, excusing its crimes and condemning antiterrorist measures. "Blind pacifism is a particularly dangerous form of moralism. For it places aggressor and victim of aggression on the same level—indeed, it accepts or even encourages the former while paralyzing the latter and making a crime of legitimate self-defense."

Taguieff's book will give the reader a clear sense of the rise of Islamic fascism, not only in the lands of Islam but in the Western world. "In the late 1990s," he writes, "at a time when global Palestinian propaganda was already conveying a culture of hatred with its characteristic demonization of Zionism, certain 'anti-imperialist' Islamist circles further spread a culture of death that celebrated the killing of infidels through the voluntary self-sacrifice of Islamic 'martyrs.'" For this new fascism, for the "Islamist-terrorist networks . . . the Jews are a people in the way and democratic culture is a poison." For Islamists, the United States and the West are Satan, and Israel must simply be removed from the map.

The alternatives confronting the Western democracies are, according to Taguieff, "theocracy or democracy: Islamic order or the republic." Meanwhile he warns that the war against intellectual or physical terrorism should not be confused with a war against Islam. He clearly sees mainstream Muslims, intellectuals or not, as perfectly capable of living and coexisting with other religious denominations in a democratic Western society in which religion remains distinct from the political state. To its credit, the French government has finally acknowledged this major problem that confronts France. As Glenn Frankel wrote in the July 17, 2003, *Wall Street Journal Europe*, "What is different these days is that the French government, after a period of almost indignant denial that the problem existed, is aggressively responding with tougher laws, uncompromising statements from leading cabinet members and stronger police presence. . . ." French Prime Minister Jean Pierre Raffarin declared on July 21, 2002, at a ceremony commemorating the deportations to Auschwitz from from *Velodrome d'Hiver* in 1942: "Attacking the Jewish community is to attack France, to attack the values of our republic where there is no room for anti-Semitism, racism, or xenophobia." The French Ministry of Education announced a new program designed to monitor and respond to anti-Semitic attacks in the French public schools, and unlike his Socialist predecessors, Nicolas Sarkozy, the French minister of the interior, issued a severe warning against anti-Semitic violence originating from Muslim communities and informed French Muslim leaders that the preaching of violence would be monitored and prosecuted.

As the former left-wing member of the Spanish parliament Pilar Roha has written, "Judeophobia is not an historical accident, limited in time and space, but a fundamental culture which explains the whole history of Europe. In a certain way the hatred toward the Jews founded Europe. . . . It is Europe that is responsible for the creation of Israel. It is Europe that created the need for this state as a last chance for survival. . . . It is Europe that invented Auschwitz, the last railway station, and it is Europe that invented Israel, the extreme solution. . . . Europe committed the worst crime: the industrial extermination of a people and a culture; and in spite of everything it did not succeed in vaccinating itself against its old hate. Europe liberated itself from most of its Jews but not from anti-Semitism. This explains its pro-Palestinian hysteria, its ferociously anti-Semitic left, its macabre banalization of the Holocaust. . . ."

While Pilar Roha is correct in her assessment, American readers of Pierre-André Taguieff's book should not feel self-righteous simply because an ocean separates them from Europe, or because America is a victim of the 9/11 mass murder. The seeds of hate are already planted in American soil. Occasionally elected officials remark that there is too much Jewish influence in the U.S. decision-making process. A movie inspired by the Bible revisits some classic elements of anti-Semitism, and the Catholic church refuses to distance itself from it. A newly elected governor seems to have been an open admirer of Adolf Hitler. Muslim charities are indicted for fund-raising for overseas terrorists, and imported extremist Islamist ideologies make inroads in mainstream American Muslim communities. The "new" Judeophobia may not be as far from these shores as we would like to believe.

RADU IOANID

Washington, D.C.
January 2004

"He who hates endeavors to remove and
destroy the object of his hatred. . . . Hatred is
increased by being reciprocated, and can on the
other hand be destroyed by love."

—Spinoza, *Ethics*, Book 3

Rising from the Muck

Introduction

Not since world war ii have anti-Jewish expressions had such currency in France among so many social groups, or met so little intellectual and political resistance as they have since the fall of 2000. Not since the war have there been so many anti-Jewish incidents affecting individuals or institutional symbols (the burning of synagogues and Jewish schools, verbal or physical attacks on people as Jews) without prompting anti-racist demonstrations and firm public condemnation from political and media elites. Things have reached the point where we might reintroduce the old term "banalization." It is exactly as if many different attitudes and manifestations of Judeophobia had become banalized, as if they fitted so well into the ideological scenery that they were no longer perceptible.

The France of reality television and popular concern with the stock market wished to continue dreaming in peace; a controlling optimism held sway over dormant hearts and minds. As for the *bien-pensant* elites, comfortable in their orthodox indignation, they concentrated on their consensus problems and on well-defined categories of victims. What is certain is that Jews no longer appeared anywhere on their list of accredited victims. But then, not without some hesitation, it was discovered that on the threshold of the twenty-first

century Jews had become a suspect group, more and more often the object of targeted acts of violence. It had become dangerous to call yourself a Jew, or even to look Jewish, in some
suburbs or "sensitive" areas of large French cities. Even in
France, Judeophobia was back.

This recent wave of Judeophobia is part of a discourse of
ideas—designed to attack Jews and mobilize action against
them—that has been spreading throughout the world.[1] We
find in this discourse a number of words and themes handed
down from various anti-Jewish traditions, but also new in-
dictments in which "Israel" and "Zionism" serve as repulsive
myths. To get to the heart of the matter, we might say that its
general form of argument is as follows: "Jews are all more or
less crypto-Zionists. Zionism is a form of colonialism, imperialism, and racism. Therefore Jews are colonialists, imperialists, and racists, whether overt or covert."[2] By presenting
"Zionism" as the incarnation of absolute evil, an anti-Jewish
vision of the world reconstituted itself in the second half of
the twentieth century. Like the old "anti-Semitism," in the
strong sense of the term,[3] it is characterized by an absolute
hatred of Jews as representatives of a single, intrinsically negative entity or exemplars of an evil force—that is, a total hatred in which Jews are "considered in themselves as endowed
with a malign essence."[4] Two ideas are regularly combined:
the Jews are everywhere ("nomadism"), and everywhere they
support one another (perhaps forming a worldwide group of
conspirators). The charge that Jews have a will to dominate,
or are involved in a "plot to conquer the world," is recycled
in this fantasy, as is the long-stereotypical rumble of accusation: "The Jews are guilty," which for more than half a century has been repeatedly translated into "the Zionists are
guilty," " Zionism is guilty," or "Israel is guilty."[5]

Variants of these anti-Jewish themes have spread to every
country without exception—one perverse effect of the new

information and communications technologies. Not surprisingly, the accusations may be found in neofascist, xenophobic-nationalist, traditionalist, or fundamentalist Christian circles of the far right. But today they are mainly purveyed by the propagandists of political or radical Islam (the various currents of Islamism[6] or "Islamic radicalism"[7]); by the humanitarian neo-Christian movement which, in its twin demonization of America and Israel, is succeeding revolutionary anti-imperialist Third Worldism; by a section of the elites, both left and right, liberal and social democratic, which advocates moving beyond the nation-state and preaches the messianic utopia of a postnational world (for which the Israeli nation-state represents intolerable resistance to globalist injunctions[8]); by the new anti-imperialists coming from a Communist or leftist (anarcho-Trotskyist) tradition, who tend to reduce their struggle against "neoliberal" globalization to a simplistic anti-Americanism;[9] and, of course, by the whole of the Arab world, whose constituent dictatorships and reactionary plutocratic regimes are looking for ways of deflecting mass anger onto external enemies and have cynically made the Palestinian cause the absolute cause, a major symbolic issue. For all these producers of ideological discourse, the amalgam "Israelis-Zionists-Jews" operates as a representation of the absolute enemy, worthy of absolute hatred.

This cluster of negative stereotypes falls within a more wide-ranging demonization of America, for radical anti-Americanism has indeed been the transnational political orthodoxy of the post-1989 world. Combined with the mythical figure of the American hyperpower, itself the latest recycling of "imperialism" or "American imperialism," the repulsive category of "Israelis-Zionists-Jews" makes it possible to pass off accusatory expressions as a kind of causal explanation. This amalgam is the basis for the common or garden-variety "anti-Zionism" observable in the Arab-Muslim world since the 1950s, with Christian Arabs not exactly lagging behind in this respect. The statements of the Jordanian minister for social affairs, Emile Algohri, are sufficiently explicit not to require further comment: "It is our firm belief that there is no difference at all between Jews and Zionists. All Jews are Zionists and all Zionists are Jews, and anyone who thinks otherwise is not thinking logically. We consider world Jewry our adversary and enemy, as we do imperialism and all the pro-Jewish powers."[10] In essence, everything is here explained and illuminated by making two forces jointly responsible for all the ills of the world: for injustice and inequality, oppression and exploitation, bloody conflicts and genocidal massacres. All these unnatural catastrophes, evils, and plagues are put down to the activities of Israel and the United States, or, most often, the two together. The resulting vulgate almost covers the range of beliefs deriving from Third Worldism. Demonization of "Zionism" or its worldwide "influence" is central to most of the formulations in question. Thus, in an "open letter to Western nations and governments" issued by Saddam Hussein on October 29, 2001, the dictator declared: "The security of America and the security of the world might be achieved if . . . America shook off its baneful alliance with Zionism, which has been ceaselessly plotting to exploit the world and plunge it into blood and darkness, using America and certain Western countries for this purpose."[11]

Now, though we can note many points of intersection or confluence of anti-American, anti-Israeli, and anti-Jewish themes, it would be the kind of excess typical of a political tract to suggest that all three are identical. Let us be still clearer: not all anti-Americans are anti-Jewish, not all anti-Israelis are anti-Jewish, and not all anti-Jews are anti-American. We must avoid giving a further boost to polemical compounds that have already become all too commonplace. But this should not prevent us from identifying the ideological and rhetorical twin-ning. In what I have called the new vulgate, there is a core be-lief that those really responsible have been caught, that the guilty ones have been found. American Jews, Jewish Americans: they remain guilty in their very essence, even when they are victims of murderous attacks. Hence the return, in various forms, of the "Judeo-American" amalgam: from "Jewish America" or "Jew York"[12] to "American-Zionist imperial-ism." The fact remains that Jews in Israel or Europe are more vulnerable—far less numerous, wealthy, and powerful—than Americans in general (including Jews). This makes them ideal targets for demonizers of all persuasions. Israel is inherently culpable, the only nation-state guilty by its mere existence: such is the matrix of the new anti-Jewish configuration.

In this book, therefore, I argue that what we are seeing to-day in Europe, and evidently in all the Muslim countries, is a wave of Judeophobia unprecedented in scale or intensity in the post-Nazi period. I shall try to demonstrate this in the face of a number of received ideas—especially the widespread be-lief that anti-Semitism is in irreversible "decline" and its "withering away" inevitable, in short, that it is "a thing of the past," one area among others for historical research.[13] This thesis of the gradual extinction of anti-Semitism is often com-bined with another idea, which we may quote here in a for-mulation by the late American Palestinian intellectual Edward Said: "The transfer of a popular anti-Semitic animus from a Jewish to an Arab target was made smoothly, since the figure was essentially the same."[14] I shall therefore be responding to a view that feeds precisely on denial of the global reality of the phenomenon. I approach this task without illusions, be-cause the clichés and slogans that replace thought in these matters are bound up with strong passions and powerful in-terests; you cannot persuade active militants and partisans

that their commitment or ideological convictions are hallucinatory in character.

One of my interpretive hypotheses is that the most recent
mutations of Judeophobia answer, with remarkable symbolic
efficiency, the demand for meaning and the mobilization of
causes felt by all those orphans of "revolution" who continue
to think and find guidance in the traditional Communist element of revolutionary myth, in one of its many Marxist
(Leninist, Trotskyist, Third Worldist) or anarchist (neoleftist,
"neoradical") variants. For these "radical" milieux, and for
all the far-right groups (which was not the case before the late
1960s), Israel is the devil incarnate, "Zionism" the absolute
enemy. And behind these visible figures and these utterable
denunciations, Jews are perceived as disturbing, malign, and
fearsome creatures.

I shall also show that the set of Judeophobic themes, inserted into the "anti-imperialist" illusion, constitute a bridge
between the neorevolutionary milieux and the various movements of "radical" Islamism. This is why I repeat Hannah
Arendt's particularly lucid warning: "What I wrote may
shock good people and be misused by bad ones."[15] My pessimistic view of humanity does contain certain nuances, however. I assume that, apart from the large number of stupid or
ill-intentioned people impressively distributed across the
frontiers, there are others more sensitive to rational argument
and open to criticism of their own certitudes.

ONE

Surveying the Landscape: Figures of Contemporary Judeophobia

To AVOID possible misunderstanding, especially the kind of questioning of intentions that is all too common in these matters, I should at once make it clear that I advocate a negotiated solution to the Israeli-Palestinian conflict. More precisely, I would support a political solution based upon the principle of two independent states, one Israeli, one Palestinian, existing alongside each other and open to federation at some time in the future; the return of the State of Israel to its 1967 frontiers, with a clause providing for the division of Jerusalem; an end to the occupation of the West Bank and the Gaza Strip; and the dismantling of the Jewish settlements. If it is to succeed, such a peace process will require the Palestinians to recognize Israel's legitimacy and right to existence, as well as an end to anti-Israeli terrorism—hence the de-Islamization of the Palestinian national movement. It is important to draw a critical balance sheet of the negotiations so far, whose breakdown has largely been due to mounting suspicions on both sides.[1] In my view, then, the failure of the

Oslo peace process during the talks at Camp David (July 11–24, 2000) and at Taba (January 21–27, 2001) is only temporary,[2] and the Mitchell Report (published on May 21, 2001) opens the way to a resumption of negotiations.[3] The principal task is to restore or create mutual trust between Israelis and Palestinians.

Although an agnostic and a firm defender of the principle of secularism, I respect all religious beliefs. I try to apply this to Islam—the various Islams—as much as to Judaism (which may also be put in the plural) and the many different forms of Christianity. But I strongly oppose the political use of religion, which turns social and political conflicts into religious or pseudo-religious wars. This is why it seems to me that no weakness or concession should be displayed in combating Islamism. I stress that I am speaking here of Islamism, not Islam; this *ism*, in which obscurantism merges with terrorism, is today the main vehicle lending fresh fanaticism to Judeophobia. In fact the premise of this book is that, after a period of calm, anti-Jewish imagery again came under the sway of ideological fanaticism, only this time not on an ethnic-racial basis but on a distinctive religious basis involving improper or distorted references to Islam.[4] For me this came as an intolerable discovery. As a citizen I felt I should do everything to limit the force of this new wave of Judeophobia and to stop it from spreading; as an academic researcher (one of whose fields is precisely the study of racism and ideologies of rejection) I felt I should try to describe the ways in which it manifests itself and to advance hypotheses and interpretive models to account for its appearance. My published work and my interventions in the public arena are thus intended to desacralize the conflicts in question, to demystify their causes and content, to retranslate them into the language of politics.[5]

In the new international context, the question of terminology has acquired a meaning and a value that are historical

no less than sociological. If, to denote intellectualized or ideologized hatred of Jews, I use the neologism "Judeophobia"
rather than the current term "anti-Semitism," if I prefer to
use the epithet "anti-Jewish" or "Judeophobic" rather than
"anti-Semitic," this is because the terms "anti-Semite" and
"anti-Semitism"[6] (which presuppose an old theory of race
and particularly a racialist distinction between "Semitic" and
"Aryan/Indo-European"[7]) today strike us as ill-suited for a
fruitful conceptualization of the anti-Jewish phenomena now
observable in the world.[8] Post-Nazi Judeophobia is grounded
not upon the vulgar racialist theories of the late nineteenth
century, with their myth of a "race war" between two imaginary constructs, "Semites" and "Aryans,"[9] but upon a set of
cultural and political elements quite different from those
characterizing the anti-Semitism of the Dreyfus Affair or the
state racism of the National Socialists.

To use the term "anti-Semitism" today would be to give a
new lease on life to a number of vague and ambiguous rep-
resentations, which in turn may suggest various misleading
notions. By avoiding this term, we will save ourselves the
trouble of having to refute those in the Arab world and elsewhere who, though proven to be anti-Jewish by their words
or deeds, defend themselves with the standard sophism: "We
cannot be anti-Semitic since, as Arabs, we too are Semites."[10]
The black American leader of the Nation of Islam, Louis Farrakhan (Abdul Haleem), whose repeated anti-Jewish outbursts have brought upon him the charge of "anti-Semitism,"
once allowed himself the indulgence of retorting, with a fantasy etymology and semantics in support, that he was incomparably more "Semitic" than the European Jews and that the
accusation against him therefore made no sense:

"The word itself, Semitic, deals with Afro-Asian people.
If I am anti-Semitic, I am against myself. You have Arabs,
and they are called Semitic people. *Semi* means half. They

are in between. There is a mixture of the blood of Africa and Asia and Europe in there, and you have what you call a Semitic people. . . . Now, most of those who call me anti-Semitic are not Semites themselves. These are Jews that adopted the faith of Judaism up in Europe; they're called *Ashkenazi* Jews. They have nothing to do with the Middle East—they're Europeans."[11]

Let us therefore endeavor to make the term "anti-Semitism" obsolete and marginal—except, with certain precautions, in scholarly historical discourse relating to the anti-Jewish ideologies and actions of the second half of the nineteenth century and the first half of the twentieth. For, during that period of approximately one hundred years, Judeophobia really did find its concepts and its expression within the ideological space of a racially grounded anti-Semitism mainly oriented to nationalist goals.[12] The Islamization and, in some respects, re-Islamization of Judeophobia, which have been peaking in the 1990s and the first decade of the 2000s, in no way exclude the formation of themes deriving from earlier anti-Jewish traditions. The Saudi paper *Okaz*, for example, in its issue of April 30, 1987, published an article prophesying that the heroic Hitler's failed program to exterminate the Jews would be carried through by Allah in person:

"The influence of the Jews has constantly grown in modern Europe, to the point where they are in a position to trample the innocent under foot. This situation caused a reaction in Germany, with the rise of the party of the Third Reich led by Hitler. He became the leader of the anti-Semitic movement and attempted to liquidate the Jews. In the end he failed. [. . .] But God himself will fight the Jews and keep his promise to crush and destroy them."[13]

But the stereotypes and accusatory themes that have become more and more widespread since the 1970s, in the

French public arena (my main field of observation, interpretation, and intervention, as both citizen and researcher) as well as in the West more generally, were originally drawn from the traditional discourse of Palestinian nationalism, the only nationalism deemed fully respectable by the intellectual and political elites. For a nationalist movement that has not actually created a nation-state is likely to attract the sympathy of elites as a national liberation movement, even if it has recourse to terrorism. The good terrorist, mainly by analogy with the struggle against Nazism during World War II, is the one thought of as a "resistance fighter," or as a combatant for the "liberation" of a people or a land. Having previously worked for the benefit of *fedayeen* who hijacked airplanes or committed spectacular bloody attacks, the transfiguring label today operates in relation to the "human bombs" of Hamas or Islamic Jihad, who blow themselves up in public spaces in Israel, indiscriminately killing as many people as possible—suicidal attacks that have been taking place since 1994 and are often, more or less justifiably, described as "blind."[14] This type of terrorist or "Islamikaze" joyfully accepts self-sacrifice in and through murder; he or she belongs to the category of "cerebral killer," for whom the act of killing has a value and a meaning as a proof of religious faith, and whose self-justification invokes the function of "punishing a corrupt and unjust society."[15] To kill oneself while killing others is to take the side of right, to enforce justice. It is as if the indoctrinated terrorists were drawing the ultimate conclusion from what Gauguin once said: "Life being what it is, one dreams of vengeance."[16] But we should note in passing just a couple of counterexamples: neither the Tibetans—long plundered, discriminated against, and massacred by the Chinese regime—nor Christians persecuted by the same totalitarian system have carried out bloody terrorist actions or enjoyed the same ideological compassion as the Palestinians,[17] not to speak of the financial aid that has served mainly to enable PLO leaders to keep their bank accounts in good shape. The exposure of this latter fraud—which may be analyzed sociologically as a classical case of a ruling elite of spokesmen and leaders who become autonomous and cynically exploit the people they are supposed to represent, enlighten, and guide—in no way means that we should neglect the sufferings of the majority of the Palestinian people, or, to be more precise, of those who recognize themselves as Palestinians, as members of that special "imagined community" postulated by any nationalist movement, with its founding and mobilizing mythology of Blood, Land, and the Dead.

To glorify the actions of a terrorist as those of a hero or martyr,[18] it is necessary to adopt the formula dear to revolutionaries that "the end justifies the means." The end that here gives absolute justification is the sacred cause, open to various interpretations within the perspective of Palestinian national Islamism but often reduced to the goal of the series of terrorist actions: that is, "driving the Jews" from the "Sacred Land," either through terror (involving not a decisive battle but a gradual intensification of the conflict resulting in discouragement and despair) or through extermination in a *jihad* that mobilizes all the Muslim countries around the world. A good way of grasping the different levels of meaning of the term "*jihad*" (holy war) within Islamic fundamentalism is to examine the following definition from a text by Hassan al-Banna, one of the men who founded the Muslim Brotherhood in Egypt in March 1927. He is addressing "combatant" members of the Brotherhood, its militarily trained elite:

"What I understand by holy war [*jihad*] is the duty lasting until the day of resurrection that is envisaged by the words of God's messenger (may God's peace and blessing be upon him): 'He who dies without having fought a campaign, or had the intention of fighting a campaign, dies a death from the days of paganism.' The first degree of holy war consists in driving evil from one's own heart; the highest degree is armed struggle for God's cause. The intermediate degrees are combat through words, through the pen, through the hand, and through the word of truth addressed to unjust authorities. Our apostolic movement can live only through combat. Commensurate with the sublime character and vast horizons of our apostolate will be the grandeur of the struggle we wage for it, the size of the price that must be paid to sustain it, and the greatness of the reward for those who have labored well. 'Fight for the cause of Allah with the devotion due to Him' (*Koran*, 22:78). Then you will know the meaning of the watchword that you must always retain: 'Holy war is our path.' . . ."[19]

Someone who has understood the lesson knows that *jihad* has several degrees, which stretch from efforts to spread Islam by word of mouth through armed struggle in the form of holy war against infidels.[20] In short, the end that justifies the means is worldwide Islamization; this is the final goal of the various movements associated with Islamist activism.[21] The means employed, however, may be interpreted quite differently by non-Muslims disposed to find more prosaic justifications in revolutionary ideology or, more recently, in the slogans of anti-globalization. It is sophistical reasoning of this type that sought to "explain away" the suicide attacks of September 11, 2001: to destroy the twin towers of the World Trade Center was to destroy the symbol of American financial capitalism, or even of globalization. We are reminded of some of Lenin's or Trotsky's arguments, according to which any action that furthers the revolution is good or justified. Here is one of Trotsky's last messages: "Only that which prepares the complete and final overthrow of imperialist bestiality is moral, and nothing else. The welfare of the revolution—that is the supreme law!"[22] Terrorist "bestiality" can be justified in this way as a counterbestiality: frenetic anti-globalizers can be happy at the spectacle of acts of violence deemed to be revolutionary;[23] they are making the same journey in celebration of total hatred that one finds elsewhere in the revolutionary tradition. Take, for example, this little piece of bravura from the writings of Che Guevara: "Hatred as an element of the struggle, a relentless hatred of the enemy, impelling us over and beyond the natural limitations that man is heir to and transforming him into an effective, violent, selective, and cold killing machine. Our soldiers must be thus. . . ."[24]

Such is the permanent temptation for those who slide from criticism, even radical criticism, of free-market society toward total hatred bent on destruction of its object, including other humans. The means might be blind terror or unclaimed massacres, without definite or credible aims, carried out even if they might lead to a third world war. *Fiat justitia, pereat mundus* (Let there be justice though the world perish). At first, considerable care is taken to dissolve the terrorist act into its context or its economic, social, or psychological causes, by referring, for example, to "U.S. bias toward Israel and the embargo against Iraq," or perhaps to the "despair of the masses"; then attempts are made to present the ends in question as absolutely good. It might be argued, for example, that the poor and oppressed victims, especially if they invoke such great or sublime goals as justice or freedom, have every right to kill "innocent people" or civilians as a way of rebelling against injustice or expressing their desire for a "better world." To explain and understand the acts of violence is thus supposed to justify them. Monique Canto-Sperber has lucidly shown the sophistical nature of such arguments, whose traces are repeatedly found in commentaries on terrorist outrages. "No explanation in terms of social or psychological causes," she writes, "no explanation in terms of a goal, can alter the moral quality of what is an act of lynching or murder. . . . The desire to understand should . . . remain critical. It must not stop describing the deeds of the oppressed for what they are. It must not feed the idea that the poor of the earth have a legitimacy that excuses everything. It must denounce the ideals of supposed liberation when these are no more than myths through which violence is constantly sustained, transferred, and reproduced. It must refuse to excuse acts of indiscriminate or aimless terror by diluting them in social and political ills."[25] As for the disturbing silence of the terrorists who have not explicitly or directly claimed responsibility for the attacks of September 11, 2001, we are entitled to take up André Glucksmann's suggestion and to interpret it as an attitude very close to that of the Nazis in the death camps: "*Hier ist kein warum*" (Here there are no whys or wherefors).

The spread of so-called "anti-Zionist" rhetoric now affects all Western countries, not only France. If it is here appropriate to put the term "anti-Zionist" in quotation marks, this is because it refers both to an expression of propaganda and to an ideological-political project which, with a few tactical and strategic intermediate stages, is nothing other than the destruction of the State of Israel or (in Israelophobic Newspeak) the "removal of the Zionist entity." In Israelophobic polemics, a number of different metaphors from pathology, ranging from "cancer"[26] to "chancre," are used to characterize this "entity," and they conjure up solutions from the realm of surgery: excision, removal at the roots, elimination, and so forth. We may define anti-Zionism in the strong sense of the term as "the strategy seeking the elimination of the State of Israel."[27] Such "anti-Zionism" may be interpreted as the most recent form of what some historians call "eliminationist" anti-Semitism[28]—which, in reality, is inseparable from any variant of "redemptive" anti-Semitism.[29]

This simple definition of anti-Zionism may be cogently illustrated by numerous passages from Palestinian schoolbooks, where the war against Israel is transfigured into *jihad*.
Here are three characteristic examples.

"Learn, my son, that Palestine is your country . . ., that its
pure soil is soaked with the Martyrs' blood. . . . Why is it necessary for us to fight the Jews and to drive them from our
land?"[30]

"Remember: the inevitable final result will be the victory
of the Muslims over the Jews."[31]

"This religion will vanquish all other religions, and—
through the will of Allah—it will be spread by the Muslim *jihad* fighters."[32]

From the 1960s to the 1980s this radical "anti-Zionism"
was ideologically received and politically expressed only by a
majority of Third World countries (beginning, of course, with
the Arab countries) and the Communist world. It made a career for itself mainly on the left, in "progressive" Communist
and far-left circles.[33] Here, for instance, is the final sentence
of an article by the Palestinian militant Mounthir Anabtawi,
a member of the Institute for Palestinian Studies in Beirut,
which appeared in 1967 under the title "Zionism: A Colonialist, Chauvinist, and Militarist Movement": "The Arabs'
demand concerning the recovery of Palestine and the *sup-
pression of Israel's existence* [emphasis added], while expressing their wish to respect the principles of justice and
human rights, represents a positive contribution to the solution of the Jewish problem as it presents itself today."[34]

The fall of Soviet communism between 1989 and 1991 in
no way impeded the attractive power and persuasive force of
this "anti-Zionism." After the brief episode of the Gulf War,
it spread into cultural and political circles that had previously
seemed impervious to it. There was even a universalization of
the vague idea that most of the ills affecting humanity were

somehow linked to the Israel-Palestine conflict, and that the fault for this lay with Israel. "Anti-Zionist" themes formed a stock list of accusations, whose target was always the same even if its precise name differed: "Zionism," "Zionist imperialism," "American-Zionist imperialism," and so on. We may conclude that, by the late 1990s, PLO propaganda had largely achieved its objective of saturating international public opinion with its vocabulary and its imagery, of imbuing the most diverse national aspirations and sentiments with "anti-Zionist" convictions inseparable from, and intensified by, an unconditionally anti-Israeli, pro-Palestinian reflex of indignation. The intended result was to monopolize legitimate appeals to right and justice in an international context where the sway of a peculiar mixture of moralism, legalism, and humanitarianism effectively depoliticized the approach to political conflicts.

It needs to be understood, of course, that the "Zionism" targeted by "anti-Zionism" is an imaginary construct, a fiction. If Zionism had not existed,[35] the "anti-Zionists" would have invented it. They did in fact reinvent it, constructing a totally repulsive entity out of rumors, prejudices, stereotypes, and legends, an entity meant to be totally rejected and ultimately suppressed.[36] This is why the term "anti-Zionism" now operates in most contexts as a euphemism—that is, to use a classical dictionary definition, "a milder expression of an idea whose direct expression would be in some way disagreeable."[37] The euphemistic use of "anti-Zionism" involves substituting this milder term for another that would be condemned as too explicit or "direct." Since 1945, in the public discourse of pluralist democratic societies, no one has called himself "anti-Semitic" or "anti-Jewish." But a growing number of individuals do declare themselves to be "anti-Zionist." Analysis of the contexts as well as the (usually veiled) intentions leads one to believe that the target of this "anti-Zionist" expression is less and less "Zionism" or "Zionists" and more and more Jews as such.[38]

Furthermore, this Judeophobic discourse, coupled with a new, post-Communist version of anti-Americanism more adapted to the psychology of anti-globalization,[39] is both promoted and intensified by the ongoing process of Islamization. For Islamization reformulates and recycles the stock of anti-Jewish stereotypes, accusations, and rumors stemming either from the Koran and other fundamental texts of Islam[40] or from local traditions in the Arab-Muslim world.[41] These unfavorable or hostile images and beliefs have been hardened by doctrinaire Islamists and inserted into the all-powerful framework of a world conspiracy.[42] The theory of a plot is an all-purpose theory, which makes it possible to denounce invisible, hidden, masked, lying enemies and to impute to them unspeakably criminal actions. It is a Manichean vision, based upon a simplistic (and paranoid) reading of all events, so that the demonic causality of "international" or "world" Zionism is present everywhere as the new key to history. For example, an Algerian Islamist belonging to the FIS (the Islamic Salvation Front) observed in early 1990: "France has become the essential crossroads for international Zionism, its favored den in the Diaspora operating the world of finance and the main Western media, which uses this power to manipulate world opinion as it pleases."[43] The same Islamist added to his denunciation of "Zionized" France the inevitable twin charges: "incitement to hatred against Islam, its principles and all its faithful believers"; and insidious and pernicious Islamophobia[44] on the part of the "hypocrites" (bad and/or false Muslims), whose minds have been poisoned by the secular culture of France, an inherently colonial power:[45]

"In tune with this campaign of hate against the entire Muslim world, an echo reverberates among us from a class of intellectuals trained overseas in Marxist-Leninist or Judaist [*sic*] milieux. It is an echo that uses a language so hostile and so brazen that it causes the most virulent enemies of Islam to blush. . . . Some well-known news media . . . have gone so far as to open their columns to representatives of Jewish councils with which they have very extensive relations. . . . In the name of 'tolerance,' these defenders of free expression and opinion even set themselves up as reformers of Islam. . . . Their (highly simplistic) idea of Islam coincides with the one formed overseas. . . . It is what the French call integrationist Islam, as opposed to fundamentalist Islam. And the principle of secularism contained in their Constitution, which they want to introduce at any price into Algerian society, is neither more nor less than a new kind of colonization. . . . In seeking to create scapegoats within Muslim milieux, . . . these enemies of Islam—whether Marxists, supporters of secularism or Judaism, or the product of other imported ideologies— today stand exposed. They are the real enemies of the whole of Algeria."[46]

Anything other than the Islam of the Algerian Islamists is therefore rejected as an "imported product," a form of cultural or political colonialism, an expression of a "poisonous cultural invasion." A war of cultures is declared: "The real weapon with which to confront the French cultural invasion is Islam."[47] Anti-French xenophobia here goes hand in hand with anti-Zionism and anti-Judaism, against a background of phobic rejection of "modernity," "modernism," "Western civilization," and "the hybridized and pretentious West."[48] Centeredness upon the Arab-Islamic world can often look like cultural anti-Western xenophobia. Ali Belhadj,[49] for instance, a FIS preacher, objects to the very word or idea of democracy as something alien to Islam and as a dangerous product of Western culture whose importation is part of a plot against the

Islamic Umma[50] by its many enemies ("Judeo-Masonic forces," "Zionists," "atheists," "Communists," etc.), whose puffed-up claims have always been relayed by "Orientalists."[51]

"The democratic idea," Belhadj continues, "is one of those pernicious intellectual innovations that haunt people's minds. They hear it from morning to night, forgetting that it is a lethal poison whose basis is impiety. . . . Democracy is a Greek word, unknown in the language of the blessed century. . . . It is therefore a word born in the land of impiety, corruption, and tyranny. Brothers in Islam, you should know that we ruthlessly reject any impious democratic dogma. . . . The word 'freedom' is understood in conflicting ways in liberal thought, existentialism, and Marxism. These three Western ideologies, which claim to uphold total freedom, are driven by a number of dangerous hidden aims, the worst of which is the victory of materialism, Marxism, and licentious atheistic propaganda. All this corresponds to the objectives contained in the *Protocols of the Elders of Zion*. As the first protocol states, 'We were the first to call upon the nations in the name of *liberty, equality, and fraternity*.' These words have been continually parroted right up to the present day; they have corrupted the world as they have corrupted the true freedoms of the individual. The word 'freedom' raises up human groups against all authority, even the divine Sunna. . . . The word 'freedom' is one of those Masonic and Jewish poisons that are intended to corrupt the world on a large scale."[52]

During the mass demonstrations organized by the FIS in August 1990, in a context heavily marked by the Gulf War crisis, its orators not only ritually denounced "the plot being prepared against the holy sites"[53] but spoke in the most violent terms against the demonic Jewish enemy, "the Jews" and "international Jewry." The "Zionists" were forgotten"![54] And at a large Islamist rally in Constantine, on August 17,

1990, the most widely heard slogans were: "Allah Akbar!" and "Down with the Jews!" while the "coordinator" shouted: "Allah O Akbar, let us crush the Jews. The soldiers of Mohammed will return. The Umma is one and indivisible. We won't allow a single hair of a Muslim to be touched, whether in Palestine, Saudi Arabia, Afghanistan, Iran, or anywhere else. . . . Rise up, Muslims, the Jews are in Haramein [the holy places of Jerusalem, Mecca, and Medina]. Jews, the army of Mohammed will return. Down with every infidel, long live every Muslim! . . . Let us brandish the flame of Islam. Let us brandish the *jihad*. Down with the valets of colonialism!" Then Sheikh Ben Azouz, FIS vice president and director of *El Mounquid*, declared from the platform: "We have tasted the bitterness of the Crusader invasion, since the day of the Revelation and up to the present day. . . . Yes, we shall go and fight the Americans; it is a holy war, against the Jews [shouts from the crowd], against France, Great Britain, and the Crusaders who want to humiliate Muslims in their own lands."[55] One thing is sure for the Algerian Islamists: the Jews "are everywhere hatching their plots."[56] In an interview published in September 1989, Ali Belhadj spoke most soberly about whether there could be "peaceful coexistence" of Muslims and Jews: "Our relationship with the Jews can only be one of war, of *jihad*—full stop, period."[57]

The Islamist identification of democracy with the enemies of Islam implies a blanket rejection of the principle of secularism—that is, of any separation between religion and politics. Secularism must therefore be fought for the same reasons as democracy, and, for Ali Belhadj, the struggle must be waged against Christians as much as Jews, the propagators, exploiters, and profiteers of "secularism."

"Impious democracy," he argues, "considers that man builds his destiny independently of his creator. The immoral formula, 'Render unto Caesar that which belongs to Caesar

and to God that which belongs to God' is at the origin of the
principle of separation of religion and the State, the philo-
sophical basis of democracy. . . . Secularism is really the hard
core of democracy. . . . In fact, the apostles of secularism are
applying, consciously or unconsciously, the world policy of
the Jews. They care little about their affiliation to Islam and
set to work in the Muslim countries in general and Algeria in
particular. I have written elsewhere that the separation between religion and the State exactly corresponds to the claim
of the Jews and Christians to cut life off from religion—
which God has formally condemned."[58]

The FIS leader constantly argues that the *sharia*, or religious law, must be opposed to the "dogma of democracy"
and the "secularist poison" used by Christians and "Judeo-
Masons" against Islam: "For us in Islam, . . . freedom is cir-
cumscribed by the *sharia*, not by the law or, as they say, by
the concern not to harm others. . . . The people have a right
to choose only the Muslim sovereign who will rule in accordance with the *sharia*. . . . Unlike the infidels, we denounce
democracy in the name of the rules of the *sharia*, and the
mass of Muslims has learned the one that puts Jews and
Christians in the wrong. . . . This is why we reject democracy,
that dogma of the impious West."[59]

It should be clear, then, that Islamists promote and defend
a political project belonging to what the Egyptian philosopher Fouad Zakariya has rightly called "an authoritarian
mode of thought," where a phenomenon or a problem "is
confronted not directly but in relation to what has been said
about it previously by the holy texts and scholars with recognized authority," so that any approach diverging from
them is liable to be "condemned as heretical or blasphe-
mous."[60] Contrary to the claim of Islamic "fundamentalists"
that Western secularism is the expression and instrument of a
("Jewish" or "Judeo-Masonic") plot,[61] the secular principle

may be seen as a universal, or anyway universalizable, ideal, "an extremely broad intellectual framework allowing arbitration among all kinds of political and ideological positions." Zakariya, a theoretician of the Arab secularist current, argues that "Islam is nothing other than what Muslims make of it"[62]—and this leads him to challenge any essentialist vision of the Islamic set of beliefs, to insist that it should remain a religion governing the salvation of believers and make no claim to solve all the problems facing humanity. The actual diversity of Islam[63] is an argument in favor of this nonessentialist conception: "The intellectual, political, social, and religious diversity of the contemporary Muslim world shows that, far from conforming to a supposedly authentic Islam, each of the forces that employ it presents a version conforming to its own genesis, interests, and ambitions."[64] The "hard core" of Islam, the "essence" of Islam, "authentic Islam": these are so many fictions, so many abstractions functioning as illusions. This is why nothing prevents Muslim societies from being governed by secular and pluralist norms,[65] in the way that the Islamists—from simple fundamentalists to *jihad* "revolutionaries"—totally reject.

In the late 1990s, when global Palestinian propaganda was already conveying a culture of hatred with its characteristic demonization of Zionism, certain "anti-imperialist" Islamist circles further spread a culture of death that celebrated the killing of infidels through the voluntary self-sacrifice of Islamic "martyrs." One large calendar bearing a portrait of Osama bin Laden, printed in Pakistan in 1999, carried a verse from the Prophet calling for the "expulsion of Jews and Christians from the Arabian peninsula" as well as the slogans "*Jihad* is holy war against America" and "Allah is the only superpower."[66] In early October 2001, bin Laden's chief lieutenant made the significant statement, in the form of a threat, that there were "as many young Muslims who loved death as young Americans who loved life."[67] This merely repeated what was said by the Egyptian fundamentalist leader Rifa'i Ahmad Taha, a disciple of Sheikh Omar and instigator of the massacre in Luxor on November 17, 1997, which left fifty-eight foreign tourists dead, some of them disemboweled and dismembered. On November 12, 2000, Ahmad Taha had written: "Faced with American nuclear weapons, we have our faith. America cannot live peacefully out of reach of the Muslim peoples, because a nation cannot be defeated so long as its youth are ready to die while their young enemies live in shame and sin, even if they possess weapons of destruction."[68]

Following Gilles Kepel, we should note that, apart from the special meaning in the practice of mystics (the effort that each believer makes in relation to himself to be the best Muslim possible), the term "*jihad*" denotes the effort to spread Islam. This takes two distinct forms. First is what is called "offensive *jihad*," referring to situations where Muslims attack non-Muslim territory and thus fulfill an obligation that concerns only the commander of the faithful (the head of the community) and the armed fighters. An example of this form of *jihad* was the attack on the World Trade Center. Second is "defensive *jihad*," in which all believers have a duty to participate—by fighting, giving money, and praying—as soon as the Umma (the community of believers) is judged to be in danger. The motive for "defensive *jihad*" is thus a feeling of solidarity with fellow Muslims under attack—a feeling that bin Laden sought to arouse by declaring *jihad* against the Americans on the grounds that they were occupying the sacred land of the Holy Places, in this case in Saudi Arabia.[69]

This indoctrination and fanatical conditioning of "believers" has had terrifying effects everywhere, from the Middle East to the United States, including sub-Saharan Africa, Central and Southern Asia, and Indonesia. A communiqué issued by the Islamic Jamaa Mujahedeen contained the following

instruction: "All French people in Morocco must be elimi-
nated, and anyone who speaks French in public must be
killed."[70] In the same communiqué the Islamic Jamaa stated
that it "will not tolerate a single Jew remaining in the country," and informed Mohammed Abdul Raouf (alias Abu
Amar, or Yasser Arafat) that "the struggle against the Jews is
a sacred duty, even if they leave Greater Syria [the territory of
the State of Israel and the territories under the control of the
Palestinian Authority], until they leave the planet Earth and
their property goes to Muslims."[71]

The belligerent Islamist call to universalize a purifying *jihad* is perfectly symbolized by the creation of the World Islamic Front for Jihad against Jews and Crusaders (made
public on February 23, 1998), whose founding charter is
signed by Osama bin Laden as well as his right-hand man,
Dr. Ayman al Zawahiri (head of the Egyptian group Al Jihad), and various leaders of small Islamist groups in the In-
dian subcontinent.[72] Inevitably the charter denounces the
"crusader-Zionist alliance" (or alliance "of the Crusaders
and Jews") and issues a *fatwa* "to kill the Americans and
their allies, civilians and military," as "an individual duty for
every Muslim who can do it in any country in which it is possible to do it."[73] On August 7, 1998, two deadly attacks soon
attributed to bin Laden destroyed the U.S. embassies in
Nairobi (Kenya) and Dar es Salaam (Tanzania).[74] Then the
terrorist spectacle of 9/11 revealed the vulnerability of the
American hyperpower and led even the most skeptical to
recognize the reality of the Islamist threat, including the
ideological-political project to conquer and destroy the modern non-Muslim world before reconstructing it on a fundamentalist basis. The Islamist war on the West appears to have
been immediately taken up in the form of what is usually
called bioterrorism.[75] For the fanatics who wish to eradicate
all traces of "impiety" from the face of the earth by waging

nuclear, chemical, or bacteriological warfare,[76] the concept of "crime against humanity" is nothing more than a Western concoction. Everything technically possible is Islamically necessary to "cleanse" the planet or to bring humanity back to (Islamic) normality.

A catechism lauding the grandeur of *jihad* tells us: "If, to kill infidels, one kills their wives and children at the same time, that does not matter."[77] Nor are there to be any limits on violence, since it is perpetrated in the name of Allah and the one true religion, Islam.[78] Pascal warned us of this long ago: "Men never do evil so completely and joyfully as when they do it out of religious conviction." And if the twenty-first century will be the century of biology (or biochemistry), it will come as no surprise if the new Islamist "cleansers" of humanity let loose bacteriological warfare. The fundamentalist doctrinaires consider that the "infidels" are almost a race apart, an inferior, "degenerate" subspecies of humanity. That is the great polemical unity: the absolute enemy is also subhuman. Islamist propagandists tirelessly identify Islam as the only true monotheism,[79] banishing Christians and Jews to the fringes of the human race, and so it follows that conversion to Islam is the only way in which an individual can become truly human. The most honorable Hani Ramadan,[80] director of the Islamic Center in Geneva, delivers this message in professorial style: "Whatever their race or color, men can really become human only if they choose to conform to this divine will."[81] On the same Francophone internet site of the Islamic Center in Geneva, the preacher Yakoub Roty spells things out: "Whoever denies God denies the essential truth, and is therefore only a being in a state of ignorance, not a man in the full sense of the word. . . . The word '*kufr*' [impiety, lack of belief] denotes the state in which the human mind is in shadow, the state of fallen man."[82] Since Islam is supposed to be the perfect religion and the only genuine monotheism,

Muslims are the only fully human beings; they embody the equivalent of a "superior race." One Algerian Islamist, presented as a "doctor of philosophy," described as follows the "modernism" that he regards as another name for Western civilization:

"Modernism is a direct revolt against religion and the spiritual values it represents. This phenomenon goes back to the Renaissance. . . . From its bastion in the West, this malignant tumor has spread like wildfire to the whole planet, annihilating on its way the local cultures of Asia and Africa. . . . Modernism appears with the most diverse labels: communism, socialism, capitalism, pragmatism, positivism, fascism, Nazism, Zionism, Arab nationalism, Berberism, and so on. . . . The main dogma of modernism is the rejection of an afterlife. . . . All modern ideologies are characterized by the cult of man, often beneath a cloak of Science. . . . The low value that modernist ideology attaches to family ties and domestic life is another of its fundamental characteristics. . . . The emancipation of women has indisputably been the most effective means in this open war on the family. . . . The malaise of Western civilization is no accident. . . . Western civilization is loathsome in theory and in practice."[83]

The West, then, is rejected as a sickness endangering Muslims around the world. The incurable disease of "Westitis" threatens to infect the community of believers, the Umma, with the viruses or toxins borne by "Crusader Christianity," "Judaist and Judeo-Masonic circles," atheists, licentious elements, feminists, and so on.[84] In 1990, Tunisian Islamists denounced "Western society" as "a society of homosexuals and lesbians," a "stinking" society that has hatched a "plot" against Islam by spreading the germs of its culture to the Muslim world, via "our Westernized intellectuals" who claim that "Islam too contains democracy and human rights," whereas in reality "it is completely incompatible with them."[85] To prevent this Westernization of the Islamic world, Islamists should eliminate those responsible for it; the minority of "true believers" has "the right to fight and kill them until the evil is rooted out."[86] This vision, from which the project of Islamicizing modernity or the West is derived,[87] is far from being held only by Islamists who totally reject any modernization, reform, or Westernization of Islam. At the Islamic congress held in Lyons in December 1985, for example, the Muslim convert Roger Garaudy—the "great professor, thinker, and philosopher Raja' Garaudy"—offered a "message of the Unity of Religions" while actually presenting the struggle for Islam as the positive face of the battle against an inherently oppressive and alienating "modernity," itself crudely conflated with capitalism or "Western civilization."

"The same struggle for justice and peace is being waged by Christians in the grassroots communities of Latin America, by Muslims in the Afghan resistance, and by the resistance fighters in Palestine and South Africa. The message of Islam is a liberation theology. . . . To answer the challenges of our time—the blind, godless growth that the superpowers and multinationals seek to impose, the nationalist wars and conflicts, the nuclear threat, and the unequal exchange between North and South—to answer these problems requires us not to modernize Islam but to Islamicize modernity. To modernize Islam, in the view of many of our contemporaries, would mean abandoning the goals of Islam and guiding ourselves by those of a Western civilization that is seriously adrift. . . . Each one of us is personally responsible for the blossoming of this meaningful life and this God-filled world."[88]

The superiority of Islam may thus be asserted as self-evident at the same time as the messianic program of the Islamicization of modernity moves ahead. The influence of well-known intellectuals like Roger Garaudy, who converted to Islam and became lecturers-cum-preachers in its cause, is far from insignificant. It has helped to create what certain specialists since the 1980s have called the phenomenon of "anti-Western militants"—most often, intellectuals or students living temporarily in France who support a political Islam conceived as both "victim and enemy of the West."[89] The Palestinian cause is here "the main instrument whereby anti-Western militants try to raise political awareness among all Muslims, and especially the Muslims of France."[90] It allows the construction of "a form of global Islamic opposition or resistance to the West," as we may see from the following testimony of a thirty-two-year-old man of Tunisian nationality who had been living in France for fourteen years and held a master's degree in economics.

"I am involved with Islam in France for two reasons: because I am interested in my own country and in the Muslim countries more generally. Islam is currently going through a kind of renaissance. . . . I am also interested in Islam because it is being attacked by the Western countries. . . . Before, I wasn't interested in it directly. Only after the invasion of Lebanon, when I saw that the Arabs were powerless to do anything about it, was my direct interest in Islam awakened. One day, in a paid advertisement in *Le Monde*, I read what Roger Garaudy and a French Catholic had written in support of the Palestinian cause—at a time when the Arabs were not reacting—and for the first time in my life I opened my checkbook to send some aid. . . . Second-generation children are more French than they think, and it is because they are not integrated that they experience a crisis of identity. . . . Our role is to help them find themselves, and to increase their awareness of causes like that of the Palestinians."[91]

In addition to this religious-cultural imperialism and political-religious neoracism, whose basic postulate of superiority results in discriminatory norms,[92] we also find among less cautious Islamist preachers a good old-fashioned appeal for extermination of the subhuman "infidels": "We ask Allah to come to our aid and clear this planet of all the *kufars* [unbelievers], so that only Muslims are left on it."[93] In their own ways, Islamist theoreticians and preachers are thus returning to the paths of exterminatory racism that Europe followed in the late nineteenth century and the first half of the twentieth. In practicing intellectual terrorism and calling for terror against "infidels," they show that, in spite of themselves, they are good disciples of the worst racist ideologues of modern Europe.

It is an evasion to counter this by arguing that political Islam is no more than "a form of deviance spread by atheists,"[94] for that would amount to saying that an imposing majority of the Muslim world—varying in size with the norms of the period—should be consigned to the darkness of atheism! In any event, the transnational reality of political Islam means that we are a long way from the politically correct cliché of a "religion of peace and toleration." That "peaceful" Islam exists only as the ideal Islam of UNESCO and the Islamic-Christian dialogue of the 1960s and 1970s,[95] which was later promoted as an attractive "spiritual" product able to adapt to the planetary superideology corresponding to a metapolitics of peace and human rights, as well as to consumerist expectations. This Westernized Islam, secularized and respectful of individual liberty (especially religious liberty), shorn of its embarrassing aspects and implying the exercise of critical reason, fully exists only as a project in the minds of reformist Muslim thinkers, even if it is also present, more hazily, in the minds of certain experts with apologetic tendencies, or of journalists and political figures eager not to shock their readers or electorate.

It is still important to point out, however, that any form of xenophobia or racism, involving differentiation or inequality, is in principle contrary to the universalist message of

Islam. Historically this requirement of universality—in Islam as in Christianity—has not been applied in a strict or harmonious manner: practices involving slavery, for example, based especially upon racial categories, still exist in certain countries with a Muslim culture,[96] as they long persisted in the Christian West. Hence the paradox that has been the norm for more than half a century: the only just wars are launched and conducted in the name of the pursuit of peace. In reality, Islam presents a face quite different from the ideal Islam that is dreamt of and glorified by those who have an interest in doing so. It oscillates between, on the one hand, the private practice of religion by a majority of Muslims who may be truly described as "moderate" (the "pietist" pole)[97] and, on the other hand, the Islamist fanaticism of a minority that involves indoctrination (with Islam as a self-sufficient dogma), recruitment into a militant network, and availability for total commitment to *jihad*. The radical message of Osama bin Laden, who calls upon Muslims everywhere to make a total commitment to "the struggle against the international *kufar*," is heard by millions of "believers," or at least by those who have access to television and the internet. It is a fact that a not insignificant part of this mass is very sensitive to the appeal for "holy war." But the destructive force of terrorism, illustrated by the "spectacular" attacks on the American hyperpower, fascinates just as large a number of Western nonbelievers.[98] An aesthetic, amoral gaze can always be directed upon the "spectacle" of the 9/11 attacks, which for some seem to demonstrate the truth of an aphorism inspired by Anaximander: "Human order always emerges out of chaos and returns into chaos."[99]

At the beginning of the third millennium, we have before us a repugnant spectacle that teaches us that History is again on the move, though hardly in the direction of peace and harmony. The tragic, insurmountable conflict of values is suddenly and brutally making itself felt. We were, so to speak, anesthetized by the converging utopias of indefinitely rising consumption, communication covering more and more of the planet, and technology holding out fabulous promises of things to come. Comfortably installed in a compartment on the great train of indefinite and irreversible Progress, seduced and distracted like tourists by the passing countryside, we were happy to be alive in the age of globalization as we headed into a future that could only be better than the present. Nations, states, and even civilizations seemed to us things of the past, regrettable traces of the past left behind in the present. The global village, pacified, egalitarian, and festive, seemed to be within reach of the rising generation. We imagined a radiant future, seeing the unwholesome clouds of the present as those of a purely transitional epoch.

But this utopian dream broke up on contact with the harsh reality of destructive and murderous violence, which was supposed to derive its meaning from the terrible project of which it was part. The angelic society of global communication vanished like a mirage, having been inordinately exploited for propaganda purposes by the exalters of globalization. Our eyes were opened as kamikazes acting in the name of Allah made acts of murder a routine occurrence in the orbit of transnational Islamic terrorism—whether in the shape of Hamas's "human bombs" in Israel, or of aircraft in the hands of fanatical *mujahedeen* trained to operate as suicide pilots. The call for a *jihad* against "the Jews," "the Americans," and "the infidels," which Osama bin Laden and his spokesman issued on October 7, 2001, is not just a racist incitement to hatred and violence, even if its racelike categories jumble together ethnic, religious, and civilizational criteria.[100] The message is clear in an Islamic Liberation Army communiqué of December 12, 1998: "To fight against the

United States and its allies, the Jews of Israel, is a life-and-death struggle."[101] Let us note in passing that the leader of global Islamic terrorism speaks of the Jews without recourse to the lexicon of euphemism: he does not use the classical codeword "Zionists" but names the Jews directly and calls for hatred and violence against them.

Bin Laden is by no means alone in pursuing this warlike mobilization. The Venezuelan terrorist Vladimir Illich Ramirez Sanchez, a "revolutionary" who converted to Islam in 1975 and is better known by his *nom de guerre* Carlos, straightforwardly declared in an interview on October 21, 2001, that the terrorist attacks of 9/11 "hit the command centers of Yankee imperialist aggression against the peoples of the world: military in the case of the Pentagon, speculative-financial in New York." And he added: "The dead are nearly all enemy soldiers, wearing a uniform at the Pentagon or a tie in New York." The terrorist, who claims to have remained a Communist despite his conversion to Islam, does not conceal his sympathy for the "revolutionary" struggle of bin Laden: "The struggle of Sheikh Osama bin Laden to liberate the three occupied holy cities, Mecca, Medina, and Jerusalem, is also my struggle." After asserting his fervent commitment to the Palestinian cause, Carlos ends with the statement that "Bush, Jr. has launched a crusade against the Muslim people of Afghanistan," and that "*jihad* is the response."[102]

In Saudi Arabia, Sheikh Hamud al-Shuaibi—the author of a *fatwa* condemning the American attacks in Afghanistan—gave a simple answer on the internet to the question of whether a holy war was permissible: "*Jihad* is allowed against infidels like the Jews, Christians, and atheists."[103] This is a call for a new-style global war, pitting against each other not two coalitions of states but two civilizational blocs: the modern Western (or Westernized) world and the Muslim world, but also, within the latter, "true Muslims" and "hypocrites and traitors." Islamic terrorism represents the first real attempt to implement the pessimistic culturalist vision of "international relations" for which Samuel Huntington in 1993 drew up the model.[104] His "clash of civilizations" thesis is translated by "anti-imperialist" Islamists into the code of religious warfare, where it takes on the summary features of Manichean dualism. Mullah Omar, "supreme leader" of the Taliban, declared shortly after the start of American bombing: "This is not a war between Mullah Omar and America; it is a religious war."[105] The statement by bin Laden broadcast on November 3, 2001, was quite unambiguous in this regard:

"This war is fundamentally religious. . . . Those who try to cover this crystal-clear fact . . . are deceiving the Islamic nation. . . . The masses which moved in the East and West have not done so for the sake of Osama. Rather, they moved for the sake of their religion. This is because they know that they are right and that they resist the most ferocious, serious, and violent Crusade campaign against Islam since the message was revealed to Mohammed. . . . Bush openly and clearly said that this war is a crusader war. . . . Those who claim that they are the leaders of the Arabs and continue to appeal to the United Nations have disavowed what was revealed to the Prophet Mohammed. . . . This is the United Nations from which we have suffered greatly. Under no circumstances should any Muslim or sane person resort to the United Nations. The United Nations is nothing but a tool of crime. . . . Our brothers in Kashmir have been subjected to the worst forms of torture for over fifty years. . . . As for what is taking place in Palestine, [it] cannot be tolerated by any nation."[106]

To this simple vision of a "clash of civilizations," however, Islamist terrorism adds a neoracist program for extermination of the two figures ostensibly resisting the Islamicization of the human race—that is, "the Jews" and "the Americans" (or, in some versions, "the Christians").

This kind of demagogy is capable of seducing minds molded by Communist propaganda, which in turn are able to sway large numbers of people well beyond the residual circle of Communist militants. The historian Annie Kriegel once postulated that "anti-Zionism is to communism what anti-Semitism was to Nazism."[107] Today this needs to be revised: ideologies that criminalize Zionism and demonize America are to neocommunism and neoleftism what redemptive anti-Semitism was to Nazism. Islamist discourse plays the role of translating and exposing the "anti-Zionism" of circles that still think of themselves as progressive: the real content of "anti-Zionism" is an exterminatory Judeophobia. This genocidal program also includes fragments of the anti-globalization that has become the fashionable common sense. Thus, in a communiqué issued in the 1990s, the Islamic Jamaa Mujahedeen declared that they were rising up against "world Judaism," the IMF, and the World Bank.[108] All that is missing is the World Trade Organization. . . .

Despite the nakedness of this repulsive message, it is noticeable that radical milieux opposed to globalization have been sliding toward an absolute anti-Westernism. In this vision a demonized United States and Europe are considered guilty for their respective past histories—hence the injunction to repent and the demand for financial reparations for slavery and colonialism, or even the "genocide" of the Africans—while similarly the image of Israel tends to become indistinguishable from that of Islamist propaganda. The West, being inherently guilty, is required to show infinite repentance.[109] The West embodies evil, as in a Gnostic view of the world. A new wave of anti-Westernism accompanies the critique of "neoliberal globalization," to the point where it actually becomes part of the vulgate of the "new radicalism" [*les nouvelles radicalités*[110]]. Since September 11, 2001, this hold of Gnostic anti-Westernism has been especially striking, in the way the accusatory finger has been pointed both at Islamist terrorism and at the Western riposte, on the assumption that anti-American terrorism is the product of an American imperialism that is itself a kind of proto-terrorism. The terrorist evil thereby becomes a derivative evil, fully explicable in terms of its causes, whereas America and the West in general embody the original prototype. With a revolutionary perspective more or less discreetly abandoned,[111] the anti-globalization movement has constructed a set of heroic figures of "resistance" along the lines of the Proletariat (which has nothing and is therefore a bearer of hope): the Unemployed, the Unregistered Immigrant, the Homeless, the Imprisoned, the Palestinians. The West as demonic original cause appears in the following awkward and confused statements by a doctrinaire Third Worldist who does not dare say what she really thinks, or everything that she thinks:

"It has often been said that the 5,500 deaths on September 11 were the bloody bill paid by the United States for its arrogant hegemony over the weakest people on earth. In fact, the thread leading to this carnage goes back further, and does not concern only the American hyperpower onto which Europe rather too hastily unburdens its own misdeeds. . . . The West cannot be held alone responsible for the identity convulsions of its designated Others, who wish to remain other. But nor can it be totally exonerated of them. It is there that we should seek the reasons why the blood of September 11 did not cause a general outcry in the South, among those who believe—wrongly—that the American dead can serve as a balm for their wretched lot. . . . Does not Islam inspire fear because its very closeness brings phantoms back to life? It is a unique Other, offspring of the same Abrahamic matrix, herald of the same monotheist revelation that for centuries has set absolutes in competition with one another around the Mediterranean and its outer fringes. It is capable of the same messianic totalitarianism of which Christianity was guilty in its time, and which can be found again in today's Israel."[112]

A stream of similar appreciations has thus tended to dilute the category of "terrorism" into something more general, with the aim of placing an equal sign between Islamist terrorism and all forms of counterterrorism deployed by Western states and Israel. The latter, in particular, is accused of inheriting the accursed past of "Christianity" (what confused shorthand!), of being the living incarnation of "messianic totalitarianism." Imperceptibly, this declaration of equivalence turns into unequal treatment: whereas the Third Worldist ideologue of anti-globalization consents to recognize the existence of "extremists" in the "Arab-Muslim world" and to allow them numerous mitigating circumstances, she denounces "messianic totalitarianism" as an invention of the Christian West, now taken up and continued by Israel. The attitude of "repentance," which affects only Western countries (with France and Germany as the most willing), forms the basis for a retrospective demonization of the West (Israel included). Bin Laden's video statement of October 2001, which was intended only for al-Qaeda sympathizers, exploits the widely held favorable view of "good" terror used in the name of resistance to American or "Zionist" imperialism: "Bad terror is terror practiced against our people by the United States and Israel. What we practice is good terror, which will prevent them from doing what they do."[113] In the new world climate following the 9/11 attacks on America, which has brought forward extremes and introduced a period of hazily defined wars, the symbolic "striking power" of this Islamized Judeophobia can only become stronger.

TWO

Israelophobia and Palestinophilia: The Paths of Hatred

THERE ARE MANY indications that since the late 1990s, specifically with regard to France, the question of anti-Semitism—a term I consider imprecise but use here and there to reflect current usage—has again been seriously posed. The year 2000 saw a sharp rise in the number of incidents of anti-Semitic violence reported by the Ministry of the Interior (a total of 116, up from 9 the year before), as well as of anti-Semitic threats (up from 60 to 603).[1] In October 2000 acts of violence increased, at a time when Israeli-Palestinian clashes linked to the second Intifada were receiving high media attention. From October 1, 2000, until the beginning of November 2001, nearly 200 attacks on Jews were recorded in France.

The power of images worked against Israel in that fall of 2000, as television showed over and over again the unbearable sequence leading up to the death by gunfire of the child Mohammed, and the enormous compassion of viewers toward that incident intensified the image of Palestinians as victims. The idea of the innocent victim could not have found better media support; the image of the Palestinian became one with that of a child martyred by a pitiless army. The legend of ritual murder, with its stereotype of the "cruel and bloodthirsty Jew," provided an interpretive schema in which Tsahal, the Israeli defense force, became an army devoted to the butchering of innocents. This was enough to erase the images of *fedayeen* attacking kibbutz day nurseries in the 1970s, and to cast in a milder light the many indiscriminate attacks on Israeli civilians by suicide bombers, or the jubilant lynching of Israeli soldiers.[2]

Early in October 2000, the synagogues at Les Ulis and Trappes (both south of Paris) and at Bondy (east of Paris) were set on fire;[3] there were also reports of firebomb attacks on other synagogues (most notably at Villepinte, Clichy-sous-Bois, Creil, Colombes, Longjumeau, Garges-lès-Gonesses, and Chevilly-la-Rue), the use of cars as battering rams at synagogues, and physical assaults on individual Jews. Threatening phone calls increased, as did anti-Jewish graffiti in the suburbs of Paris and Lyons as well as in Strasbourg, Annemasse, and Toulon.[4] On December 23, 2000, fire devastated a Jewish kindergarten in the 4th arrondissement of Paris.

These acts of violence and threats against Jews, little reported or even hushed up in the media, did not end with the new year.[5] Here I shall just mention a few examples. On February 25, 2001, at Sarcelles in the northern suburbs of Paris, an explosion due to a firebomb seriously damaged a building at the Tifferet-Israel school. On May 5, 2001, one hundred religious objects were stolen from private individuals living in the same block, and then burned. On the night of August 6–7, 2001, also in the Paris region, an arson attack took place at the synagogue in Clichy-sous-Bois; on September 12 a lock was forced at the main door of the Pantin synagogue, while the police at Villeneuve-la-Garenne responded to a bomb warning at the local synagogue (they found a gas canister with an explosive device but no actual fuse); on September 15 a group of youths insulted and threw stones at worshipers on their way to the evening service at the Clichy-sur-Seine synagogue, more stones were thrown at the synagogue in Massy, and similar attacks took place against the synagogues in Garges-lès-Gonesse and Villepinte; and on October 6 a Molotov cocktail caused a fire at the synagogue in Stains. More disturbing still was the arson attack on October 28 that partially destroyed a Jewish nursery and primary school in Marseilles,[6] whose main building was covered with anti-Jewish inscriptions: "Death to the Jews!", "Long live bin Laden!", "Bin Laden will conquer!"[7]

Furthermore, we should bear in mind the growing number of minor anti-Jewish incidents. Here we shall just mention a few examples, which are representative of ordinary Judeophobia. Fall 2000: "You bunch of dirty Jews!" a telephone caller said menacingly on October 2, in a call to the Parisian synagogue on rue Gresset where an incendiary bottle was thrown; "You dirty Jew, we'll have your hide," were the words spoken to a young Jew on October 8 as he was being beaten in the street in Belleville; on the night of October 11–12 the police in Puteaux found anti-Semitic graffiti ("Death to the Jews," "Long live Palestine," "Death to Barak") on the shutters of several shops and a bank in the city center; on October 28 a boy aged twelve and a half, who was on his way to the "8 Mai 1945" synagogue in Créteil, was attacked by a man (whom he described as being of North African appearance) who twisted his arm, punched and insulted him: "You dirty Jewish son of a bitch, I'm gonna kill you. And if you blabber about it, I'll come and kill you." Fall 2001: on September 10 the president of the Drancy synagogue received a letter containing the phrases "Death to the Jews" and "Hell is awaiting you"; on September 11, while scenes of jubilation in Barbès (18th arrondissement of Paris) greeted news of the attacks in the United States, a thirteen-year-old boy was insulted and beaten up as he left a Jewish school at Aubervilliers, and a young Jewish girl was run over by a car (which then sped off) as she left the Ozar Hatorah school at Sarcelles; on September 12, "Long live bin Laden" and "Death to the Jews" were found on the walls of the Turgot Lycée in Paris; on September 21 some fifteen second-generation North Africans shouted, "We're gonna kill your mother and father" at a rabbi in Villepinte; the next day two men with knives (described by witnesses as "Arabs") threatened worshipers at a synagogue in the 19th arrondissement of Paris; on September 27 a man put a rifle to his shoulder and made as if to open fire on the synagogue at Vitry; on October 18 pupils at a Jewish school in Saint-Ouen were chased and roughed up; and on October 24 some individuals shouted "Death to the Jews" in front of a kosher butcher's shop in the 19th arrondissement of Paris.[8] These incidents seem retrospectively to give the character of prophesy to Heinrich Heine's irony: "Judaism? Do not speak to me about that, doctor, I would not wish it upon my worst enemy. Insults and shame are all it brings: it is not a religion, it is an affliction."[9]

An analysis of opinion poll results in 1988–1991 and 1999–2000 shows that the proportion of Judeophobes in the French population has remained more or less stable, with a hard core of approximately 10 percent, but that the numbers who are ashamed of their anti-Semitism are smaller than in the past. Similarly, it is noticeable that anti-Jewish prejudices and stereotypes are less and less disguised, more and more overt. The stereotypical image of Jewish power and domination ("Jews have too much power") was endorsed by approximately 20 percent of respondents in 1988 and 1991, by 31 percent in 1999, and by 34 percent in 2000.[10] Judeophobia, then, is expressed more and more directly and clearly.

But the weakening of the prohibition on anti-Jewish utterances (the "lifting of taboos," as some would put it) does not exclude the appearance of new, euphemistic forms of Judeophobia, expressed indirectly or symbolically[11] through various attributions of praise and blame: demonization of "Zionism" and "Israel" (as incarnations of "world Judaism," Jewishness, or "the eternal Jew"), and glorification of the supposed "victims of Zionist imperialism" (Palestinians, Arabs, Muslims).

In France, Judeophobic attitudes (views expressed, insults, threats, etc.) have been carried along by the dominant Israelophobia and largely incorporated into the field of the ideologically acceptable. Even certain kinds of Judeophobic behavior (physical assaults on individuals seen as "Jews," punitive strikes, arson attacks on synagogues, Jewish schools, etc.) fail to prompt "anti-racist" demonstrations or to arouse a sense of outrage among those who specialize in outrage over acts of "discrimination." For a number of years in France, organized anti-racist militants have been passionately campaigning against the selective ban on young people of North African or black African descent at certain discotheques and nightclubs. The method of "testing," designed to reveal actual discrimination at the door of certain establishments and thus to enable legal action, has mainly been used by an organization called SOS Racisme. In my view, the only reason for the emphasis given to this minor form of anti-racist struggle is that it is easy to organize.[12] It does highlight the practice whereby "bouncers," more or less on management instructions, treat different groups of young people selectively, often with reference to their facial appearance but also to their clothing. But discrimination in employment and housing, which is more difficult to prove, is both more serious and more significant.[13] "Testing" thus threatens to become a diversion, feeding the illusion that it will gradually erode racism.

We find nothing similar when the victims of ethnically motivated violence—for example, children on their way to school—happen to be Jewish. It is a strange anti-racism that carefully separates good from bad victims of stigmatization and discrimination, or that considers only young people "of immigrant descent" to be potential victims of "racism" or "exclusion."[14] Here, understandably enough, the standard image of the "young person" as a "victim"—a "young person" being a euphemism for anyone between about twelve and twenty-six years of age, vaguely perceived as "Arab" or African by facial appearance[15]—finds acceptable concrete expression.[16] Other forms of stigmatization and discrimination, especially those affecting Jews, leave these anti-racists cold, incredulous, or embarrassed. Their anti-racism is selective in its compassion, which is triggered only in campaigns on behalf of "the excluded." For this pseudo-anti-racism, Jews are no longer—or by nature never have been—excluded, dominated, or subject to discrimination; they are not victims, and so it is permissible to place them among those who exclude, dominate, and discriminate. This leads to a denial that any form of anti-Semitism exists in France, at the very moment when a new wave of Judeophobia is sweeping the country. Often the denial is self-interested, being itself one of the symptoms of the phenomenon whose reality is denied.

The recent wave of Judeophobia is not mainly an endogenous phenomenon: it does not involve a resurgence of nationalist or racist anti-Semitism *à la française*[17] but rather an adaptation to contemporary French political culture of an anti-Jewish imaginative complex that is quite widespread in today's world. A repulsive myth has been constructed on an international scale over the past half-century, in which the demonic figure of "Jews-Israelis-Zionists" serves as the basis for a Manichean opposition between bloodthirsty butchers and innocent victims (Palestinians/Arabs). Compassionate pro-Palestinism is thus combined with compulsive anti-Israelism. To achieve maximum effectiveness, this propaganda theme links up with a string of polemical equations: Jews = Zionists (= Israelis); Zionism = colonialism, imperialism, and racism; Sharon = Hitler (or a fascist); Israelis = Nazis (or fascists).[18] In "anti-Zionist" propaganda, references to the person of Ariel Sharon are in themselves an accusation, since they do not name the Israeli prime minister as the man behind a reprehensible or dangerous policy but evoke a repulsive myth centered on a demonic "Nazi" type.

Two decades of Palestinian and (ostensibly left-wing) pro-Palestinian propaganda have built up Sharon into a kind of Hitler substitute. No sooner said than done: the mere mention of Sharon's name has a performative value, involving a *reductio ad Hitlerum*[19] based on polemical identification of the Israeli general as "the butcher of Sabra and Shatila" (a massacre itself wrongly characterized as a micro-genocide, so that Sharon's "Nazification" can be given a whiff of the obvious).[20] The deliberate misinterpretation of the massacres at the Palestinian camps of Sabra and Shatila—in fact a savage act by Lebanese Christians bent on avenging the many Palestinian exactions on their territory[21]—cleared the way for a series of polemical constructs: Sharon the "butcher," the Israeli army as killer of innocents, the "terrorist" State of Israel. The result is a paradoxical and intellectually monstrous inversion: in a part of the world where nationalist or Islamic-fundamentalist dictatorships of a military or military-police character abound, the only pluralist democracy, the State of Israel, is likened to a military regime over which the devil incarnate presides in the person of Ariel Sharon. The central concept may be illustrated by an extract from a Palestinian "anti-Zionist" pamphlet, written before the Islamization of the Palestinian cause and widely distributed until the 1990s:

"Apart from its vital links with imperialism, and the fact that by nature it is inevitably alien to the Middle East in which it has chosen to establish itself, the political embodiment of Zionist colonialism (that is, the Zionist colonial state of Israel) has three essential characteristics: 1) *Its racial content and its racist line of conduct*; 2) *Its inclination to violence*; 3) *Its expansionist tendencies.* . . . Racism is not an accidental feature of the Zionist colonial state, nor a passing or temporary aspect of Israeli life; it is innate, essential, and permanent, because it is inherent in Zionist ideology itself as well as in the motives behind Zionist colonization and the creation of the Zionist state. . . . Zionist racial identification has three corollaries: *racial self-segregation*, *racial exclusivism*, and *racial suprematism*. These are the basic principles of Zionist ideology."[22]

In the new intellectualized discourse of Judeophobia, terms such as "genocide," "ethnocide," or "apartheid" are systematically used to pillory all manner of Israeli policies. Propagandists and others seeking to influence people on behalf of the Palestinian cause try to spread the idea of a basic "asymmetry between the Palestinians (the occupied) and the Israelis (the occupiers),"[23] and to stigmatize the "apartheid system" or "racial segregation" supposedly established by the "Zionist racists." One of those who have put forward this view is Marwan Bishara, in his *Palestine/Israel: Peace or Apartheid*, a book of propaganda that serves to mobilize French left-wing opinion against Israel and to sow in people's minds the premises for a final solution to the conflict through the dismantling of the Jewish state. For if the State of Israel really is a "racist" state that has institutionalized "segregation" and "apartheid,"[24] it is an urgent necessity to destroy it, just as the apartheid system was abolished in South Africa in May 1994. Repeated analogies of Israel and South Africa[25]

are part of the basic vocabulary of anti-Israeli Newspeak.[26]
The old "anti-racist," "anti-colonialist," "anti-imperialist,"
and "anti-fascist" rhetoric is here used to construct an absolutely Satanic composite of "United States/Israel/the West."
Islamic revolutionaries have been taking up the old anti-
Zionist clichés: Sulaiman Abu Ghaith, for example, who is
presented as the spokesman for al-Qaeda, speaks of "America and its ally, the Zionist entity."[27] We recognize here the
new populist grand vision in which the evil "rich" are ranged
against the good "poor." For some in the West, through the
workings of a warped Christianity, this transfigured and
transfiguring poverty seems to bestow the right to hate, or
even to kill. It creates the basis for the mobilizing revolutionary myth of the "just struggle," which in its Islamist version
becomes "holy war." But Marxists and neo–Third Worldists
do not lag behind, as we may see from the title of a freneti-
cally "anti-Zionist" and reverently pro-Palestinian essay, Le
Péché originel d'Israël (Israel's Original Sin).[28] The charge is
drawn up in theological-religious terms: Israel embodies the
stain of a primal wrong that inaugurated its illegitimate political existence; the State of Israel is inherently guilty; its guilt
is self-grounding. Israel's "original sin" is its very birth.

On October 10, 2001, a member of the French Socialist
party revealed his deep convictions when he referred to the
American strikes against the Afghanistan of the Taliban and
bin Laden: "After all, Islam is the poor. And hitting out at
the poor makes you puke!"[29] Rich against poor, Westerners
(and "Zionists") against Muslims who are, "after all," supposed to be poor (poor Osama bin Laden, poor Prince Abdullah ben Abdalaziz al-Saud). And, well, a Socialist prefers
the poor; someone on the left should choose the party of the
poor against the party of the rich. The cliché about Islam as
the religion of the underprivileged, resting upon a Third
Worldist ideology, is capable of seducing followers of a

purely compassionate Christianity or a sentimental form of socialism. A left-wing identity can be rebuilt around sympathy for an ideologically transfigured Islam. The same is true of Christian identity, for dissatisfied Christians. This road of conversion to Islam is well marked: it was out of solidarity with "the religion of the vanquished, the poor, and the colonized" that the Catholic writer and Arabist historian Vincent "Mansour" Monteil converted to Islam as long ago as 1977. In a lecture in Tunis on February 15, 1978, he tried to justify his conversion by listing the "good causes" in which Islam would involve him:

"Faced with the two antagonistic and complementary imperialisms, with predatory neocolonialism and the permanent Zionist aggression, the decision to be a Muslim is for me a choice of camp. The Muslim camp, from Senegal to Indonesia, largely coincides with the Third World. It is the camp of the Palestinians, the most impoverished, most abandoned, most betrayed of human beings, victims as much of some of their brothers as of a racist Zionism whose very nature does not allow anything good to be expected of it. And it is the camp of the immigrant workers, those new slaves of our time."[30]

In this vision, "Muslims" in general are not only poor but are especially persecuted and exposed to attack and bombardment. This makes it possible to construct a figure of the essential victim, the victim by nature, as well as a corresponding figure of the aggressor with a "Zionist" or "American" face. The victims of "American-Zionist" aggression are therefore in a position of legitimate self-defense, so that all enemies of the "Zionists" are at the same time enemies of the "Americans"; they are nothing but "victims" (the "oppressed" and "humiliated," in Islamist rhetoric) or their spokesmen, "innocents" in justifiable revolt against the "infidels" and "hypocrites." It is a rough-and-ready dualism: on one side the dominating/arrogant West, on the other side

those who are intrinsically humiliated, exploited, and oppressed. The demonic polarization also occurs at the heart of
the Western democracies, between "pro-American Zionists"
and angelic neo-Third Worldists—a seductive Manichean vision for those who, in confusing a Christian moral disposi-
tion with the conditioned reflex of sentimental victimhood,
like to think of themselves as being always on the side of "the
victims." Thus, in the common sense of Palestinophilia,
where "anti-Zionist" propaganda has successfully written its
themes into the space of what is considered the right thing to
believe, every Palestinian comes to be seen as a symbol of
Christ, a legitimate inheritor of the Galilean, while the Jews
are rejected as intruders. Roger Garaudy should be acknowledged as having made a noteworthy contribution to this conversion of the Palestinians into Christ-like figures. In 1981,
for example, the former Stalinist wrote:

"It is therefore symbolic that, after the Six Day War, the
world discovered Palestinian—or, more precisely, Galilean—
poetry, one of whose noblest representatives, Mahmud Darwish (born in 1941), grew up in the very land where Christ
lived out all his dreams; he writes there today the poetry of
Calvary and the Passion, having composed in prison his 'To
my Mother . . .'."[31]

This play of symbols is not exhausted by its ludic function: it serves a propagandist purpose. By means of comparisons, analogies, and approximate identifications, the
"anti-Zionist" propagandist aims to convince his audience or
readership that today's Palestinians are in the same position
as Jesus and the early Christians—in short, that they are being persecuted and "put to death" by the Jews. This revives
the old charge of deicide, through various reformulations
("ethnocide," "genocide," etc.) that adapt it to the contemporary context. If the Palestinian is made into a convincingly
Christ-like figure, Palestinocide becomes a form of deicide!

It is important to establish the truth about the way in which the "international community," at least as it is embodied in the United Nations, uses double standards in its treatment of Palestinians and Israelis—or, if one prefers, Palestinian nationalism (an inspiring liberation struggle) and Jewish nationalism (a deplorable leftover from the nineteenth century, or a form of "racism" and "fascism"). For the truth can be reached here only by overturning the clichés that ideology makes appear obvious. On the one hand, those confirmed as "victims" in the imagination of the epoch have an interest in benefiting as much as they can from this image, and hence in not risking its cancellation through the creation of a Palestinian state that would make the Palestinian people appear ordinary. On the other hand, the Jewish people, with its back to the wall, is searching for peace accords that will offer it not subsidies but respect for its right to exist. In one indispensable work, the historian Shlomo Ben-Ami, formerly Israel's foreign minister in the Barak government, puts his finger on the essential point:

"Contrary to the stupid anti-Semitic cliché of 'Jewish power,' the Zionist movement has always been the national movement of a Jewish people deprived of support, a hunted people, a victim of genocide, which risked annihilation if it made a mistake at the hour of historical decision. The Palestinians, seemingly the weakest side in the conflict, have never acted as the Zionist movement did because of its lack of other options. History has known only very rarely, if at all, situations where a national movement has 'suffered' from such a surplus of international support as the Palestinian movement. At each decisive historical crossroads, the international community has given them the sense—and this is evidently true concerning the Arab world—that they have a right to expect more. . . . The way in which the Palestinian national movement has been pampered by the international community is without precedent in modern history, and no less important is the fact that this has continued to pose an obstacle to any agreement."[32]

This analysis allows a redistribution of arrogance and vulnerability, of refusal to accept a negotiated solution and eagerness to define the conditions for a lasting peace.[33] The main hindrance to mutual recognition of the two peoples, and therefore to any political agreement without reservations, is the establishment of the Palestinians in the transfiguring posture of oppressed victims, either in the Marxist utopia of the proletariat as the class bearing the future of the world, or in the Islamist mythology of the *jihad* victoriously waged by true believers against the modern/Western world of infidels.

Radical Islamism is the anti-capitalism of visionaries turned fanatical by resentment against the West (including the "Zionist entity"), whose de facto hegemony they see as a profound humiliation or even an unbearable provocation. In the Islamist movements, Islam is not reducible to a political ideology in the Western sense, or to a "secular religion" such as nationalism or communism;[34] rather, it is an inexhaustible stock of answers to every imaginable question. The memory of the role played by Islam in anti-colonial struggles is revived and acted out again, prompting its transformation into a kind of cultural resistance to the hegemony of the West or "the rich countries of the North." The stereotype of the "rich Jew," once recycled in this way, blots out the reality of the plutocratic circles that finance Islamist networks and various terrorist organizations in the Arab-Muslim world. Islamist leaders, in a great variety of contexts, continually reassert and reformulate the notion of a worldwide Jewish plot. Thus, in an appeal dated November 12, 1982, which immediately reached a wide public on the occasion of a large Islamist rally in Algiers, Sheikh Abbassi Madani (an Islamic preacher and official spokesman of the FIS) and other signatories set forth a conspiracy theory as a way of explaining events—in particular the violent clashes of November 2 at Ben Aknun University. In time-honored fashion, the appeal reduced all figures of the enemy to a single identity:[35]

"There is not a shadow of doubt that all these incidents have been provoked by the cartel of international communism, freemasonry, Jewry, and American imperialism, with the collaboration of its agents propagating communism, racism, and Baathism. The aim is clear: to involve the wheels of state in executing a plot that follows in a direct line from the appalling massacres of Muslims in Lebanon, Palestine, and elsewhere in the Muslim world."[36]

The new anti-Jewish mythology is based on a Manichean dualism that structures the opposition between two entities: the intrinsically evil Jews and the intrinsically innocent Palestinians. The two types are further interpreted according to various antitheses that lend themselves to narrative illustration: butchers and victims, colonizers and colonized, dominators and dominated, oppressors and oppressed. This set of opposites is currently acquiring a religious coloration from the "Muslim/non-Muslim" schema, which makes it possible to establish an Islamist-style antithesis between "Westerners" and "believers," or "infidels" and "Muslims." The struggle against "Israeli-American imperialism," formerly conducted by the nationalists and Marxists of the Arab world, may thus be translated into Islamist Newspeak and celebrated as the final battle against the "Jews and Crusaders." The growing Islamization of the Intifada is evidence of this process:[37] Hamas and Islamic Jihad, following the model of Hezbollah in Lebanon,[38] are becoming the spearhead of Palestinian nationalism, which seems to be gradually dissolving into the Islamist cause.[39] "Hezbollah" is literally the "Party of God."

What appears to be emerging is a kind of national-Islamist synthesis; the growing Islamization of the Intifada goes hand in hand with its militarization.[40] The Palestinian cause, a mobilizing and rallying symbol in the world arena, is becoming the banner for all the varied enemies of the West—or, to be more precise, of the "Jewish" and "American" forces of evil. In this move toward neo-Palestinism, or pseudo-Palestinism, the ethnonym "Palestinian" operates as an eponym or pseudonym for every supposedly (or self-styled) innocent victim. Here "the West" should be understood as referring to a heterogeneous entity, an ideological hodgepodge produced by hostile passions in which the rejection of modernity en bloc merges with a challenge to liberal-democratic regimes and a blanket demonization of Christianity, Judaism, atheism, and secularism.[41]

It should be said that war might be declared on the West as it is either for (partly) good reasons or for monstrous reasons. For, of course, the West as it is does not embody perfection. One might, for example, honestly and legitimately raise questions about the foreign policy of the United States, which for so long aided and encouraged Islamist movements in the world, handled Saudi Arabia (the main hideout of the sponsors of Islamist terrorism) with kid gloves, and until the summer of 2001 continued to negotiate with the Taliban.[42] This is why, when one takes up the defense of the West, one must also now and then take the time, as good Westerners, to defend the West against itself—so that it tones down its arrogance, so that it does not show itself too naively self-satisfied or think of itself as perfectible. Although the West is valued for its singularity as the cradle of universal (or universalizable) legal ideas, it should be added at once that the West has not made those ideas a reality; liberty, truth, justice, or equality, for example, remain regulative ideas in the Kantian sense of the term. The West as it is, then, may and should be criticized, but it cannot be the only civilization that is made the object of a radical and comprehensive critique.

In any event, it is clear that the professionals of Islamist propaganda use now banal and widespread Manichean clichés as fuel for their incitement (their calls for *jihad*, or rather a new-style *jihad* involving suicide bombings),[43] and more generally as justification for their struggle to establish a worldwide Islamic state based on Islamic law ("the banner of Islam will fly all around the world," as a Pakistani mullah prophesied on October 8, 2001). This enables them to pass off their delirious will to conquest and their various terrorist enterprises as a just struggle on behalf of the underprivileged.

The Palestinian cause has become the main alibi for bin Laden–style terrorists with a gift for global communication. In the mid-1990s, bin Laden himself strongly condemned the *fatwa* issued by Mufti Ben Baz legitimizing the normalization of relations with Israel: "The Jewish enemy has not established himself in his country of origin. . . . But he is an enemy who has violated sacred Islamic land. . . . *Jihad* is a legitimate duty with regard to Palestine—*jihad* waged by the Umma to liberate that territory."[44] The reader will note that the "Zionist enemy" has here given way to the "Jewish enemy": the Islamization of radical anti-Zionism has the advantage that the absolute enemy is now clearly designated. Often, however, in Islamist texts of the 1980s and 1990s, Marxist-Leninist language denouncing "Zionist imperialism" exists alongside explicitly anti-Jewish language drawing upon the *Protocols of the Elders of Zion* or derivative conspiracy-theory pamphlets, livened up with quotations from the Koran.

This kind of ideological code-mixing marks Mohammed Yacine Kassab's *L'Islam face au nouvel ordre mondial* (Islam Facing the New World Order),[45] which presents itself as a handbook of geopolitics for a readership close to the FIS, the

Algerian Islamic Salvation Front. Israel, we are told, owes its existence to a "vast Judeo-Christian conspiracy,"[46] and the State of Israel plays an essential role in the Christian plot against Islam. The Algerian Islamist does not mind borrowing from a Marxist-style analysis of the "Zionist state" as a tool of the "imperialists," but his main inspiration is the global conspiracy theory to be found in anti-Jewish literature: "The Western world is dominated by a largely Jewish-controlled financial system and banking structures."[47] Jews operate "as an abscess that infects the body at the first opportunity."[48] To justify his denunciation of the "Judeo-Christian plot," Kassab quotes from the Koran (5:51): "Believers, do not ally yourselves with either Jews or Christians; they are allied with one another."[49] And he comments: "The affinities between Jews and Christians are so great that their complicity becomes total in relation to Islam."[50]

The call for *jihad* often appears in contexts where medical or pathological metaphors are used to stigmatize Jews, or where Jews are likened to animals. In a communiqué issued on March 17, 1997, the Egyptian Al-Jihad group (led by Ayman al-Zawahiri) and Tala'i al-Fath[51] declared: "The only way to recover our rights is the way of sacrifice and martyrdom, the one followed by the Jordanian *mujahed* who fired a whole round into the chests of the offspring of apes and pigs [Israeli schoolchildren!]."[52] The imam cited in the previous note glorified the Palestinian cause as "the Cause that most preoccupies Muslims . . ., the Cause of Palestine, Muslim, *mujaheeda* (combatant), and voluntary." And, addressing his "fighting brothers," he added: "You who find yourselves in the land of Palestine, the Palestine that struggles and resists, the land of pride and honor, the land of sorrows, sacrifice, struggle [*jihad*], and rejection, . . . your cause is our cause . . ., the strength of your intifada deeply moves us. . . . You are heroes in God's eyes, you have given hope back to our Umma, . . . our soldiers will conquer, we thank you for offering your lives to God . . ., do not despair, victory is near; in fact, the two sheikhs have reported in their *Sahih* that the imam of the Mujahedeen [the Prophet Mohammed], blessed be His name, said: 'The time is near when Muslims will fight the Jews and kill them, when the Jew will have to hide behind a stone or a tree, and the stone or tree will say to the Muslim: "You Muslim, you slave of God, there is a Jew hiding behind me, come closer and kill him." God is great! . . . My God, come to aid Islam and Muslims, . . . and destroy the enemies of religion, the Zionist Jews.'"[53]

On October 7, 2001, in a prerecorded video broadcast on the Arabic news channel Al Jazeera[54]—unwisely shown by other TV channels around the world—bin Laden called for *jihad* and justified the murderous attacks of September 11:

"There is America, hit by God in one of its softest spots . . . thank God for that. When the sword comes down [on America], . . . hypocrisy rears its ugly head. They deplore and they lament for those killers, who have abused the blood, honor, and sanctuaries of Muslims. The least that can be said about those people, is that they are debauched. They have followed injustice. They supported the butcher over the victim, the oppressor over the innocent child. May God show them His wrath and give them what they deserve. . . . I swear by God, . . . neither America nor the people who live in it will dream of security before we live it in Palestine, and not before all the infidel armies leave the land of Muhammad."[55]

In invoking the Palestinian cause to justify their program of terror and murder, the radical Islamist leaders convert the struggle against Israel into a final battle with the "infidels." Saddam Hussein already attempted a similar use of the Palestinian cause at the time of the Gulf War, without really making himself credible. But the polemical argument continually recurs in Islamist discourse, where it acquires its full meaning

and its maximum force. In an interview in March 1997, bin
Laden justified his *jihad* against the United States:
     "We declared *jihad* against the U.S. government, because
the U.S. government is unjust, criminal, and tyrannical. It has
committed acts which are extremely unjust, hideous, and
criminal, whether directly or through its support of the Israeli
occupation of . . . Palestine. And we believe the U.S. is directly responsible for those who were killed in Palestine,
Lebanon, and Iraq. . . . The U.S. government abandoned even
humanitarian feelings by these hideous crimes. It transgressed
all bounds and behaved in a way not witnessed before by any
. . . imperialist power in the world. Due to its subordination
to the Jews, the arrogance . . . of the U.S. regime has reached
the extent that they occupied the *qibla* of the Muslims [Ara-
bia], who are more than a billion in the world today."[56]
     Clearly, by exploiting the strong emotions invested in the
Palestinian cause, the demagogues of radical Islamism hope
to trigger a movement of international Islamic solidarity.
There are a number of converging signs that such solidarity
did indeed develop after September 11, 2001, even though
leaders or states that have been responsible, directly or indirectly, for anti-American or "anti-Zionist" terrorism issued
statements rhetorically denouncing the wave of terror. The
September attacks were greeted with displays of joy in Pakistan and the territories controlled by the Palestinian Authority; violent demonstrations in support of the Taliban and bin
Laden took place in many Muslim countries (from Pakistan
to Indonesia), and calls for *jihad* had a considerable reso-
nance. As Olivier Roy noted, bin Laden "knew how to Is-
lamize a latent anti-Americanism."[57] Those who justify 9/11
have often done so, directly or indirectly, in the name of the
Palestinian cause—especially when their words have been intended for Western consumption. On October 11, 2001, the
Arab League's ambassador in France admitted, with the usual

caution of his post, that "solidarity with the Palestinian cause" existed in every Muslim country, and he thought he could justify this by presenting it as a "transnational solidarity of identity."[58] The dangerous implication that there is a single Islamic civilization, a vast symbolic or imagined community with a basic underlying consensus, is not far from Samuel Huntington's postulate of a "clash of civilizations."

As skilled propagandists, the Islamist video demagogues can risk inverting responsibilities in response to an ideological demand. Since Israel or the West is ultimately to blame for everything, the military operations or acts of legitimate self-defense carried out by the victims of Islamist terrorism (whether Israel or the United States) can be condemned in turn as "terrorist"! The struggle for monopoly rights over the word "terrorism" is thus waged first and foremost by the terrorists themselves, or, to be more precise, by their unavowed spokespersons. If we are to believe them, Islamist terrorism is merely a just response of indignant Muslims to the unjust treatment of the Palestinians at the hands of "American," "Zionist," or "American-Zionist" imperialism. The sophistry becomes manifest as soon as attempts are made to apply this explanation or justification for Islamist terrorism to the Algerian situation: the terrible massacres committed by the Islamists of the GIA (Armed Islamic Group) have nothing to do with the Israeli-Palestinian conflict; they are not motivated by defense of the "just struggle of the Palestinian people"; and any demagogic presentation of them in this way lacks all credibility.[59] Palestinian adulators of the suicide-bomber "martyrs" who kill large numbers of Israeli civilians have no compunction about denouncing Israel's "terrorist state" or "state terrorism" when it eliminates an Islamist planner and organizer of a murderous attack. In a televised sermon on August 3, 2001, at the Sheikh Ijlin mosque in Gaza City, Sheikh Ibrahim Madhi openly called upon Muslims (beginning with

those in Palestine) to commit themselves to *jihad* against the
Jews: "A young boy told me: 'I am fourteen years old, and I
have four years left before I blow myself up among the Jews.'
I said to him: 'O my son, I pray to Allah to offer both you and
myself martyrdom.' The Koran is very clear on this point: the
worst enemies of the Islamic nation are the Jews, may Allah
fight them. All our spears should be pointing at the Jews, the
enemies of Allah, the nation that was cursed in Allah's Book;
Allah described them as apes and pigs, idolaters and worshipers of the calf. . . . The Jews fight you, but Allah will give
you sway over them. . . . Let he who attacks a soldier be
blessed. Let he who raises children in the spirit of *jihad* and
martyrdom be blessed. Let he who keeps a bullet to fire into
a Jew's head be blessed."[60]

The Taliban, for their part, will denounce the "terrorist
bombing" of their own terrorist bases or those they protect
in an Afghanistan they have subjected to their dehumanizing
dictatorship. The inversion of responsibilities is clearly illustrated by a letter from Osama bin Laden to his "Muslim
brethren in the chaste land of Pakistan, both civilians and
military," which was received on November 1, 2001, by Al
Jazeera television:

"The crusade against Islam has intensified and the killing
of the followers of Muhammad . . . has spread widely in
Afghanistan. . . . The world has been divided into two
camps: one under the banner of the cross, as Bush, the head
of infidelity, said, and another under the banner of Islam.
The Pakistani government has fallen under the banner of the
cross. . . . O supporters of Islam, . . . whoever believes in
God and Doomsday must not rest at ease until he upholds
right and its supporters and until God defeats falsehood and
its backers."[61]

In this international context, I would defend the following position. As it has been known throughout the world

since mid-September 2001, through reports in all the media, that Osama bin Laden's twofold message is, in essence, "Kill Americans and Jews wherever they are," any public identification or expression of solidarity with bin Laden implies approval of his anti-Jewish positions. This applies to the displays of joy or solidarity that the 9/11 attacks in America triggered in most Muslim countries, or to the celebratory shouts of "Osama! Osama!" that were heard in certain suburbs in France after September 2001, and that set up the terrorist leader as an avenging hero, a victorious figure in the revolt of humiliated Muslims against their ostensible enemies (the Great Satan or Little Satan). Bin Laden, head of the "Arab Afghans," is seen here as having devoted his life and wealth to *jihad*, a kind of "Che Guevara of Islam"[62] who is restoring the lost honor and dignity of the Muslim masses. Although Islamism and pro-Islamism thereby function as the new socialism of fools (or the imaginary socialism of the new fools), they are today also one of the most common indirect forms of Judeophobia.

THREE

Construction, Content, Functioning, and Metamorphoses of the "New Anti-Semitism": Toward the Islamization of Absolute Anti-Zionism

A CASE HAS BEEN rightly made that, after the Six Day War of June 1967, a "new anti-Semitism" began its worldwide career.[1] It centered on a mythical conspiracy theory that I have called absolute anti-Semitism,[2] with its two main bases in the Arab-Muslim world and the Soviet empire.[3] A number of traditional anti-Jewish themes have clustered around the demonical figures of Israel and a fantasy-world "Zionism": Jews plot together; Jews seek to conquer the world by all means; Jews are cruel and bloodthirsty by nature (hence the reactivation of old legends of "ritual murder"[4] or the poisoning of food and water supplies); Jews are "imperialistic," and so on.[5] In addition, there is the literature of Holocaust denial, with its claim that the genocidal gas chambers never even existed.[6] Its "popular," or anyway "popularizable," conclusion is that the Jews and their "allies" invented the "tall story" of their own extermination, and that they are therefore guilty of "the biggest lie ever"[7]—itself a recycled version of the old stereotype of Jews as "liars by nature." One is reminded of Hitler's homage to Schopenhauer in *Mein Kampf*:

"One of the greatest thinkers that mankind has produced has branded the Jews for all time with a statement which is profoundly and exactly true. He called the Jew 'The Great Master of Lies.' Those who do not realize the truth of that statement, or do not wish to believe it, will never be able to lend a hand in making Truth prevail."[8]

The charge of mendacity is at the heart of Holocaust denial, assuming as it does that—to quote Robert Faurisson's strong formulation—"Hitler never ordered nor admitted that anyone should be killed on account of his race or his religion."[9] Anyone who argues the opposite is therefore a liar. In a text dated June 16, 1978, Faurisson summarized his positions, in which a radical anti-Zionism is uppermost:

"The alleged 'gas chambers' and the alleged 'genocide' are one and the same lie. . . . This lie, essentially of Zionist origin, permitted a gigantic politico-financial swindle whose principal beneficiary is the State of Israel. . . . The principal victims of this lie and swindle are the Germans and Palestinians."[10]

The denial argument has subsequently made considerable headway in the Arab-Muslim world, especially through the efforts of Roger Garaudy,[11] who has been feted as a hero there since the appearance in 1996 of the original French edition of his *The Mythical Foundations of Israeli Policy*.[12] Thus in the May 1999 issue of a Palestinian periodical, we read:

"No one in the West dares to speak out against the fiction of a Nazi holocaust of the Jews in Europe. Since the end of

the Second World War, the victors have imposed their hegemony on history: they have created the legend of the Holocaust in order to fleece the whole world by using the image
of the terrible Nazi. . . . The legend of the Holocaust . . . has
had to face the powerful winds of truth, which have had no
difficulty in uprooting it. Dozens of Western intellectuals and
politicians . . . have refuted false assertions of this legend
. . .; the renowned French intellectual Roger Garaudy . . . has
laid bare the founding myths of the State of Israel, particularly the myth of the Holocaust."[13]

The many "updated" editions of the *Protocols of the Elders of Zion*, and their widespread distribution since the fall
of 1967, testify to the emergence of this Judeophobic configuration.[14] There is a tendency nowadays to forget the extreme virulence of anti-Israeli propaganda at the time of the
Six Day War, when Arab radio stations regularly broadcast
calls for murder such as the following little ditty:

"Slit their throats, slit, slit, and show no pity.
Slit, slit, slit, and throw their head in the desert.
Slit, slit, slit, as much as you like."[15]

The defeat of the Arab armies in June 1967 marked the
beginning of the decline of that pan-Arab nationalism of
which Nasser had made himself the undisputed head. It left
behind, however, an attachment to "that inseparably cultural, historical, and political Arabism which has haunted
[public opinion in the Arab countries] since the earliest days
of the independence struggles against the Ottomans and then
against the British, the French, the Zionist movement, Israel,
and finally 'American imperialism' [always described as
linked to 'international Zionism' and Arab 'reaction']."[16]
The Israeli invasion of Lebanon, in the summer of 1982, provided the opportunity for Israel's enemies to launch another
propaganda barrage of accusations of imperialism, conspiracy, and cruelty. From the fall of 1982, both the Palestinians

and all the Arab-Muslim countries made massive symbolic use of the massacres committed by Lebanese Phalangist units in the Palestinian camps of Sabra and Shatila between September 16 and 18, 1982.[17] "Anti-Zionist" propaganda then gained fresh impetus by playing up the Palestinians who fell victim after the first Intifada was launched in December 1987. The youngest stone-throwers, aged less than eighteen, were glorified as "heroes" or "martyrs," and in the following years a popular political religion took shape around the figure of the supposedly martyred *shahid*.[18] Since the late 1980s, Islamist circles have had little trouble integrating this political-religious theme into their calls for mobilization.

It is no exaggeration to suppose that, since the mid-1990s, a second wave of the "new anti-Semitism" has been sweeping the planet, affecting Africa and Asia, making Judeophobic themes more extreme, and hastening their shift from the left to the right of the spectrum. At the same time these themes have been "Islamized," as the leaders of radical Islamism have reformulated the old idea of a Jewish world plot in the form of a "Zionist" or "Western" conspiracy against "Muslims." The Hamas charter is evidence of this: "The Zionist plan is limitless. After Palestine, the Zionists aspire to expand from the Nile to the Euphrates. . . . Their plan is embodied in the *Protocols of the Elders of Zion*, and their present conduct is the best proof of what we are saying. . . . There is no way out except by concentrating all powers and energies to face this Nazi, vicious Tatar invasion. . . . The Islamic Resistance Movement considers itself to be the spearhead of the circle of struggle with world Zionism."[19]

After the suicide attacks of 9/11, Hani Ramadan inverted the responsibility for them and called for a mobilization against the impious West: "As for us, dear brothers in Islam, it is important to become aware through these events that the Western world is organizing against us, and that it is organizing against the danger represented by Islamism."[20] Nor did bin Laden fail to denounce the machinations of impious Westerners against good Muslims: "The nations of the *kufar* openly admit their conspiracies against Muslims."[21] As Michèle Tribalat has shown in her recent work, this propaganda exerts its persuasive power especially over young Muslims. Here, for example, is the reaction of one young candidate for *jihad*, who does not conceal his enthusiasm and impatience, nor, of course, his image of the absolute enemy: "There is a need for leaders, for training places. For me *jihad* takes place on all fronts; all resistance movements must get organized, for the enemy is one and the same in Palestine, Chechnya, Afghanistan, etc.: it is ZIONISM. I know all the *jihad* speeches, but I hope soon to hear something like: go to such and such a place, undergo training, then go to such and such a front, in such and such a way. It is not only me but thousands of young Muslims who are waiting."[22]

At a demonstration in Islamabad for peace and against terrorism, organized in support of Pakistani President Pervez Musharaf, a journalist asked a schoolgirl: "What do you think about coexistence with the other religions: with Jews or Christians?" And she answered: "The Jews want to rule over Muslims, to rule over the Third World. But Muslims are strong. They will prevail. . . . When Islam conquers, there will be peace for the whole world."[23] Nor should we forget to mention that Syrian President Bashar al-Assad, in a speech welcoming Pope John Paul II to Damascus on May 5, 2001, thought it a self-evident fact that the Jews "try to kill all the principles of all religions, with the same mentality that made them betray and torture Jesus Christ, and in the same way that they tried to betray the Prophet Mohammed."[24] The new Syrian dictator was expressing the state Judeophobia that has long been part of the scene in most Arab and Muslim countries.

The main features of the new global Judeophobia are the following:

(1) Massive and virulent use is made of anti-racism for anti-Jewish purposes. A monstrous example of this occurred at the World Conference against Racism, organized by the United Nations at Durban, South Africa, between August 31 and September 8, 2001,[25] when "Zionism" was again identified, more viciously than ever, as "a form of racism and racial discrimination."[26] (Compare the sadly famous Resolution 3379, passed with an overwhelming majority by the UN General Assembly, on November 10, 1975.[27]) At a deeper level, the charge of "racism" (and therefore of "apartheid," "genocide," etc.) turns against Jews-Zionists-Israelis the old negative interpretation of the election of Israel: that is, the denunciation of the "chosen people" as a people giving itself every right to dominate, conquer, oppress, and destroy.

(2) Images and arguments associated with Holocaust denial become a banal feature of discourse (denunciation of the "Holocaust industry," doubts about the number of victims, historical relativism ending in the equation of Western democracies with totalitarian regimes, and so on).[28]

(3) Modes of legitimation are borrowed not only from the old Third Worldist anti-imperialism, pious anti-colonialism, and demonological anti-Americanism but also from radical critiques of neoliberal globalization (some of whose high-profile leaders are open enemies of Israel).

(4) There is massive dissemination and uncritical reception of the myth of the intrinsically "good Palestinian"—innocent victim *par excellence*, descended from all previous figures of the victim in world history, beginning with Christ. A shift of historical identities takes place, such that "today's

real persecuted Jews are the Palestinians"—a role reversal making them victims of "genocide" committed by "the Jews."

(5) The imagination and affects mobilized by new "all-is-woe" demagogues are reinvested in radically Israelophobic and Palestinophiliac discourse. Since the 1980s these demagogues, following in the wake of Abbé Pierre,[29] have politically and morally perverted the Christian imperative of charity into a denunciation of "rich" individuals and countries, and justified calls for intifada against all institutions and their representatives.

(6) Interaction takes place in various ways with the Islamist (let us say, pan-Islamic) view of the world, whose branding of Israel as "little Satan" combines with Western-style demonization of "Zionism."

Denunciation of a "Zionist" plot is the first step in an argument leading to the conclusion that it is necessary to strike back at the conspirators, and therefore to calls for a *jihad*. Jewish nationalism,[30] unlike Palestinian nationalism (a "just liberation struggle"), is accused either by turns or altogether as a form of colonialism, imperialism, racism, and fascism! Similarly, Israeli policy is regularly described as racist, colonialist, and genocidal. The aim is to monopolize the words "racism" and "genocide," so that the only symbolic beneficiaries are Muslim, Arab, and especially Palestinian "victims"; monopolizing the legitimate use of these highly emotive terms thereby delegitimizes any application of them to the Nazi genocide of European Jews. It is a theft of memory, an obliteration of history, an improper solicitation of an affective legacy. In his opening address to the International Symposium on Zionism and Racism (Tripoli, July 1976)—which was attended by Edward Said,[31] among others—the president of the Libyan Bar Association, Abdullah Sharafuddin declared:

"Our world is now faced with the emergence of a new type of Nazism whose followers claim that their doctrine goes back a long way in history. The truth is that they have departed from the laws of Abraham and Moses so far as to adhere to the devilish doctrine of, 'I am better than others; I was made of fire, and they were made of clay.' Zionism, with its inhumane ethnic, racist principles, with its devilish schemes which generate chaos all over the world, with its dangerous plans to dominate, . . . and with its beastly octopus which has almost a decisive role in directing the policies of the greatest countries in the world, cannot be viewed as a threat to this region alone, but to the whole world."[32]

Zionism, then, is a new "Nazism" threatening to dominate and destroy the whole of the human species.[33] For the Islamist rhetoric of the late twentieth and early twenty-first centuries, the targets of attack are the threats supposedly directed against Muslims. Thus, in a context where Western elites never tire of calling for the avoidance of "Islamophobic" utterances,[34] the head of the Islamic Center in Geneva, Hani Ramadan, coolly denounces "the genocide being organized against Muslims."[35] Not to be outdone, bin Laden has remained true to character with his colorful hyperbolic denunciations based on crude anti-Western slogans: "The genocide of Muslims is a legal act under the world charter of the United Nations. . . . Not one square inch of the Muslim Umma remains unpierced by the poisoned arrows and swords."[36] This rhetoric appeals entirely to emotions triggered by the use of such terms: it does not encourage critical analysis of the relationship of forces but seeks to arouse indignation, compassion, sympathy, or empathy with the supposed victims. It is the politics of tears and rage, cynically conducted.

An intellectual version of this Islamist monopolization of victimhood may be found in the writings of those doctrinaires who try to present a face more culturally acceptable to the Western public.[37] Tariq Ramadan, for instance, a charming

Islamist born and settled in Switzerland, elegantly denounces "Islamophobia" or "what certain British sociologists call 'anti-Muslim racism,'" with the authority of a highly respectable "lecturer" (in philosophy and Islamic studies).[38] Here I will make just one remark: these British sociologists are contributing, as "useful fools," to the dogma of multiculturalism (or, more precisely, multicommunalism), which prohibits any criticism of the many forms of Islamism that have found especially favorable soil in Britain. Today's neoleftist social scientists, in London as in Paris, often function as "useful fools" for Islamism (which does not mean they cannot give their consent, and therefore their complicity, without taking the slightest risk). In the name of absolute respect for religious pluralism, London has thus become one of the main reference points in Europe for Islamists of all persuasions.[39]

The declaration of the NGO Forum, adopted on September 2, 2001 (a week before 9/11) at the World Conference against Racism in Durban, again hauled the State of Israel before an imaginary Nuremberg Tribunal and defined it as an inherently racist entity. Delegates from Jewish NGOs were booed, and shouts of "Death to the Jews!" came from all sides. Following on from the UN resolution of November 10, 1975, more than four thousand humanitarian and charitable NGOs from around the world, with a few noteworthy exceptions, revived the link between Zionism and racism, branded Israel a "racist state" conducting an "apartheid policy" against innocent Palestinians, denounced "acts of genocide" by the Jewish state, and even accused it of "crimes against humanity."[40] Here are a few quotes from this delirious document: "The Palestinian people . . . is subject to . . . racist methods amounting to Israel's brand of apartheid and other racist crimes against humanity" (para. 98); "A basic 'root cause' of Israel's . . . acts of genocide and practices of ethnic cleansing is a racist system, which is Israel's brand of apartheid" (para. 99); "We declare Israel a racist, apartheid state in which Israel's brand of apartheid [is] a crime against humanity" (para. 162).[41]

The criminalization of Israel has gone hand in hand with the criminalization of the whole West: the history of the West is said to have been nothing other than one continuous crime, the moving picture of an eternal, unmoving essence of Evil.[42] The two figures of Satan, the West and Israel, are therefore an unwelcome presence in a world of Others made up of devout believers, pure revolutionaries, and generous humanists—in short, angels and archangels become human. At the Durban Conference the Arab Lawyers Union put this view into its brochure:

"Israel is the perfect example of a complex large-scale racism. This state is in fact the embodiment of the distinctive racism underlying Zionism, and it makes Israel the last incarnation of a somber history that has witnessed the sufferings of humanity due to the aggressiveness of racism and its vile discrimination among human beings. . . . The UN General Assembly Decree No. 3379 of November 15 [sic], 1975, which asserts the racist character of Zionism, was a genuine expression of the experience of the international community and of how it sees the fruits of Zionism in Israel and the discriminatory, aggressive policy of Zionism toward the Palestinians."[43]

Caroline Fourest, who was attending the Durban Conference on behalf of the French Pro-Choice NGO, did not conceal her horror at what she saw in this "world of hate and slogans":[44]

"From the beginning of the Forum, anti-Zionist slogans forced themselves on everyone's attention: 'Free Palestine! Butcher Sharon! Zionism Is Apartheid!' Facing them were another group, some wearing kippahs: "Give Peace a Chance! End the Violence!" Soon the Arab Lawyers Union stall was handing out a leaflet likening Jews to Nazis. You could see little flags there sporting swastikas on Israeli soldiers' heads. On one tract, a photo of Hitler had the following commentary: 'And what if he had won? There would have been no Israel, and no Palestinian blood would have been shed.' Gulp. The same stall had the *Protocols of the Elders of Zion* on sale for 20 rand. A strange way of starting real debate on the Middle East at a conference against racism. . . . For who are the 'Judeo-Nazis' booed by these 'anti-Zionists'? Are they hideous Zionists? Or Jewish fundamentalists? Of course not. . . . No, the targets are not Israeli but Jewish. And those who are Israeli citizens are peace activists."[45]

In Durban on August 31, 2001, the president of the Palestinian Authority, Yasser Arafat, denounced Israel's "policy of supremacy" in the following terms: "This brutality and violence [of the Israelis] is driven by an attitude of supremacy, an attitude involving racial discrimination, population transfer, cleansing, and the daily imposition of settlers on our people."[46] No one thought it a sign of a mental disorder when Farouk Kaddoumi, a high PLO official, stated that in his view "Israeli practices against the Palestinians exceed the Holocaust in horror."[47] Everything is grist to the mill in this final stage of demonic criminalization, where Israel becomes a state, the only state, in everyone's way. This manufactured image of Israel as an absolutely negative exception is a symbolic preparation for its elimination. It fits in with the revival of a charge massively leveled by anti-Jewish propaganda in the late 1930s: the charge that the Jews are a force pushing the world toward war, the ones really responsible for the coming war.[48] The kernel of the argument is that the very existence of Israel will be the cause of future bloodbaths. And, beyond the Israelis, it is Jews in general whose existence is placed in question through the central amalgam: Jews-Israelis-Zionists. Formerly accused of being the ones really responsible for World War II—as the revisionist historian Paul Rassinier proclaimed in the very title of his last book[49]— Jews are now blamed for the third world war that various authors are predicting.[50]

During the last three decades of the twentieth century, detestation of the mythical figure of "Jews-Israelis-Zionists" followed the pathways of the expansion of Islam; anti-Jewish hatred kept growing as something like a new fascination with Islam spread throughout the world. The fact that there are several different Islams changes nothing: for each Islam has its fundamentalist version, and many fundamentalisms have their pietist (or puritanical or rigorist) variants,[51] as well as their war-oriented deviations involving a "revolutionary" or "anti-imperialist" political program.[52] If the Muslim world is at once fascinated and nervous, or even filled with hatred, in relation to Western modernity, the same ambivalence may be found in the attitudes of Westerners to Islam: a mixture of seduction and fear, which may be put down to the extraordinary power of intimidation exerted by a religion that is today particularly dynamic and triumphant, and that confers on more than a billion followers their main cultural identity.[53]

Of course, a distinction should be drawn here between intellectual fascination with Islamic thought (discovered in France through the work of Louis Massignon or Henry Corbin, Jacques Berque or Louis Gardet[54]) and the actual rallying of an ever-larger number of individuals to the world's most powerful religious machine, in an age of deep disenchantment when they can no longer satisfy their spiritual needs in the culture of market-oriented, scientific-technological societies. This is the revenge and transfiguration of the cultural pessimism that lies at the origin of the Islamists, who started out from the uneasiness raised by such questions as: "Why have Muslims lagged behind while everyone else has progressed?"[55] or, a little later,

"Are we still Muslims?"[56] And we know the short answer of the Islamist doctrinaires: "Instead of seeking to prove that Islam is rational, we must proclaim loud and clear that true rationality is Islamic."[57] Thus Sayyid Qutb can affirm the principle: "We have no reason to be ashamed of Islam."[58] The author of *Our Struggle Against the Jews* justifies as follows his talk of a "Judeo-Christian conspiracy against Islam": "Truth and falsehood cannot coexist on earth. . . . When Islam undertakes in general to establish Allah's rule on earth and to free humanity from the worship of other creatures, it is resisted by those who have usurped Allah's sovereignty on earth. They will never make peace. Islam therefore sets about destroying them, in order to free men from their sway. . . . The liberation struggle of *jihad* will not end until Allah's is the only religion."[59]

The current quasi-sociological definition of Islamism refers to the sense of malaise in countries with a Muslim culture that have been subjected to corrosive Western modernity as well as to the attempt to escape it by returning to a "pure" or authentic Islam: "By Islamism we understand a type of movement, present in Muslim societies destructured by modernity, that harks back to a reactionary and anti-modern Islam."[60] In contemporary Islamophilia, then, which also affects the Western world, there is certainly both fear and fascination: a *bien-pensant* fear of appearing Islamophobic but also a more prosaic fear of being isolated and rejected in a world where Islam, beyond the limits of a religious phenomenon, constitutes a cultural, social, political, and economic force. It is an Islam and an Islamophilia that have impressed and intimidated many people since the Salman Rushdie affair,[61] especially in Western societies where the values of hedonist individualism go together with a widespread pacifism of principle. This consumerist pacifism might be expressed in a desire for submission: a Munich-style quest for peace at any price, involving agreement to negotiate with the Islamists and then bow to their conditions. This is a psychosocial, political, cultural, and geopolitical fact; the right kinds of questions need to be asked about it. It does not, of course, sanction a false and summary identification of the Muslim religion with Islamism; the latter is a fundamentalist ideological corruption of Islam and a means of politically using religious beliefs that are respectable in their own sphere. Hence the paradoxical style of many Islamist movements—traditionalist and revolutionary, hyperconservative and ultrasubversive (to the point of so-called random terrorism).

Islamism involves an ideologization and criminal politicization of a simplistic, biased reading of the founding texts of Islam. In the name of a return to "pure" Islam, it rejects the whole of Western modernity except its technology (in so far as this can be turned against the West through *jihad*). Islamism is based upon a slogan-postulate that "Islam is the solution."[62] At the very least, then, it is a kind of dogmatism— a hyperdogmatism.[63] The propaganda of the Islamists presents Islam as "a single whole, a perfect system answering all the needs of men and women,"[64] and Islamic law as "a complete system resting upon genuine sources applicable in all times and places."[65] Since the Koran is supposed to be perfect, the perfect man is a perfect Muslim. Hence there is no point in thrashing around in search of citizenship or democracy: "God alone deserves power. The Koran . . . and the Sunna . . . represent the fundamental constitution, the core of the state. . . . In Islam, the reins of power are held by God, the laws have already been passed."[66] The only legitimate regime, for a convinced Islamist, is an all-encompassing theocracy. Amar Lasfar, rector of the Lille mosque, explains as follows this inseparability of politics and religion: "In Islam the concept of citizenship does not exist, but the concept of community is very important. It expects that the Islamic community, once recognized, will have its own laws, apart from any that might be common to the *sharia* and the Republic."[67] The alternative "theocracy or democracy," then, translates as "either Islamic order or the Republic."

A quick application of comparative sociology is necessary here to locate the basis of a widespread conception of political Islam. The American legal theorist Abdullahi A. An-Na'im, a specialist in Islam and human rights, describes the present manifestations of political Islam as "regressive and hostile"; and he adds that he is "mainly alluding to the policies and practices of the fundamentalist regimes of Afghanistan, Iran, Pakistan, and Sudan,[68] and to the present or foreseeable consequences of the struggle for power by comparable Islamic movements in countries such as Algeria and Egypt today."[69] But the same author adds that "other manifestations of political Islam exist in the traditional authoritarian regimes of Saudi Arabia and the Gulf States, as well as in certain cultural institutions and certain political processes at work in other Muslim countries. For example, the fact that the monarchies of Jordan and Morocco partly base their legitimacy on religious criteria reflects another aspect of political Islam."[70] This is a distinction between the fundamentalist type of political Islam and other variants of it.

The "radicality" of what is usually called "radical Islam"[71] may thus be understood in two ways: a quest for "purity" of doctrine with a view to its strict application (implying unification of the religious and the political spheres),[72] or involvement in attempted conquest or acts of terror against "heathenism." Literalism and jihadism here underwrite the construction of a general anti-modernism, rejecting the secular principle (therefore all tolerance and pluralism) and the principle of equality (between men and women,[73] Muslims and Jews or Christians, and so on).[74] Of course, socially applied doctrinal purism may be effectively, if not always explicitly, combined with active purification through "sanctified" terrorism. A very good example of this is contemporary transnational wahhabism[75] (or, to be more precise, neowahhabism), which casts a cruel light on the ambiguities or even equivocations of Saudi Arabia, the embodiment of a contradiction in terms that might be called "moderate radicalism." The oxymoron highlights the difficulty in defining that particular Arab-Muslim country:

"On the one hand, it is a country where [the wahhabi reading of] the *sharia* is applied in the most 'radical' fashion, especially in penal matters or the status of women, and which has widely subsidized the expansion of the most radical groups all over the Muslim world; but, on the other hand, apart from the fact that the ruling dynasty mobilizes the religious referent within a perspective of legitimation, Saudi Arabia (as 'Desert Storm' confirmed) is a key element in the system for the protection of American, and broader Western, 'national interests'—which is why it may be classified among the 'moderates.'"[76]

One of the features of contemporary Islamism is that it presupposes the power wrongly accumulated by mullahs (in the Khomeini model), ulema, and imams, those doctors of law or preachers who are mostly ignorant, biased, and simplistic in their reading of the texts of Islam. Their reduction of the message of Islam to a body of systematically antimodern dogmas or precepts (especially concerning the inferior status of women), and to appeals for *jihad* against America and Israel, makes it little more than a machine for the creation of fanatics ready to kill and die for a single "devouring abstraction" (Bakunin's phrase): Allah. Islamist education is a system of indoctrination and dragooning, which entails the brutalization of children "treated" in this way, the mass production of well-groomed parrots, totally subject, conditioned, and stupefied. It is a system of totalitarian "debraining," a crime against the human spirit, a crime against the humanity in each child. The crime is committed not only by the Taliban in Afghanistan (an especially stupid and ignorant force, overthrown in November 2001), but in less caricatural forms wherever the school system is in the hands of fundamentalists. Sheikh Abd al-Aziz bin Baz—the "pope" of wahhabism and author of a book that seeks to show "that the Sun and Moon move while the planet Earth is stationary"[77]—has condemned to death "any person who asserts, without repenting, that the Sun is stationary—for that is tantamount to contradicting the words of the Prophet. In Islam, the unanimous view is that he who causes God, his Prophet, and his Book to be contradicted is guilty of impiety. He therefore deserves to be killed and deprived of his Property, unless he repents."[78] When modern science opposes the dogmas in the holy texts (which it does very often!), it must be rejected as impious.

The extreme violence of the Islamists' "terrible simplifications" is quite apparent and rightly arouses the indignation of liberal minds, but the reality of stupidity in power is more monstrous still. At the beginning of the third millennium, stupidity has taken a terrible revenge: the great struggle against stupidity, waged by Western philosophy since the ancient Greeks, here encounters an obstacle that no one foresaw. Islamism is the organized form that this stupidity assumes when it takes up battle positions. How could anyone have predicted that an absolute enemy of intelligence, critical reflection, and freedom of the spirit would develop in this form?

This mixture of mindless literalism and murderous fanaticism, tirelessly purveyed by the mullahs, sheikhs, ulema, and imams of Islamist persuasion, inspires the one-dimensional strategy of the Islamic terrorists: that is, to provoke a third world war between a unified Muslim world and the West (or even the rest of the world). Not without intellectual courage, Mohammed Arkoun has shown how orthodox Islam generally "skips over the fundamental role of Muslim philosophy," to the point that, after 1945, "the Islam that expressed itself was cut off from any intellectual input." The eminent philosopher-historian adds that "the intellect was perverted by . . . an 'ideology of combat,' a mobilization of the Arab-Islamic personality to liberate people from colonial domination."[79] There is a proliferation of subthinkers in the element of underdevelopment: the impoverished masses are particularly credulous, and their force for resentment easily mobilizable;[80] it is enough for political-religious demagogues to single out enemies for hatred and to call them "Crusaders," Jews, and so on. The perspective of these terrifying strategists may be summed up in a parody of the classical formula: *Fiat sharia, pereat mundus* (Let there be Islamic law though the world perish).[81] This is the road to nihilism—or, more precisely, to one of its elements that Nietzsche called active nihilism, though not in a form he foresaw. The man "who wants to perish," who succeeds the "Ultimate Man,"[82] reveals himself at the same time to be the man who wants to make others perish while perishing himself. Islamic terrorism is the ultimate frenzy of active nihilism.

The globalist wahhabi conception of a universal Islam (the Muslim nation: *Umma al islamiya*) legitimizes an imperialist project for forcible Islamization of the world, as illustrated especially by bin Laden's "jihadist-salafist" current.[83] In many respects we may follow Bat Ye'or's suggestion that "the war against Israel is a war against rebellious *dhimmis* to restore the supremacy of Islamic law."[84] Re-Islamization, a traditionalist response in the Third World after the failure of Western-style secular religions, may be analyzed as one form of the process of "indigenization" that Samuel Huntington describes as the expression and vehicle of postcolonial revenge,[85] implying a reappropriation of non-Western and

premodern models of society and politics.[86] This is the basis
for the kind of political, social, and religious aims that those
semi-scholars of the Islamic world pursue as they develop the
literalist commentary prescribed for revenge on the hegemonic West, thereby fueling the fanaticism of "believers" and
driving them into self-sacrifice and murder. These fundamentalist demagogues certainly cannot be held up as the only
genuine representatives of Islam. But that is not sufficient to
set our minds at rest. For the split between fanatical Islamists
bent on conquest and tolerant Muslims who accept the logic
of secularization is likely to grow more intense and hence to
strengthen the former who, as skillful strategists, seek
through terrorist and other actions to provoke a pseudo-de-
fensive mobilization by all Muslims against the Western "aggressor" countries. This is why it is so important that the
Muslim religious authorities, as well as representative intellectuals of the Muslim world, take a clear position against
Islamism and unequivocally condemn the whole Islamist-
terrorist enterprise.[87]

    There has been a most disturbing rise in the number of
grey areas where the frontier between Islam and Islamism
cannot be defined. These are also areas of sharp swings,
where convictions may be expressed in campaigns of violence
or acts of terror. This is a remarkable feature of contemporary Islam: you find certain sociological indicators both of
"moderates" (or "modernists") and of "extremists" (or "fundamentalists"), but also numerous figures of "believers" in
between. The legal theorist Mohamed Charfi, former president of the League of Human Rights in Tunisia, uses the
metaphor of a "footbridge" to describe this ever-possible
drift from moderation to radicalism, on the grounds that
there is a basic consensus about how to interpret the sacred
texts: "If there is a difference in behavior between traditional
and official Islam, on the one hand, and the fundamentalists

on the other, there is no difference at the level of analysis, theory, and foundations. Footbridges linking the two are therefore inevitably created."[88] Most significant, perhaps, are the types of interface: according to circumstances, "believers" may react either by embracing the virtue of prudence and displaying extreme moderation, or by radicalizing in the direction of *jihad*. In the case of Catholicism, the frontier between "integrism" and "non-integrism" became clear enough, albeit rather late, in the second half of the twentieth century, when a basic consensus emerged over the principle of secularism,[89] and the long exercise of free self-examination resulted in the internalization of individualist/pluralist values by the citizens of liberal democratic societies.

The most urgent task in countries with a Muslim culture is to further the transition from authoritarian or despotic regimes to law-based states that respect the separation of the religious and public spheres implicit in the secular principle and that no longer confuse education with indoctrination.[90] It is a question of society and politics rather than of different civilizations: there is no cultural inevitability that prevents religiously Muslim countries from becoming constitutional democracies in which individual freedoms are respected and gender equality is written into norms and customs. It is necessary to choose between the privatization of religion (or religious belief) and the theocratic road, between freedom of religious affiliation and the weight of inherited religious identities.[91] Cultural absolutism and an emphasis on civilizational difference are already highly debatable (in my view, indefensible) as models of interpretation, but an even greater problem is that they can justify the coexistence only of civilizations that have already been "cleansed." That is a repulsive geopolitical utopia if ever there was one.

There is only one regulative idea that can illuminate and guide a policy favoring the emergence of just (or equitable[92]) and decent societies in the so-called Muslim countries. This idea—the idea of pluralist and constitutional democracy—was born in Europe but is not the property of Europeans: it is in principle universalizable, without being linked to any civilizational imperialism.[93] Whatever theocratic and obscurantist tendencies exist in societies with a Muslim culture, there is no decisive reason why it should be impossible for them to evolve toward secular social and political orders.[94] Besides, it is a moral duty to wager on such evolution. We should recognize, however, the huge gap between what is possible and desirable in this sense and the political and social reality in most of the Muslim world. And, like Emmanuel Sivan, we fear that liberal and "enlightened" milieux will prove incapable of resisting the Islamic tide, in a situation where, to adapt W. B. Yeats, "The moderates lack all conviction, while the radicals are full of passionate intensity."[95] For even in nonterrorist variants of Islamism, there is a cultural imperialism clearly illustrated by the following oath of allegiance to the Muslim Brotherhood: "I believe . . . that each Muslim has a mission to educate the world in accordance with the principles of Islam. And I promise to fight to accomplish this mission."[96]

Mohamed Charfi puts his finger on the fundamental problem: "Democracy is not viable, or even practicable for a time, if a not insignificant section of the population thinks that it is in possession of the absolute truth, and that it has the right, or even duty, to impose it by force: that is to say, if it embraces an anti-democratic ideology. In this regard, it is unfortunately evident that fundamentalism exists, in varying degrees, in virtually all the Muslim countries."[97] What is certain is that, unlike liberal-pluralist democratic societies, and unlike authoritarian regimes with a Muslim culture that can be reformed up to a point, Islamist totalitarian societies are inherently imperfectible.

In Western democracies, however, in a kind of convergent process, the legitimate "anti-racist" defense of immigrant populations against xenophobia has surreptitiously—though, of course, only partially—turned into an uneasy indulgence of the dubious "anti-Zionist" views widespread in milieux of North African and Black African origin, an indulgence that can even go as far as empathy or design. So it is that today a significant part of the left and far left in Western countries is strongly impregnated with Judeophobia. Active sympathy for the Palestinian cause has combined through syncretism with the militant defense of immigrants from outside Europe (especially those from North Africa, who are targeted by Le Pen) and with support for the Bosnian Muslims and the Albanian UCK (KLA) in Kosovo. In the latter cases it was naive and unthinking support that led people to overlook and then cover up such facts as that some three thousand Islamist volunteers,[98] subsidized by Muslim countries or networks, arrived in the early 1990s to strengthen Bosniac forces fighting the Serbs.[99] Then, after the Dayton accords, these Islamist combatants dispersed in various European countries and elsewhere.[100] In any event, selective xenophilia is what lies behind the hardening of "anti-Zionist" demonology, especially in French intellectual circles.

We should recall here the distinction between legitimate (rationally argued) criticism of Israeli policy and an unconditional rejection of Israel based upon irrational Satanization. The category "Zionism" operates in this context as an amalgam, so that amid the confusion what is called "anti-Zionism" refers both to admissible criticism of the State of Israel in a particular conjuncture and to jihadist appeals for the destruction of Israel. Understandably enough, Léon Poliakov used to speak of "the hairbreadth frontier separating anti-Zionism and anti-Semitism,"[101] referring to a dubious radical "anti-Zionism" that constantly extended its field of

ideological influence in and after the 1960s. Over time the
"hairbreadth" has narrowed still further.

There is a certain combined way of fantasizing about
"the struggle against racism" and "the struggle against globalization" that bases itself upon a prejudice in favor of "the
victims" or "the excluded." This leads some individuals who
are carried along (without always wishing or even realizing
it) by "anti-Zionist" passions to join the new camp of the
anti-Jews, where the open affirmers are still incomparably
more numerous than the unthinking or concealed supporters. The basic argument implicit in this move may be reconstituted as follows: "If Israel did not exist, peace and justice
would reign in the Middle East"—to which is added another
claim to the effect that Islamist terrorism would then no
longer have any justification or reason for existence (which
implies that it now does have reasons for existence!). The
practical and policy conclusion can only be that Israel is "in
the way" and should disappear. In a not too distant past, we
have heard a similar argument about the Jews: "If the Jews
did not exist there would be no anti-Semitism" (which suggests that the Jews are actually responsible for anti-Semitism, as Édouard Drumont's best-seller *La France juive* was
arguing back in 1886, in the first modern synthesis of Judeophobia). And the terrible normative conclusion could be logically drawn that "the Jews must disappear" (by means that
remained to be specified!).

The leader of the onetime Palestinian progressives, Yasser
Arafat, recently put forward his own solution: a right of return for Palestinians,[102] with the eventual submergence of the
Israeli nation[103]—a solution to the Israeli-Palestinian problem that involves Israeli euthanasia. This provocative demand for a right of return for all Palestinians, which was
introduced in late 2000 just as Ehud Barak was showing a
willingness to meet the most legitimate Palestinian demands,

is acknowledged to have caused the breakdown of the negotiations. Most probably, for a number of reasons, Arafat does not want a Palestinian state alongside the Jewish state: first, because it would mean an end to his military-police dictatorship;[104] next, because the ideology of Palestinian national Islamism allows no place for the Jews and quite simply denies their historical links to the Land of Israel. In Palestinian schoolbooks, which are highly revealing in this connection, Israel does not appear on any map; what they show in its place is "Our Fatherland Palestine," or "Occupied Palestine." Israeli towns are described as Palestinian, and of course Jerusalem is glorified as "capital of Palestine."[105] We even learn that "Abraham was a monotheistic Muslim, not one of the idolaters."[106] The practical conclusion is clear: "Since the beginning of our rebirth . . . we have woken up to a harsh reality, and [to] an oppressive imperialism that we have driven from some of our lands and are on the point of driving from the rest."[107]

Total refusal to accept the existence of Israel is thus a basic premise of the "historical" education received by young Palestinians. This early indoctrination, later reinforced by "anti-Zionist" propaganda, makes impossible any honest recognition of Israel's right to exist; and it may raise legitimate doubts about the sincerity of the statements of Palestinian leaders, even when these appear to lack all ambiguity. Of course, Islamic education Palestinian-style also includes *jihad* education: "*Jihad* for Allah is one of the most important duties and commandments of Islam, whose aim is to establish the rule of Allah on earth."[108] A peculiar kind of pacifist propaganda ("Peace in the Middle East"), livened up with frenetic appeals for right and justice, may thus be used to justify a call for the elimination of Israel and, beyond the Israeli population, of Jews in general. A recent Islamist expression of this is "Every Jew is a target and should be killed"—a command whose sources can always be found in the Koran.[109] Bin Laden has been speaking in this way recently, after a long list of others. And the Communist terrorist Carlos, now a convert to Islam though still an advocate of "world revolution," declared in October 2001 that the Israel-Palestine conflict "is the epicenter of the revolutionary war at an international level," and that "the jihadist movement is the vanguard of the anti-imperialist struggle."[110] On the side of Arab "nationalism," Marshal Mustapha Tlass—the Syrian defense minister, organizer of a new edition of the *Protocols of the Elders of Zion*, and author of a book on Jewish ritual murder (*The Unleavened Bread of Zion*)[111]—felt able to say on LBC Television, on May 5, 2001: "If each Arab killed a Jew, there would be no Jews left."[112]

Such statements, which more or less openly call for extermination of the Jews, have been multiplying in the Arab and Muslim countries. Should we conclude that the Arab-Muslim world is driven by a genocidal project? Obviously not. Our intention here is not to copy the central Judeophobic amalgam, transferring it to the Arab-Islamic "entity." First of all, only the intellectual error of essentialism could ignore the wide diversity of forms taken by Islam, or even the multiplicity of Islams; but also we should not generalize by reducing the best and the worst to the identical—the bin Ladens and Tlasses can in no way be held up as paradigmatic types of Arab or Muslim elites. Nevertheless we have a right to feel astonished that so few non-Muslim (and non-Christian) Arab intellectuals are avowed or militant atheists, or, why not? anti-Muslims; or to wonder about the seemingly irrepressible hold of religious norms and the almost spontaneous upsurge of blind, compacted solidarity in milieux with a Muslim culture. It is only in these milieux that one finds today believers—even minimalist believers—who always feel in agreement with their "Muslim brothers throughout the world."

This transnational solidarity and fraternity may, of course, operate in the realm of charitable works, but they may equally aid the dissemination of Judeophobic stereotypes and rumors as well as the construction of terrorist networks in the name of the "just cause." It may be that the ever stronger Islamic transfiguration of the Palestinian struggle is to be explained by the fact that it can be presented as the main front in a war waged by "Muslims throughout the world" against the "infidels" (and their allies, the "hypocrites"), beginning with the Americans and Jews. When a preference for the Palestinian cause becomes exclusive and slides into the absolute realm of the mystical or mythical, it proves to be a vehicle for that absolute anti-Zionism which is one of the new manifestations of Judeophobia, all the more formidable because of its power of ideological persuasion.

FOUR

Silence in the Face of the New Judeophobia: Blindness, Complacency, or Design?

In FRENCH political circles, especially on the left, as well as in the media, there is a curious and disturbing blindness about the new manifestations of anti-Jewish hatred. This is most noticeable when the incidents in question are linked to the Israeli-Palestinian conflict and are prompted by groups descended from the North African and black African immigration—in short, when they appear to be a phenomenon of "suburban youth," much of which has remained impervious to the norms of integration into the French republic.[1] Although a sense of exclusion and humiliation is widespread among these sections of the population—sustained by their strangely indulgent presentation as media spectacle—and although these factors explain certain types of anomic behavior (anti-Jewish violence being only one sector), they cannot be used to justify them.

Let us start by saying that poverty or social marginalization, and, a fortiori, any easy settling into the position of victim, does not confer the right to hate, to insult and assault, to injure and kill. Yet political actors and commentators always find excuses for acts of delinquency attributable to social groups that they consider to be generally "underprivileged," "excluded," or "discriminated against," or to be driven by "despair." In such cases an indulgent attitude is de rigueur; a vaguely sociological explanation serves indiscriminately as political and moral justification. Angelic sociologism rules and keeps watch. Most of its representatives assume that the dysfunctionalities of French-style republican integration mean that it is necessary to move toward a multicultural society, and hence to replace the model of assimilation with one of multicommunalism. "Plural citizenship" then becomes the radiant horizon. An "all-is-woe" smugness ("I am a victim, I am rejected, excluded, etc.") answers the benevolent angelic gaze, one of whose most persistent themes is gentle integration of the suburbs through Islam,[2] when in fact the suburbs all too often present a landscape of devastation, disintegration, retribalization, and violence—plus, of course, Islamist indoctrination and dragooning, not due only to the effects of preaching and guided instruction. Abstract references to Islam should therefore not be used to justify the growing hold of Islamist associations and networks in certain French suburbs. The bitter testimony of Father Christian Delorme, nicknamed "the priest of the Minguettes [an eastern suburb of Lyons]," is most interesting on this point, given the success of the Union of Muslim Youth (UJM) whose star speaker is Tariq Ramadan:

"As for the UJM, it is I who first got them on their feet, in 1983. To see young people bringing spirituality into the suburbs could only fill me with joy; it was a bit like the JOC [the Christian working-class youth movement]. . . . The UJM has gone in for a reform of Islam that means affirming religion as the only truth, and it bases itself on the growing victimization of young Muslims. . . . Grassroots re-Islamization

goes hand in hand with exclusion and the rejection of difference and mixing. Above all, it has cut young people off from
their family roots, by hurling contempt at what it calls
parental Islam. . . . The Jewish community is talking of clos-
ing down the synagogues at Saint-Fond and Vénissieux, as
there are too many incidents and malicious acts. . . . Today
there is an Islam structured around organizations and movements that have a negative discourse about Christianity. . . .
They discuss Christianity only in a polemical manner. And
let's not underestimate the reach of this anti-Christian discourse in the suburbs."[3]

Similarly, it is a rare journalistic report that brings out the
scale of Islamist proselytizing in French prisons. Commenting
on the story of one nonpolitical prisoner in the Paris region,
two *Le Monde* journalists stressed the following lesson:
"Pressure on the weakest prisoners, harassment to enforce the
strict practice of Islam, anti-Semitic and anti-Western indoctrination through the circulation of prohibited books and cassettes: this man has daily rubbed shoulders, in several prisons
of the Paris region, with prisoners who practice a fundamentalist Islam and engage in more or less open proselytizing."[4]

Thanks to the black magic of the small screen, it has not
taken long for a heroic aestheticization of marginal delinquents to set in. After all, if the proletariat of European stock
has vanished from the revolutionary imagination as a figure
of promise and redemption, neoleftist doctrinaires have not
found it difficult to find substitutes for the class bearing the
"future of humanity." This they accomplish by working on
the raw material of all the underprivileged and marginalized
groups thrown up by rampant globalization. In France it is recent immigrants and young people descended from the
African immigration who have been the object of this reinvention of the proletariat: the post-1989 neorevolutionaries
found their new enemy in an "American-Zionist imperialism"

already prowling the world, and they had to locate a credible, sociologically identifiable equivalent to the Third World that had lost its symbolic force. This explains the targeted xenophilia that has become a paradoxical (anti-racist/racist) prejudice, the other side of which is a profound contempt for the pathetic "Frenchman born and bred," and a limitless hatred for "the Jews" or "the Zionists."

Francophobia and Judeophobia work in concert with each other. The Islamophilia of these circles crowns their hierarchical view of ethnic-social categories: the superior race-class is the young and handsome "interbred foreigner"; the inferior race-class is the pure "Frenchman" of European origin (for neither Italianness nor Spanishness can save the "Frenchman" from his native horror). As for the "Zionist entity" and its representatives who are "everywhere" in the Diaspora, they are outside all categories and scales of measurement: neither at the top nor at the bottom, they are simply over there, the embodiment of demonic causality.

In the imagination of certain militant elites, the leftist aesthetic theme of "hybrid beauty" and the glorification of the "mestizo type" in advertising have been compounded by an a priori sympathy for groups lumped together as victimized "foreigners" or "immigrants"—that is, those popularly known as illegal [*clandestins*] immigrants whom the new *bien-pensants* celebrate as "unregistered" [*sans-papiers*]. These individuals, defined as victims or outcasts in their very essence, are dressed up in the role of principal bearers of a subversive potential lacking in other social groups. Juvenile offenders, and terrorists in their image, for example, are thus glorified as "rebels" or "resistance fighters"—so long as they come, or are imagined to come, "from elsewhere." The Intifada can be replayed on French soil, as can the Algerian war for that matter. When a survey in 1997 and 1998 asked young people descended from North African immigrants what Palestine meant to them, they gave replies such as: "It's a country fighting as Algerians fought during the Algerian war. They are courageous, because Israel is very powerful and gets weapons and money from the Americans"; "Palestine is like Algeria in the time of the French"; "It's a country that the colonialists stole from the Arabs, where they put the Jews to get rid of them"; or "Palestine is a banner for all Arabs who want to be just and to hold their heads high."[5]

We might recall here the case of Khaled Kelkal,[6] that "young person" from Vaulx-en-Velin outside Lyons, seemingly "without a history"—in fact a petty criminal who gravitated to Islamism and was turned into a hero after his death was televised live on September 29, 1995.[7] The sad end of a pitiful criminal-terrorist linked to the GIA became the death of a brave rebel in combat, gun in hand, a hero and martyr for the cause.[8] It was a hallucinatory eternal return of Che Guevara, and indeed, since 1989, contemporary neoleftism has been living off such ersatz avengers: a guerrillero relic, a touch of Robin Hood, an Islamic martyr's look, but actually more akin to Nechaev's nihilist sect[9] than to romantic Latin American warriors. In short, whether it is out of angelism, "all-is-woe" ideologies, or heroization, the "young person" at issue is never guilty. This both covers up and sustains the acts of incivility (beginning with ritual insults) or violence toward Jews or "Frenchmen born and bred," committed by those "young people" who in some cases did not conceal, on October 8, 2001, that bin Laden had become their hero. (Among the shouts reported were: "Osama is too strong for them!"—"Osama is who I am!"—"We are all [Talibanized] Afghans!"[10])

There is nothing in this that makes France an exception. After 9/11 and the American response, public identification with bin Laden could be observed in most Muslim countries, where demonstrations took place in support of him and new volunteers went off to fight. The attacks in the United States immediately sparked expressions of joy among Palestinians, most notably in Nablus and Khan Yunes (in the south of the Gaza Strip), though the Palestinian Authority censored pictures of these incidents in an attempt to avoid any repetition of the strategically damaging errors committed during the Gulf War.[11] On October 26 the Moroccan paper *Opinion* published an editorial on the positive image that "the Muslim street" had of bin Laden, "a perception also found . . . in the slogans shouted by thousands of demonstrators: Bin Laden, avenge us! Bin Laden, strike against Israel! We are all Osamas."[12] The article continued with an account of "the pictures held up by thousands of sympathizers," testifying to a perception that had "sprung from their imagination":

"He sits astride a horse at triple gallop; his clothes are timeless, and he is brandishing a sword. He seems to spring from the earliest times of Islam, from its first battles at Badr and Uhud. He seems to spring from the desert of the Arabian Peninsula. He defies time and space. . . . The 21st century and the 6th century (1st century of the Hegira) are now one and the same. . . . This telescoping is incomprehensible for an American mental structure, but contains no contradiction or anachronism for those who support the leader of al-Qaeda. The sword against the Tomahawk—a disproportionate struggle right from the beginning. But here the sword is charged with fourteen centuries of History, with victories, defeats, frustrations, humiliations, and a wish to avenge what is seen as scorned dignity."[13]

It is impossible to overemphasize the social disintegration that is taking place in the suburbs. The provocative identification with bin Laden, the expressions of Judeophobia, the Francophobic attitudes among sections of the population who, though descended from immigrants, are French citizens— all this testifies to a failure of integration in society and

nation. The breakup of the social bond goes hand in hand
with a banalization of acts (car-burning at the slightest provocation, for example) that are both uncivil and uncivic in that
they display a profound contempt for France.[14] Aggressive
examples of this include booing the national anthem as it
is sung by French sportsmen, whistling at Zinedine Zidane
for playing on the French soccer team, flying the Algerian flag,
shouting the name of the new hero: "Osama! Osama!", or
violently interrupting a France-Algeria match that was supposed to symbolize cordial relations between the two countries (at Saint-Denis on the evening of October 6, 2001, where
a large number of Socialist and Communist public figures
were in attendance). A "spoiled festival," the naive might
say—and then move on to deplore the fading of the angelic
utopia of a "multicolored France" that appeared at the 1998
World Cup, a vision in which the "Black, White and Beur"
team (Beur referring to children of North African immigrants)
was supposed to symbolize the new "interbred" youthful citizens of "plural France." The "politically correct" attitude to
the recurrent acts of violence is to refrain from publicly commenting on them at all, and certainly not to deplore (or
"dramatize") them, because that would "play into the hands
of the far Right."[15] The identity of these "young people" is
actually a big issue, because there remains no satisfactory
answer. Hence the restless wandering from one illusory identity to another: a mythical Algerian identity (sometimes, not
unparadoxically, through the soccer star Zinedine Zidane[16]);
a marginal identity of the neighborhood delinquent (the drug
dealer as means of access to consumer society); a polemical
identity of negative or bellicose self-affirmation (against the
West, America, Israel, "infidels," and so on); an identity as
victim of the "racist French."[17]

  Police investigations have shown that, in addition to the
disturbing progression to organized crime among housing-

project delinquents,[18] the period since the mid-1990s has witnessed increasingly frequent linkups between criminal gangs and Islamist-terrorist networks (in Roubaix, Béziers, and elsewhere).[19] Once again, generalizations should be avoided: ethnic-based tribalism and Islamist terrorism are by no means the inevitable destiny of "young people" in "sensitive districts." But the fact that the xenophobic far right exploits these associations does not justify compassionate angelism in the name of anti-racism. Malek Boutih rightly remarked: "The discourse of compassion provides a justification for the young person who strips bare a motor scooter or attacks someone on their way out of school."[20] And I would add: who assaults a Jew as a Jew, or attacks a symbol of Judaism.[21] Use of the "victim" category can erase the responsibility of the young people in question, actually reinforcing their segregation and ghettoization. But the inequality of social mobility is particularly acute and is scarcely allayed by the demagogy of those who play up to young people's loutish or delinquent behavior and thereby commend individual attempts to overturn or circumvent obstacles rather than face up to them.

It can never be repeated too often that successful social integration, like the formation of citizenship, assumes a process of individualization enabling freedom of choice. We owe to an Algerian journalist the following firm and lucid comment on the interrupted France-Algeria match of October 6, 2001: "The cars they burned, the train compartments they wrecked, the Zinedine Zidane they jeered for calmly exercising his choice to be French, the racist insults they hurled at Marcel Dessailly or Lilian Thuram in the name of the Arabs' supposed superiority over Blacks: there can be no justification for any of that."[22] One wonders about the disarming ease with which one hero replaces another in the "youth planet": Zidane, once fondly known as "Zizou," the champion of successful integration, a moderate Muslim and unashamed French citizen, young, rich, and famous, finds himself forgotten, or even rejected, for the sake of the new hero, bin Laden, fraternally known by his first name "Osama."[23]

On October 7, 2000 (at the Place de la République, of all places), during a demonstration in solidarity with the Palestinians and in the name of an aberrant "anti-racism," it was possible to hear slogans such as "Kill the Jews!" or "Death to the Jews!"[24] Anyone who heard them understood that anti-Zionism and hatred of Israel are less and less of a cover for ordinary Judeophobia, whose blatant public expressions are, however, still an embarrassment for those who share it in one degree or another. Of one thing we can be sure: no responsibility will be taken for such expressions, even by those who feel responsible for establishing the ideological context that makes them seem quite ordinary and natural. Since the early 1990s certain Greens, certain Trotskyists, certain anarchists, and certain neoleftists have made a profession of defending the homeless and other "have-nots," through associations such as the DAL ("Right to Housing") or "Droits devant!" ("Rights Ahead!").[25] And these, along with anti-globalization activists such as José Bové, have helped to make Judeophobic clichés and slogans more acceptable (and eventually respectable) by extending the already banalized amalgam "Jews-Zionists-Israelis" to include the Nazis.

The "new social movements," from which some angelic sociologists expected salvation, have largely turned into semi-sectarian organizations led by "all-is-woe" agitators; the target of their indoctrination or exploitation is a mass of marginal individuals without social ties who face the dire consequences of economic-financial globalization, real victims of the disintegrating effects of what Edward Luttwak has rightly called "turbo-capitalism."[26] The negative dialectic of McWorld and Jihad highlighted by Benjamin Barber,[27] in which any increase in uniformity due to globalization triggers convulsive reactions at the level of identity, has led to a McWorldization of the whole conflict over identity, a globalization of *jihad* itself. The writer Arundhati Roy has described this process with the necessary touch of irony: "Terrorism is the symptom, not the disease. Terrorism has no country. It's transnational, as global an enterprise as Coke or Pepsi or Nike. At the first sign of trouble, terrorists can pull up stakes and move their 'factories' from country to country in search of a better deal. Just like the multinationals."[28] But there must be no slippage from comparison to equation: analogy sometimes allows us to picture something better; it is not a method for gaining knowledge, and can never be a substitute for empirical investigation or conceptual labor.

We know the main spiritual guides, the original prophets of woe, the men of God *à la française* whose emulators are now legion. There is Roger Garaudy, whose conversion to Islam included a commitment to absolute anti-Zionism and Holocaust-revisionist propaganda.[29] There is Abbé Pierre, who did not hesitate to place his media aura at the service of a demonological anti-Zionist caricature based on an old anti-Jewish catechism.[30] And there is Monseigneur Gaillot, with his aesthetic-ethnic preferences in the ultra-Palestinophile tradition started by nonbeliever Jean Genet.[31] "We are all Palestinians!" said the leftist churchman in August 2001, during a self-promoting trip to the Palestinian territories. In his eyes the Palestinians are a victim-nation, to be loved as a chosen people transfigured by injustice and suffering beyond compare. Many are those who have traveled in Genet's footsteps and shared the wonderment of his discoveries. He himself described, in 1983, the irrational reasons for his unconditional pro-Palestinian commitment:

"Since the *fedayeen* had only recently left adolescence behind, the rifle, as a weapon, was the sign of triumphant virility

and gave assurance of being. . . . Since the roads had been cut
off and the telephone was silent, deprived of contact with the
rest of the world, for the first time in my life, I felt myself become Palestinian and hate Israel. . . . The statement that there
is a beauty peculiar to revolutionaries raises many problems.
Everyone knows, everyone suspects, that young children or
adolescents living in old and harsh surroundings have a beauty
of face, body, movement and gaze similar to that of the *fedayeen*. . . . As for the very young *fedayeen*, I will meet some in
Damascus. You can select a particular community other than
that of your birth, whereas you are born into a people; this se-
lection is based on an irrational affinity, which is not to say
that justice has no role, but this justice and the entire defense
of this community take place because of an emotional—
perhaps intuitive, sensual—attraction; I am French, but I defend the Palestinians wholeheartedly and automatically. They
are in the right because I love them. But would I love them if
injustice had not turned them into a wandering people?"[32]

    We should recall, however briefly, those statements of
Abbé Pierre from 1996 to which the media gave such promi-
nence because of his personal notoriety. After denouncing the
"international Zionist lobby,"[33] he explained himself more
clearly in an interview that appeared on June 17, 1996:

    "The Zionist movement, from its base in the United
States, has worldwide ramifications. It bases itself on a verse
in Genesis that claims that Abraham heard God tell him: 'I
give you the earth, from the river Nile up to the great Euphrates river.' So the Zionist movement says: 'We don't give
a damn about Israel or the Palestinians. What we want is the
empire foretold to Abraham.' And the movement is scheming
all around the world for that."[34]

    In another text, originally written at the request of *Le
Monde* (which refused to publish it) and then passed on to
Roger Garaudy on July 28, 1996, the pious friend of the ex-
cluded had this to say:

"The 'Zionist Movement,' which has powerful leaders settled in the United States and carries great weight in every American election, is bent on gaining possession of all this territory sketched out in the Bible: from the Nile to the Euphrates. The 'Zionist Movement' has secret agents in all the strategic policy sites concerning these states, both in France and elsewhere, and their doctrine is proving to be more and more racist and imperialist with regard to the Palestinians. The methods too have been growing more and more tyrannical, since the murders of Bernadotte, Rabin . . . the massacres: Deir Yassin, Sabra and Shatila, Hebron, Cana. . . ."[35]

On August 1, 1996, the website of Radio Islam (a Stockholm-based station founded and managed by a Holocaust denier of Moroccan origin, Ahmed Rami[36]) carried an editorial under the heading "Let Us Rise Up!":

"Radio Islam fights against all forms of racism—including the Jewish racism of which the Palestinian people are the victim, and including Jewish racism against the German people, Muslims, and Arabs. Radio Islam is against all forms of violence and terrorism, physical or intellectual, including the Jewish acts of violence of which the Palestinian people are today the victim. We also denounce the Jewish intellectual violence and terrorism against free French men and women such as Professor Robert Faurisson, Roger Garaudy, Abbé Pierre, and all the French revisionist historians who are struggling against the Jewish falsification of history. We also denounce the Jewish campaign of calumny against the only free French political party, the Front National, and its leader Jean-Marie Le Pen, the only real French statesman who has dared say no to the arrogance of Jewish power. And that is no mere detail!"[37]

All these "anti-Zionist" opinion leaders, from Abbé Pierre to his Third Worldist imitators, help to banalize the stereotype of "Israel's imperialism," the myth of a "Zionist plot," the polemical equation of the Israeli state and the Nazi state. During the demonstration of October 7, 2000, in Paris, one could see an apparently devout (judging by her *hijab*) young woman holding up the following placard: "Stop Jewish Hitlerite terrorism! 1 dead Palestinian = 1,000 inhuman (Jewish) dead."[38]

And yet these and similar displays of hatred are greeted with silence, in stark contrast to the media commotion that the slightest Le Pen–style outburst of (greatly toned-down) xenophobia provoked in the media a short time ago. There are good reasons to think that this blindness of the political and media elites is usually deliberate, and that it is motivated not only by French-style "political correctness" but also by cynical electoral calculations. While the intellectual elites, with rare exceptions, have rallied to the conventional thesis that "anti-Arab racism" has generally replaced anti-Semitism, or is now the "dominant" racism and needs to be fought as a priority,[39] the political elites concern themselves more and more with the Muslim vote in France and with that of young people descended from the North African immigration.[40] Hence the disturbing silences, the "general blackout systematically obscuring the special insecurity into which French Jewry is being plunged."[41] It is exactly as if the last thing that should be mentioned were the growing number of small-scale anti-Jewish acts (threats, assaults) in the *quartiers*, as if it were necessary to cover one's ears to the shouts of anti-Jewish hate, as if it were essential not to raise the issue of the arson attacks on synagogues, Jewish schools, and so on. No synagogue burned or wrecked by "young people" arouses anything like the emotion or public demonstration that met the desecration of the Jewish cemetery in Carpentras in spring 1990, at a time when it could be attributed with some plausibility to the Front National. The only anti-Semitic actions that cause an outcry are those that can be imputed to individuals or groups on the far right. Then the standard anti-racism still operates. But silence about the growth of Judeophobic attitudes in French society beyond the limits of the far right seems to be a position that few fail to respect.[42] Investigations of the issue are rare and fragmentary. Arrests and prosecutions have thinned out since October 22, 2000, when the minister of the interior reported that fifty-five persons had been arrested since the beginning of attacks against the "Jewish community" (of whom thirty-eight were the object of court proceedings).[43] As for public condemnations and demonstrations, they have been nonexistent.

One need only switch on certain radio stations aimed at an Arab-Muslim audience to appreciate the measure of routine Judeophobia. In 2001 the Tribunal de Paris found Radio-Orient guilty of "complicity in incitement to racial hatred and violence" after it had broadcast live (on October 27, 2000) a sermon in which the imam of Mecca took up some passages from the Koran, used them to present Jews as enemies of Islam, and therefore of God, and even called for "the disappearance of Jews from the face of the earth." His justification? "Allah said: the *yaouds* [Jews] are jealous, do not go near them because they are vermin."[44] Another example, illustrating the growth of violent attacks on Jews, was the incident on Sunday, September 2, 2001, when young men of North African origin armed with baseball bats pounced on a group of Jewish teenagers at their regular meeting place in front of the Häagen Dazs ice cream parlor on the Champs Élysées. At the sight of these passing representatives of the demonic enemy, they shouted: "Jews, we're going to kill you!"[45] A pitched battle involving several hundred young people went on until late in the night: a Jewish-Arab conflict in miniature, in the heart of Paris!

Here were "young people" living in France who said they were at war with the Jews, who said they hated the Jews and—to all appearances—really did hate them. What do the new *bien-pensants* think about this? They say it is not their fault if "young people" behave that way: such attitudes or actions are, of course, regrettable, but they are also understandable if we remember that those involved are victims of "exclusion" and "discrimination." To listen to their lawyers, and sometimes members of their family, these "young people" spontaneously identify with Palestinians suffering from the arrogance and cruelty of a "racist," "colonialist," or "fascist" Israel. It is necessary to understand them, to enter into dialogue with them, and above all not to "humiliate" them—to avoid at all costs provoking their just "anger." For the "anger" of a "young person" is highly contagious: it always finds expression in the incendiary "anger" of groups of "highly volatile" (and therefore rarely seen again) "young people." Whether or not they are proven criminals, the "origins" of these "young people" or their feelings of solidarity with their "Muslim brothers" make them especially susceptible, and so they should be handled very carefully. Such an approach excuses them in advance: it always finds justification for what they do.

Some people in positions of responsibility argue that we must not "add fuel to the flames"; others insist that the last thing we should do is provoke the "sensitive suburbs" or drive them to despair. At all costs we must avoid "making waves." Indulgence therefore becomes the most widespread virtue, and it tends to lapse into a kind of hazy condonation. When we think of those who, for several weeks in the spring of 2000, frantically sought to mobilize protests against the "anti-Semitic statements" allegedly made by the writer Renaud Camus in his *Journal* of 1994,[46] we have a right to expect an unstoppable wave of indignation and a powerful public campaign whenever shouts of "Death to the Jews!" or "We're going to kill you, Jews!" are furiously poured forth in the heart of Paris. Intellectuals, writers, and journalists who usually express outrage over some vague rumor of a dubious metaphor have remained silent and extremely sparing with their signature. The media censors and lynchers see nothing and hear nothing.

This extreme reserve on the part of those who petition most actively in the world of the media and intellectual life is also commonly found among professional politicians (for whom the real question is: How many divisions of voters does Renaud Camus represent?). All try to minimize the gravity of the incidents, calmly attributing them to a "tiny minority" of the groups in question. But these are just elegant justifications for what is really an act of desertion, a cowardly neglect of a state of affairs that is simply left to rot. In the name of a (correct) wish to avoid generalization and stigmatization, everyone is left to get on with what they are doing. The end result is to cover up, and even to bless, what was at first simply tolerated. Long-term blindness to things that one totally condemns in principle is tantamount to complicity with them.

The problem is wider than one of anti-Jewish violence. Extreme tolerance is the order of the day when it comes to what is happening in the "sensitive districts"; explanations for the violence begin to look like justifications. Policemen, under constant provocation, are always assumed to be wrong. A laid-back attitude prevails in the face of the re-Islamization of "young people" in the housing projects, even though many leaders of Islamist associations scarcely conceal their optimistic prospects of advance and already classify France in the "house of Islam" (*dar al-islam*), one of the three divisions of the world alongside "the house of war" and "the house of reconciliation." Here is one French Islamist leader: "France has more Muslims than most countries in the Arabian peninsula, Libya or Lebanon. . . . And you think it isn't

part of *dar al-islam*!"[47] Another defines more precisely his
horizon of expectations: "In the beginning, [the Muslim com-
munity] had no more than a handful of believers grouped
around the Prophet; twenty years later it already encom-
passed several countries. . . . France today has three to four
million Muslims;[48] that is more than a promising start."[49]

Faced with expressions of a delirious or criminal Judeophobia, the beautiful souls come up with smooth and edifying pleas on behalf of "young people" transfigured by their
status as "victims." The pious sociologization of anomie and
violence operates through an argument referring to frustra-
tion or humiliation. We are urged to "understand," to "reach
out toward these young people," to "speak to them," to "enter into dialogue with them," in between two volleys of
stones and bottles,[50] amid burning trash bins and cars, and
attacks on firemen, ticket collectors, and bus drivers. This is
the myth of the "noble savage" which glorifies "young people" as innocents in the very act of criminality. Although the
"noble savage" lives and thinks in a constant state of war, he
appears to be projected back into what Rousseau called "the
youth of the world," the fortunate moment of the state of nature. He can innocently employ the word "Jew" (*feuj*) or
"Frenchman" as an insult, loathe policemen ("*keufs*") and
treat them as enemies to be ambushed. He can happily say he
is "*antifeuj*" and shout all around him: "I don't like the
feujs";[51] for him the "*feujs*" are the enemy, either too French
(too assimilated) or too alien ("Zionist"). He can proclaim
through shouts or graffiti his admiration for bin Laden—
most journalists will overlook it or indulgently report the
statements of others who play down its significance. "The
fact that a few teenagers shout 'bin Laden' on their way out
of school 'means nothing,' says Djamila, a mother in Ris-
Orangis (Essonne). 'They're just into a bit of stirring.'"[52] If
that is what a mother says, there is no more to be said about

it. In the protected universe of the elites, a kind of neo-Rousseauism serves as a psychosociological explanation for these irritating phenomena that jar their angelic vision. The culture of hate in the suburbs is thought of as normal: it has, so to speak, been naturalized as a general symptom of the "dysfunctionalities" of the "Jacobin" and "racist" French republic. The only violence that ever shocks these refined souls is the violence of the state—which, in a throwback to 1968, is itself still a "police state."

A number of academic studies have established that in the 1980s and 1990s there was a considerable rise in the number of violent crimes (except homicide) in France—provided that a careful distinction is made between thefts and acts of violence.[53] Yet all those who live off an angelic ideologization of the issues posed by "juvenile delinquency" have disregarded these results of in-depth studies. In the pseudo-anti-racist, "youthist" mythology that centers on the category of victim, the "young person" embodies both "the outcast," an object of compassion, and the "outsider," an object of the immoderate xenophilia that supposedly combats xenophobia by exactly inverting it. But this inversion rests upon a dangerous illusion: both xenophilia and xenophobia reduce the individual in question to his or her origins. The "young person," whether rejected or glorified, comes to be seen only through his or her status as victim and outsider. Xenophilia, no less than xenophobia, confines people to a particular situation: it too bars the way to social integration and upward mobility. Demagogic glorification does not encourage a "young person" to come outside of himself, outside of his own habits and his circle of close family and friends. It sets up pressures toward consumerism, narcissism, subsidized unemployment, and, of course, petty crime. Once again, one of the few political leaders in contemporary France to have opened some people's eyes to the disturbing social reality is Jean-Pierre

Chevènement, through his rejection both of the right's demagogic exploitation of security issues and of the left's angelic indulgence:

"If we open our eyes to reality, we see an explosion of underage crime and public anger over the growing number of acts of violence that go unpunished. The response is patently inadequate. . . . It is wrong to set punishment and prevention off against each other, for punishment that calls people to order obviously has a pedagogic dimension. Every society involves the setting of limits, and the crossing of them must be punished. . . . I know that some right-thinking people are quick to allow offenders an excuse on grounds of poverty or immigration. But to invent some kind of predisposition to crime is an insult to ordinary people and immigrant families. The truth is that in the Republic any offender must be punished, whether he is rich or poor, from the Auvergne or North Africa."[54]

Anti-Semitism and neofascist-style xenophobia against immigrants arouse violent—and justified—reactions of indignation and denunciation. But Judeophobia inspired by Islamism (or Islamic youthism) seems to have been rendered ideologically inaudible or negligible, when it is not "understandable." Everything is permitted to those who, as victims of "exclusion" over here and of underdevelopment or poverty over there, are supposed to be without hope. Their "anger" is always justified, whether expressed in incitement to hate or murder, the burning of cars or symbolic places, terrorist actions, or whatever. "Good reasons" can always be found. This is especially the case in France, where a number of spin doctors specialize in downplaying the significance of, and finding excuses for, any kind of "youth crime."[55] The "young person" is always right: such is the postulate of the professionals of youthist demagogy. Even if he lapses into criminality, the reasons for his actions are supposed to be always good reasons that merely need to be discovered. The political and media elites thereby take "young people" tempted by crime and confine them to the role of irresponsible "victims." They do not act freely but are much more "acted upon" by their social conditions of existence. The Marxist principle of social-economic determinism is saved. The result, however, is to render nonexistent all the many other "young people" in the "projects" who are neither criminals nor Islamists, young people who, in spite of a series of handicaps, respect the laws and institutions of their country, work in often difficult conditions, and do not hold the republic's educational system in contempt.[56]

But the most important, and most disturbing, aspect of this situation lies elsewhere. The video-political strategies of the Islamist demagogues make effective use of the components of this new great myth of the victim by equating the cause of the poor and underprivileged with that of the "humiliated" or "attacked" Muslims. The Islam of the Islamists thus becomes the religion of the poor, the humiliated, and the injured. The Beurs of the French "housing projects" become one with the Palestinians of the "occupied territories." Whether sincerely (and therefore illusorily) or as part of a victim strategy, they often think of themselves as Palestinians devoid of all hope.

Journalists who studied Paris housing projects in early November 2001 noted that "the main radicalism there, even more than in September, expressed itself in connection with the Middle East conflict." And they illustrated this with Thiam, "a tall Mauritanian from the Pyramides project" and a declared Muslim, who said: "The Israeli tanks . . . are shooting at Palestinian families."[57] Such is the rumor spreading around the French suburbs. It expresses a view in keeping with the Manichaeism of anti-Zionist propaganda: the coldness, harshness, and cruelty of the Israeli army, dehumanized to the point of being little more than "tanks," assaulting the paragon of innocence and human weakness that emanates from the gentleness and warmth of the family, of "Palestinian families." On the Israeli side, "tanks" have replaced "families"! The Islamist preachers hope they can cast their net wide, by assembling beneath one flag the wronged Muslim masses and the masses proletarianized by the effects of rampant globalization, with a further, not insignificant input from all manner of people discontented with their lot. This globally oriented demagogic system has already proven to have a formidable capacity for mobilization. And a subtle, indirect, symbolic Judeophobia emanates from this ideological configuration, at once Islamophile, idolatrous of the Palestinians, and "Beurophile."[58]

It is time for France's intellectual and political authorities to confront this harsh reality and to refuse to enter silently, with complacency or by design, into the logic of Judeophobia. While the conflation of Islam with Islamism (or Islam with terrorism) must be avoided at all costs, it is equally necessary to denounce the conflation of Jews, "Zionists," and "Nazis" (or "racists"). In public, however, we scarcely hear voices raised any more against anti-Jewish polemics. It is as if powerful mechanisms of intimidation were holding them back, as if, on this question alone, a particularly effective intellectual terrorism were ensuring the silence of the cultural and political elites (with some rare exceptions). These elites (in concert with the Islamist intellectuals who raise the issue) unanimously voice their condemnation of Islamophobia, and without batting an eye follow the neoleftist groups in noisily denouncing homophobia. But, with some exceptions, they keep quiet about the growing signs of a new wave of Judeophobia—as if they wished to hear and see nothing.

Today unconditional support for the Palestinians is a widespread affectation in the protected world of the cultural elites, and an easily accessible form of mysticism in the devastated world of the suburbs.[59] To denounce Israel and glorify "the Palestinians" in general has become the proper, and most comfortable, thing to do. This new political-intellectual conformism has been able to establish itself through the routinization of what is conventionally known as "the struggle against racism and anti-Semitism." The struggle against anti-Semitism, centered for half a century on the Nazi past, has fallen asleep amid commemorative speeches and the kind of edifying pseudo-anti-racism prevalent at international conferences where everyone agrees with everyone else. The so-called anti-racist organizations seem to be dreaming with their eyes open: they have become, in many respects, temples of "political correctness," one of whose new faces—Islamic correctness—is encouraged by work in Islamic studies that is almost openly apologetic even about radical Islamism.[60] Critical lucidity does not, however, consist in replacing a "positive" fixation on one's own society ("we, the best of men") with a "negative" fixation on one's own society ("they, the most human of human beings"[61]), where self-hatred is sublimated in dogmatic xenophilia. As Éliane Amado Lévy-Valensi well put it: "Systematically to espouse the other's subjectivity is no proof of one's own objectivity."[62] A hybrid political culture, compounded of neo-Christianity, anarcho-leftism, Marxist revolutionism, and Arab-Islamophile intellectual terrorism, has burrowed its way into hearts and minds. Anti-racist or human rights activists have largely internalized the ponderous truths of this combative political culture; the surrounding angelism feeds off them. The campaign to delegitimate laws and institutions finds here a permanent ideological supply of sophistical justification.

Nothing forces us to get carried away by demagogy, angelism, and indulgence; these are the first stage of submission to a new "fascism." To assert ourselves as citizens of a

democratic society means refusing to bow to the power of
the violent—and therefore avoiding certain risks, as in the
kind of emergency or crisis situation that followed 9/11,
when Islamist propaganda was able to kindle terrorist sentiments in the name of "solidarity among Muslims." This in
turn commits us to demystify the language of those who
present violent individuals in a favorable light and find excuses for them in poverty, exclusion, or despair; those whose
flattery ("the beauty of the young rebel girls") encourages
these "victims" to persist in the path of violence.

We need an adequate assessment of the international
scene in the wake of the attacks of September 11, 2001 (already prefigured by the 1993 attack on the World Trade Center). Let us say, following François Heisbourg, that we have
suddenly passed from the post–cold war to hyperterrorism,
where the two main features of the new threat are the existence of messianic movements organized into megasects (like
bin Laden's military-religious organization), and a capacity
for mass destruction designed to eradicate the representatives
of evil (the alleged anti-Muslims—a category actually referring to non-Muslims, "Crusaders" and "Jews" above all, and
to "bad Muslims").[63] When certain anti-racist and human
rights organizations follow the example of neoleftist groups
and imperceptibly turn themselves into traveling companions
of the new Islamist totalitarianism, or into vehicles of radical
Judeophobia (as at Durban), by denouncing all anti-terrorist
measures taken by the government in place, it must be clearly
said that they have embarked on an unacceptable course.[64]
The defense of immigrants (especially illegal immigrants,
who are supposed to be more "victimized" than others) and
the denunciation of Islamophobia have become a position of
principle in favor of displaced foreigners, including a ban on
any criticism of Islam as it exists (hence the new wave of "political correctness").

What is necessary is a thorough intellectual and moral re-casting of the "struggle against racism and xenophobia."[65] It is simply false to claim that "anti-Arab" or "anti-immigrant" racism has driven anti-Semitism from the scene. And it is no less false to assert that there has been a corresponding shift in the modes of stigmatization, segregation, and discrimination, away from anti-Semitism toward "anti-Arab racism." The fact that this is a widespread view does not make it true. The historical and sociological truth is quite different: anti–North African xenophobia (directed against certain groups of im-migrants and their children or grandchildren) has not supplanted but exists alongside Judeophobic attitudes (preju-dices and negative stereotypes), ideology (conspiracy theo-ries, etc.), and behavior (acts of violence, etc.).[66] Only preexisting bias could invent some scale of "gravity" on which to weigh these two forms of heterophobia. For, in the universalist perspective that I share, which is inseparable from a republican view of the political order, the task is to combat the one as much as the other. And I would add that the only realistic response to the seductions of Islamism—that is, of a politicized Islam opposed to republican values and institutions (and, more broadly, to everything "West-ern," including democracy)—is a campaign to promote an Is-lam of France,[67] an Islam organized in an atmosphere of openness that respects the principle of secularization, an Islam with its own places of worship and representative in-stitutions, which firmly and explicitly condemns the funda-mentalist demagogy of *jihad*. In France and Western Europe the number of "well-integrated and secular yet religiously ob-servant Muslims"[68] is sufficiently high to offer reasonable hope that Islam will have a Vatican II of its own—or, more modestly, that a French Islam will be built by applying the principles separating church and state to the specifics of the Muslim religion.

But let us return to the present. Since the 1960s the gradual worldwide establishment of an anti-Jewish mythology
centered on the demonization of Israel and "Zionism"—
a mythology now conveyed by transnational Islamist
milieux—should be a major focus of anti-racist vigilance and
investigative research. The duty and work of remembrance
are legitimate in their way, but work and reflection are also
necessary to confront the newly emerging threats, so that
things can be done about their causes and contextual factors
and ways be found of limiting their destructive effects. It is
unbearable to see so many people with refined souls and
consciences allowing it to be said, or themselves implying,
that all the ills of the world are due to the existence of Israel.
It is intolerable that Israel should go on being denounced as
"the source of our evils" (to quote the title of an early edition of the *Protocols of the Elders of Zion*).[69] For a long time
Israel has been in the front line of the struggle against Islamist terrorism.

Today's fine hearts and minds, in France but also in Italy
and Germany, for example, say they are opposed to terrorism, but they also speak out against the struggle *against* terrorism. And, not surprisingly, we hear the traditional refrain
from the *gauchistes* of the golden mean: "Neither an imperial
crusade nor Taliban terror!"[70] And, of course: "This war is
not our war." After criminalizing the Western response to
acts of terror, the text of this appeal from Trotskyist and
Communist circles indicates the urgent (and staggeringly
naive!) measures required "to avoid the traps set by the logic
of war and to cut the ground from under the feet of religious
fanaticism": "It is urgently necessary to lift the embargo on
Iraq, to demand Israel's unconditional restoration of the territories it has occupied since 1967, and immediately to recognize a sovereign Palestinian state." Indeed, why not? The
creation of a Palestinian state seems to me both necessary and

urgent. But this set of propositions acquires its real meaning in a context where the supreme leader of Islamist terrorism, for whatever deeper reasons, is raising the same kinds of demands. The program of the Trotskyist and Communist "pacifists," therefore, whose legitimacy and credibility derive from the shining deeds of their ancestors since the time of the Bolshevik Revolution, comes down to an elegant relaying of bin Laden's argument, a translation of it into a softer version.

Of course, this is not the first time we have seen such ideological soup, where all sorts of opposite values and contradictory principles float alongside one another, and whose only function is to justify a lack of action or, in the case of the fall of 2001, a lack of reaction to terrorism. Devoid of a credible revolutionary horizon, the various families of neoleftism can produce only a moderate extremism in keeping with today's parameters of ideological acceptability. Some of their Middle Eastern counterparts, in suggesting ways to deprive terrorism of its breeding ground, go further than the creation of a Palestinian state—which would have the disadvantage of recognizing the right to existence of the Jewish state. They propose instead the creation of a binational state[71] as a way of achieving the panacea of a multinational society (which would differ in little but name and a few minor inflections from a multicultural, or multicommunalist, society). The problem is that this model has been historically tested more than once, and all the tests have ended in failure. In an extreme example of abstract utopianism and blind angelism, supporters of this path sing the praises of the multinational model at a time when all multinational states (from the USSR to Tito's Yugoslavia) have been collapsing and giving birth, through bloody conflict, to ethnically cleansed nation-states.

We can be sure that, in the rational and reasonable world of which our gentle utopians dream, the fine measures they propose would be enough to end Islamist terrorism. But in the terrible world in which we actually live and think, Islamist terrorism is a political and religious project for conquest and domination that must be combated in quite a different manner. If we think that the removal of mere pretexts for terrorist action will actually eradicate Islamist terrorism throughout the world, we delude ourselves and remain in the shadow of Islamist influence, by giving pious answers to the questions it asks and disseminates. This does not at all mean, however, that it is illegitimate to demand an end to the embargo against Iraq if the dictator Saddam Hussein is driven from power;[72] or to consider that the American bombing riposte in Afghanistan,[73] while legitimate in itself, has not taken the form most appropriate to a conflict that is not actually a war between states.[74] But we must avoid mixing everything up. Islamism needs to be taken seriously, as the main threat weighing upon free societies, for it might well prove to be the "communism" of the twenty-first century. (Perhaps this is why it is so seductive for Leninism-Trotskyism, as Islam was seductive for Stalinists of Garaudy's ilk.[75]) And this "green" (Islamist) neototalitarianism might well herald, through its calls for "holy war," a new era of massacres in the name of the sacred cause. Jews, "Crusaders," and "infidels," but also "apes" and "pigs," represent a new variant of the enemy, treated as a type of "noxious insect" (Lenin) of which the world should urgently be rid.[76] The sacred cause of extirpating evil is held up as a universal mission for the cleansing of the human species; the imagery of "holy war" merges with redemptive purification. The core of this new totalitarian vision contains a project for a thoroughgoing purge, with an implication of total control, total Islamist normalization. Antiglobalization activists should urgently put their own house in order, for a tempting anti-Americanism plus a drift into Judeophobia, held securely together by total rejection of the West, threaten to undermine their legitimate and respectable struggle and to open a royal road to Islamist illusion.[77] A royal road to darkness and oppression, to stupidity and murderous violence. Blind pacifism is a particularly dangerous form of moralism. For it places aggressor and victim of aggression on the same level—indeed, it accepts or even encourages the former while paralyzing the latter and making a crime of legitimate self-defense. Inability to recognize and name the enemy, to dare mobilize against him—that is the nadir of politics. It is also the nadir of geopolitics. Let us find the courage (without mirror-image demonization) to recognize the persistent reality of violence and to call the emerging enemy by its name. The enemy is the transnational Islamist-terrorist network, for which the Jews are a people in the way and democratic culture is a poison. This identification of the Islamist enemy Diaspora—at once internal and external, we might say—does not mean that we should avoid criticizing the policies of the world's only hyperpower: we should not lazily oppose Gnostic anti-Americanism with an enraptured, artificial pro-Americanism, as too many intellectuals in a hurry are inclined to do. We should read Max Weber again on this: "Whoever wants to engage in politics at all, and especially in politics as a vocation, . . . lets himself in for the diabolic forces lurking in all violence."[78]

The struggle against the new "networked" global terrorism cannot be reduced to the elimination of this or that organization, for the Islamist networks are only the hard core of an expanding ideological-political field. This affects in varying degrees the Muslim masses of the whole world, who are sensitive to the propaganda of the Islamist leaders. And these leaders, in turn, spotlight and skillfully exploit popular causes in the Muslim world (the Palestinian cause, the struggle against the embargo on Iraq, the "liberation" of the "holy places" in Saudi Arabia). Special attention should be paid to the arguments of the Islamist terrorists, which—with the distinctive addition of *jihad*, of course—take up most of the predominantly anti-American themes that structure the discourse of neo–Third Worldists and doctrinaires of anti-globalization, and similarly denounce the evil works of the World Bank, the IMF, and so on. Thus, in a communiqué issued on August 12, 1998, by the Islamic Liberation Army, we read:

"Given the American and Jewish occupation of the area around the Al Aqsa mosque, given what the Jews are doing in Palestine (destruction of houses), given the death of more than a million Iraqis, given the imprisonment of the ulema in America and U.S.-dominated countries, and given the theft of the wealth of Muslims through the extraction of petroleum, this forces us into a worldwide *jihad* at every moment."[79]

At the opening of the third millennium, the culture of hate and death has imperceptibly become an international social movement, with a *jihadist* vanguard at its head that lacks all scruples. The politicization of death and criminal suicide emerges from the obliteration of politics: "The failure of politics reflects on religion and makes the sacred a bearer of death."[80] Massacres and wars of extermination invoke sublime ideas and the loftiest values, or one particular figure of the Absolute. Today's Islamist warriors relate to Allah as a new idol in whose name they kill to live post mortem, and give up their own lives in order to kill others. But we should never tire of pointing out that the first victims of Islamist terrorism were and are Muslims, as the massacres in Algeria (mostly committed by Islamists trained in Afghanistan) vividly demonstrate.[81] A division pregnant with bloody conflict is thus observable at the very heart of the Muslim world, where genocidal Islamist totalitarians are pitted against "enlightened" Muslims who reject the madness of war, pursue a path of dialogue and cooperation with non-Muslims, and wish to have for themselves what seems positive in Western modernity (science, liberal-pluralist democracy, the principles of free enquiry and free discussion, etc.). When he was asked about the American air strikes in Afghanistan, the mufti of Marseilles, Soheib Bencheikh, did not beat about the bush: "This military action does not trouble me at all, because it is aimed at liberating the Afghan people from a cruel and tyrannical regime. . . . I therefore strongly dispute all the interpretations thrown up here and there by a peace movement whose indulgent attitude fills me with dread. . . . Muslim societies should be helped to rid themselves of fundamentalism."[82] It is important that Islam's religious authorities and the intellectual elites of Muslim countries, as well as representative Muslim figures in all countries around the world, speak out as clearly against the new Islamist totalitarianism.[83]

Contrary to what bin Laden's propagandists keep trotting out, the war against Islamist total terrorism does not belong to the category of religious war—for the simple reason that only the Islamist fanatics engage in bellicose invocations of Islam. But the distinction in principle between Islam and Islamism can be eroded by a self-fulfilling prophecy: that is to say, constant assertions of a religious war between Muslims and the "Judeo-Crusaders" are always liable to find expression in behavior that conforms to the prophecy. This is why a many-sided cultural war should accompany the military intervention, countering the power of Islamist demagogy to persuade and mobilize the masses. We might begin by challenging the smugly "revolutionary" interpretation of terrorism: "Once," Walter Laqueur noted in 1977, "it was the strategy of the poor and weak used against ruthless tyrants; today its more prominent representatives are no longer poor, and modern technology is giving them powerful weapons."[84]

The Islamists are not alone in their enterprise of terror and destruction against the West and the pluralist democracies (Israel included). The imagination of those obsessed with

a Jewish or Zionist plot knows no bounds. And all these mot-
ley hallucinators can recognize themselves in the wildest accusations issued by the fanatics of "Salafism-jihadism."
When Mullah Omar, the "supreme leader" of the Taliban,
was asked about the 9/11 attacks on America, he did not bat
an eyelid as he hinted at some fiendish manipulation: "I am
convinced that those who committed these attacks come
from inside America itself. . . . Why have the American investigations paid no attention to the fact that 4,000 Jews
working at the World Trade Center were not there on the day
of the attack?"[85] The trained eye of an Islamist is capable of
detecting a Jewish cause behind every event. But the Islamist
visionary is here only the most visibly grotesque figure of an
army of anti-Jewish hatemongers. Ideologized Judeophobia
leads them to see Jews everywhere: to spot Jews at work in
the shadows, to imagine them busily in pursuit of world
domination, to suppose them capable of anything and therefore of the worst.[86] In France, as in other European countries,
certain fanatical anti-Americans and anti-Israelis (mostly on
the far right or the Communist or neoleftist "left of the left")
have played the role of traveling companions and auxiliary
legitimators in the total war unleashed by the 9/11 attacks.
By way of illustration, I will mention a highly synthetic text
of October 7, 2001, signed by the sociologist Bruno Roy, director of Fata Morgana Editions. Addressing his fellow academics, he writes:

"Some humanists hoped that, because of its moderate
character (5,500 dead, or less than one per cent of the total
number of victims caused by the blockade of Iraq), the just
warning of September 11 would lead the United States to
change its policy. This proved a vain illusion. The worst of
the terrorist states, itself established on the basis of genocide
and grown rich through slavery, prospers only by means of
crime: from Mexico to Hiroshima, from Guatemala to Viet-

nam, from Colombia to Palestine. Today, when the Afghan people is the direct victim of the bombing (and Palestine the indirect victim, with the Zionist regime profiting from the situation to intensify the massacres), we can all the less remain indifferent in that the French government, a valet of the Americans, seeks to implicate us in the crime. What can academics do? In response to the government lies and media disinformation, we can try to make the truth known, to oppose the war, and to display our solidarity with the victims."[87]

On reading such a hate-filled text (the 9/11 massacre a "just warning"!), which colludes with the enemies of all freedom, one cannot help thinking of Orwell's observations on the singular penchant of intellectuals for totalitarian dictators: "Intellectuals are more totalitarian in outlook than the common people"[88]; "What is sinister . . . is that the conscious enemies of liberty are those to whom liberty ought to mean most."[89] Yet it is necessary to resist the calls for hatred, and the hatred of those who hate—to retreat from the vicious circle of mimetic hatred, to refrain from the "pathos of the victim" and the "vehemence of the avenger." This is one of the lessons I learned from *If This Is a Man*, Primo Levi's great work, which in 1976 limpidly answered one of the questions that his readers had repeatedly asked:

"I must admit that if I had in front of me one of our persecutors of those days, certain known faces, certain old lies, I would be tempted to hate, and with violence too; but exactly because I am not a fascist or a Nazi, I refuse to give way to this temptation. I believe in reason and in discussion as supreme instruments of progress, and therefore I repress hatred even within myself: I prefer justice."[90]

There is no destructive violence that does not try to justify itself by referring to strong beliefs, and these beliefs are further strengthened by the acts of violence they motivate and conceal. Zygmunt Bauman has described this vicious circle of

beliefs and violence: "Like vampires, values need blood to re-
plenish their life juices. And the greater the number of dead,
the more splendid and divine grow the values on whose altar
the lives had been burned."[91] But the terrible logic is not in-
escapable. The Sisyphean task of politics is precisely to define
the conditions that allow us to escape this vicious circle, by
establishing an order in which plurality does not exclude
unity. Faced with combat groups whose declared aim is to
win over, or win out over, the "infidels," to conquer recalci-
trant nations or delete them from the map, pacifist angelism
is simply not an option. It is no more than the smiling and ac-
quiescent face of defeatism. We are embarked on a war, and
in that war we have to choose our camp, the camp of liberty.
Ibn Warraq concluded his book as follows: "The final battle
will not necessarily be between Islam and the West but between those who are and those who are not prepared to pay
a price for liberty."[92] Let us just slightly correct this: there
will be no final battle.

In France, the nation that has dreamed of itself as the moth-
erland of human and civil rights, it has become necessary for
people of all beliefs and origins who reject intolerance and fanaticism to open their eyes to the present situation. They must
consider what is to be said and done to prevent the banalization of the terrible mental sickness of anti-Jewish hatred[93]—
a sickness whose ideological mutations continually give it fresh
life, in a new context where transnational Islamist terrorism
conveys and intensifies it. "Intolerance breeds intolerance,"
noted Leroy-Beaulieu in 1897, in the troubled context of the
Dreyfus affair.[94] The expansion of the Enlightenment has not
caused intolerance or religious fanaticism to disappear.[95] Nothing in man can ever be totally eradicated. What we see in history is a succession of unpredictable ebbs and flows,
disappearances and reappearances. Anti-Jewish passions never
ceased to be reborn in the twentieth century, in forms that no

one had foreseen. And in the last three decades of the century, Judeophobia based on racism and nationalism gave way to Judeophobia based on anti-racism and anti-nationalism, or even anti-globalism. It was a tragic reversal of the "struggle against racism," which since the end of the nineteenth century had included the struggle against anti-Semitism.

These are times of mutually reinforcing hatreds. Intellectualized hatreds accompany the spread of a technological neobarbarism that aims to bring every nation into line, and of its "jihadist" reverse side that pours forth calls for herdlike submission, blind obedience, and the holy extermination of satanic enemies. Martyrs are in plentiful supply. Yet, as Nietzsche suggested, martyrs prove nothing about the truth of a cause: "Blood is the worst witness of truth; blood poisons and transforms the purest teaching to delusion and hatred of the heart."[96] Everyone—consumer, stockholder, or suicide—is looking for happiness. Even the "Islamikaze" killers are in search of paradise. May I perhaps quote André Breton here? "To reduce the imagination to slavery, even for what is crudely called happiness, is to hide from every element of supreme justice that you find deep down inside yourself."[97] What is distinctively human in man is the act of wagering on a possible world where hatred does not have the last word. Love remains our utopia. Love wedded to intelligence.

Notes

Introduction

1. In the 1980s I began to analyze this worldwide anti-Jewish configuration as it was taking shape, and I thought fit to publish a long synthetic article on the phenomenon, "La nouvelle judéophobie: Antisionisme, antiracisme, anti-impérialisme" (*Les Temps modernes* 520, November 1989, pp. 1–80). The present book continues the work of description, interpretation, and conceptualization that I began in the early 1980s, and of which that article from 1989 was a provisional balance sheet.

2. It should be made clear that this is not a quotation but my own reconstruction of a common line of argument that does not always appear in such developed and explicit form.

3. It is important to distinguish at least three degrees or levels of anti-Jewish attitudes, in ascending order of intensity and intellectualization: (a) a vague xenophobia, involving diffuse antipathy toward "outsiders" or "foreigners"; (b) hostile reactions to people thought of as disturbing and threatening, and therefore as potential adversaries; and (c) negative images, organized as an ideological system, in which the Jewish people appear as an evil force and a figure of the absolute enemy. This ideological phantasm assumes a high degree of intellectualization of anti-Jewish passions and appears only at the third level. For a model that seeks to grasp the phenomenon in a similar way, see Michael R. Marrus, "The Theory and Practice of Anti-Semitism," *Commentary* 74/2, August 1982, pp. 38–42.

4. Maxime Rodinson, "Sur les visions arabes du conflit israélo-arabe" (1969), reprinted in M. Rodinson, *Peuple juif ou problème juif?*, Paris: François Maspero, 1981, p. 351, n. 14.

5. "The Jews are guilty, the punishment is coming," thundered Joseph Goebbels in 1931. Quoted in Saul Friedländer, *Nazi Germany and the Jews*, vol. 1, *The Years of Persecution*, London: Weidenfeld and Nicolson, 1997, p. 111.

6. The use of such descriptive terms may be at least minimally clarified by the following brief summary: "Islamism designates the political uses of Islam. It should be distinguished from fundamentalism, which may be defined as a return to the founding texts, the Koran, and the tradition of the prophet Mohammed that tries to be as close as possible in its everyday practice to the initial spirit of the Revelation. Fundamentalism becomes Islamism when it is used as an ideology in the competitive political arena, with the aim of transforming society and the state in order to bring them into line with the Koranic message (which then functions as a political ideal)." (Bernard Botiveau, Jocelyne Cesari, *Géopolitique des islams*, Paris: Economica, 1997, p. 95.) There is something to be said for Maxime Rodinson's concern that diffuse use of the term "Islamism" or "Islamist" carries the risk of confusion with "Islam" and "Islamic"— hence his preference for the term "Muslim fundamentalism" (*intégrisme musulman*), with its suggestion of the possibility of comparative analysis. See *L'Islam: politique et croyance*, Paris: Fayard, 1993, then Pocket edition 1995, pp. 231–295, 301–330.

7. When Olivier Carré began employing the category "Islamic radicalism" in the early 1980s, he wanted to highlight both the "return to roots" and the extremism—that is, the two characteristic features of the political Islam which, since the 1970s, had been "rising like a groundswell throughout the Muslim world" (Olivier Carré and Gérard Michaud [Michel Seurat], *Les Frères musulmans, Égypte et Syrie (1928–1982)*, Paris: Gallimard/Julliard, 1983, p. 205). See Olivier Carré, "Essai de typologie descriptive des mouvements radicaux d'inspiration musulmane," in Olivier Carré and Paul Dumont, eds., *Radicalismes islamiques*, vol. 1, Paris: L'Harmattan, 1985, pp. 5–21. The "integrist" dimension (a term freely borrowed from Émile Poulat), which may be expressed in a demand for cultural authenticity or in literal adherence to certain texts, coexists in Islamism with a maximalist or extremist tendency that takes on fanatical features, especially in the bellicose form of "jihadism." Furthermore, a number of researchers have demonstrated a tension throughout the Muslim world between a pole of political Islamism, geared to the conquest of state power,

and a pole of conservative neofundamentalism, whose aim is to reform society and morals by Islamicizing, or re-Islamicizing, cultural practices. See Gilles Kepel, *Prophet and Pharaoh: Muslim
Extremism in Contemporary Egypt*, Berkeley: University of California Press, 1985; Olivier Roy, *The Failure of Political Islam*,
Cambridge, Mass.: Harvard University Press, 1994; Olivier Roy,
The New Central Asia: The Creation of Nations, New York: New
York University Press, 2000. Bruno Étienne, in a work first published in 1987 (*L'Islamisme radical*, Paris: Hachette, 1987), sets
out to study this "reappropriation of politics" through Islam, and
immediately makes it clear that the term "radical Islamism" should
be taken both "in the primary sense of the *root* doctrine of Islam,
and in the American sense of politically radical, almost revolutionary Islam" (quoted from the "Biblio Essais" series edition, Paris,
1989, p. 21; cf. p. 335, n. 15).

8. Thus, in anti-Jewish mythology, a new version of the paradoxical posture of the modern Jew accuses him of being both glob-
alizing and territorially grounded, or of being "too globalist" (or
"imperialistic") as well as "too Zionist" (or "nationalist"), hyper-
cosmopolitan and hyper-rooted. This new pairing of seemingly contradictory charges is tending to supplant the one that was for long
uppermost in Judeophobic visions: namely, the pairing of "Judeo-
bolshevism" and "Judeo-capitalism," which laid the main stress on
the accusation of "rootlessness" and/or nomadism, supposedly
shared by the two components of the pair.

9. Vulgar Americanophobia is only a derivative opiate (and a
dangerous ideological outgrowth) of something I consider both legitimate and absolutely necessary: a properly argued critique of the
technological, market-centered globalization that is destroying the
political and cultural foundations of democracy and eliminating nations (as communities of citizens) for the benefit of ethnic groups
and transnational networks. See my book *Résister au bougisme.
Démocratie forte contre mondialisation techno-marchande*, Paris:
Mille et une nuits, 2001.

10. Quoted by *Al Hayat* (a newspaper published in Beirut), 17
August 1969. See my book *Les Protocoles des Sages de Sion. Faux
et usages d'un faux*, Paris: Berg International, 1992, vol. 1,
pp. 327–328, n. 19. It should be remembered that the *Protocols of*

the *Elders of Zion* were introduced into the Middle East in the early 1920s, by Christian Arabs who were the first to translate and adapt the well-known anti-Jewish forgery (ibid., pp. 295f.).

11. Quoted from *L'Arche* No. 524–525, October–November 2001, p. 42. The pro–Le Pen press in France obligingly reproduced the bulk of this "letter" from Saddam Hussein: see "La réflexion de Saddam Hussein sur les attentats du 11 septembre," *National-Hebdo* No. 905, 22–28 November 2001, p. 9.

12. See, for example, Paul Morand, *New York*, London: William Heinemann, 1931, first published in French as *New York*, Paris: Flammarion, 1930; Louis-Ferdinand Céline, *L'École des cadavres*, Paris: Denoël, 1938, p. 28 ("the utterly Jewish United States"), pp. 44–45 ("Yid-American warmongering propaganda"), p. 66 ("Judeo-Americans—in short, the whole of America"); Pierre-Antoine Cousteau, *L'Amérique juive*, Paris: Les Éditions de France, 1942; Henry Coston, *L'Amérique. bastion d'Israël*, Paris: C.A.D., 1942.

13. What may be considered established, with regard to the positions of the Catholic church, is that during the period from the courageous initiatives of John XXIII and the Second Vatican Council (1964–1965) to the numerous interventions of John Paul II in the 1990s there was a gradual erosion of anti-Semitic traces "in the doctrine of Christian instruction, in theology and apologetics, preaching and liturgy" (Solemn Declaration of the French Episcopate, Drancy, 30 September 1997). This makes it possible to envisage an end to "the teaching of hatred." See Pierre Pierrard, *Juifs et catholiques français. D'Édouard Drumont à Jacob Kaplan 1886–1994*, Paris: Éditions du Cerf, 1997; Paul Giniewski, *L'Anti-judaïsme Chrétien: la mutation*, Paris: Éditions Salvator. For a less optimistic perspective, see Georges-Elia Sarfati, *Le Vatican et la Shoah, ou comment l'Église s'absout de son passé*, Paris: Berg International, 2000.

14. Edward W. Said, *Orientalism: Western Conceptions of the Orient*, London: Penguin Books, 1991, p. 286. In Said's view, this process of slippage or displacement became apparent after the 1973 war (ibid.).

15. Hannah Arendt, "Reflections on Little Rock," *Dissent* 6/1, Winter 1959, p. 46.

Chapter 1. Surveying the Landscape

1. See Franck Debié and Sylvie Fouet, *La Paix en miettes. Israël/Palestine, 1993–2000*, Paris: PUF, 2001; and Ilan Greilsammer, "Il faut se batter pour la paix!" (remarks recorded by Alex Korbane), *Regards* [Brussels] No. 508, 13–26 November 2001, pp. 14–15.

2. See the testimony and analysis of Shlomo Ben-Ami, the former Israeli foreign minister who was present alongside Ehud Barak during these negotiations: "End of a Journey" [interview with Ari Shavit], *Ha'aretz*, 14 September 2001. This leading Israeli politician of the left repeats here that "the establishment of a Palestinian state is a moral and political necessity."

3. See Michel-Yves Peissik, "Le rapport de la 'Commission Mitchell' parviendra-t-il à réconcilier Israéliens et Palestiniens?," *Revue Politique et Parlementaire* No. 1012, May–June 2001, pp. 77–89.

4. I am not forgetting the existence of Judeophobic deviations among Christian Arabs, who are nevertheless themselves victims of religious persecution (especially at the hands of Islamists) in a number of Muslim countries in the Middle East.

5. See my *Résister au bougisme*, op. cit., pp. 52–64.

6. The term *Antisemitismus* was introduced and established in Germany by the Socialist journalist Wilhelm Marr (1819–1904) toward the end of the 1870s, to designate a "nondenominational" rejection of Jews and "Judaism." Marr himself was the author of an anti-Jewish pamphlet published in Berne in February 1879: *Der Sieg des Judenthums über das Germanenthum. Vom nicht confessionellen Standpunkt aus betrachtet* [The Victory of Judaism over Germanism, Considered from a Non-denominational Point of View], which was so successful that it was reprinted eleven times within a year of publication. A few months later, in the fall of 1879, he founded the League of Anti-Semites (*Antisemiten-Liga*). See Léon Poliakov, *History of Anti-Semitism*, vol. 4, *Suicidal Europe 1870–1933*, London: Routledge & Kegan Paul, 1985, pp. 16–18; Jacob Katz, *From Prejudice to Destruction: Anti-Semitism, 1700–1933*, Cambridge, Mass: Harvard University Press, 1980, pp. 1, 260f.; Helmut Berding, *Moderner Antisemitismus in Deutschland*, Frankfurt-am-Main: Suhrkamp, 1988 [French trans. *Histoire de l'antisémitisme en Allemagne*, Paris: Éditions de la Maison des

sciences de l'homme, 1991, p. 91]; Robert S. Wistrich, *Anti-semitism: The Longest Hatred*, London: Thames Methuen, 1991, pp. xv, xxiv, 57, 252. See also Mosche Zimmermann, *Wilhelm Marr: "The Patriarch of Anti-Semitism,"* New York: Oxford University Press, 1986. The terms "antisémitique" (or "anti-sémitique") and "antisémitisme" (or "anti-sémitisme") became current in French in the early 1880s: see Jeannine Verdès-Leroux, *Scandale financier et antisémitisme catholique. Le krach de l'Union Générale*, Paris: Éditions du Centurion, 1969, esp. pp. 118ff.

7. See my book *La Couleur et le Sang. Doctrines racistes à la française*, Paris: Mille et une nuits, revised and expanded ed., 2002.

8. In the late nineteenth century some of the so-called anti-Semitic literature was, in varying proportions, both anti-Jewish and anti-Islamic (or anti-Arab). See, for instance, two successive books published by an avowed Greek "anti-Semite" under the pen name D. Kimon: *La Politique israélite: politiciens, journalistes, banquiers. Étude psychologique*, Paris: Albert Savine ("Bibliothèque antisémitique"), 1889; and *La Pathologie de l'Islam et les moyens de le détruire*, Paris: D. Kimon, 1897. On the first of these, see Marc Angenot, *Ce que l'on dit des Juifs en 1889. Antisémitisme et discours social*, Saint-Denis: Presses universitaires de Vincennes, 1989, pp. 36–40. See also Maxime Rodinson, *Europe and the Mystique of Islam*, London: I. B. Tauris, 1988, pp. 67 and 142 (n. 123); Jean-Louis Triaud, "L'Islam vu par les historiens français," *Esprit* no. 246, October 1998, p. 111, n.2.

9. See Bernard Lewis, "Semites and Anti-Semites," first published in *Survey*, 1971, and reprinted in Lewis, *Islam in History. Ideas, Men and Events in the Middle East*, London: Alcove Press, 1973, pp. 138–157; and Bernard Lewis, *The Multiple Identities of the Middle East*, London: Weidenfeld & Nicolson, 1998, pp. 42–46. See also the observations in Olivier Carré, *L'Islam laïque ou le retour à la Grande Tradition*, Paris: Armand Colin, 1993, p. 27.

10. See the remarks in Bernard Lewis, *Semites and Anti-Semites: An Enquiry into Conflict and Prejudice*, London: Weidenfeld & Nicolson, 1986, pp. 16–17, 117f. Rodinson, for his part, having reduced the meaning of the word "anti-Semitism" to "hatred of Jews," notes "the emptiness of the argument of certain Arabs, to the effect that we cannot be anti-Semitic because we too are Semites." *L'Islam: politique et croyance*, op. cit., p. 351. If I propose to drop

the current term "anti-Semitism," it is precisely to avoid the contradiction between its etymological meaning (hostility toward Semites) and its semantic usage (hostility toward Jews).

11. Louis Farrakhan, in *Independent Black Leadership in America: Minister Farrakhan, Dr. Fulani, Rev. Sharpton*, with an introduction by William Pleasant, New York: Castillo International Publications, 1990, pp. 43–44. For a contextualization and commentary, see Gilles Kepel, *Allah in the West: Islamic Movements in America and Europe*, Stanford, Calif.: Stanford University Press, 1997, pp. 91f.

12. For a more precise characterization, see my introduction to the collection I edited, *L'Antisémitisme de plume 1940–1944. Études et documents*, Paris: Berg International, 1999, esp. pp. 30–44.

13. Quoted in Michel Gurfinkiel, *Israël. Géopolitique d'une paix*, Paris: Michalon, 1996, p. 19.

14. On April 13, 1994, a suicide bomber killed five people on a bus at Hadera; on October 19, 1994, another caused twenty-one deaths on a No. 5 bus in Tel Aviv. See "Les attentats-suicides du Hamas," *L'Arche* No. 524–525, October–November 2001, p. 65.

15. Roland Jacquard, *La Tentation nihiliste*, Paris: Presses universitaires de France, 1989, p. 34.

16. Quoted in ibid.

17. Nor have the "noble consciences" mobilized in support of the Christians and Southern animists of Sudan, where an Islamist dictatorship has been persecuting non-Muslim minorities and covering up the practice of slavery. We could provide many other examples of this kind, which would show that the Palestinians have a privileged place among recognized victim-groups. They enjoy special treatment and many advantages deriving from the public sympathy of elites, recognition of the legitimacy of their nationalist struggle, and financial assistance from the major powers.

18. On the uses of the figure of the martyr (the one who falls on God's path and thereby becomes a "witness" or *shahid*), see "La maladie de l'Islam. Entretien avec Abdelwahab Meddeb," *Esprit* No. 278, October 2001, pp. 87–89.

19. Hassan al-Banna, "Lettre des enseignements" (1943), quoted in Carré and Michaud, *Les Frères musulmans*, op. cit., p. 44. The Sunni theoretician Hassan al-Banna summarized as follows

his general conception of Islam: "Islam is ideology and faith, fatherland and nationality, religion and state, spirit and action, book and sword" (quoted from Rochdy Alili, *Qu'est-ce que l'islam?*, Paris: La Découverte & Syros, 2000, p. 323). The same thinker maintained that "Islam is an all-inclusive order that has a bearing on every aspect of life" (quoted by Mohammed Arkoun in M. Arkoun and Louis Gardet, *L'Islam, hier, demain*, 2nd ed., Paris: Buchet-Chastel, 1982, p. 157; and by Olivier Roy in *The Failure of Political Islam*, op. cit). This vision of Islam as an all-inclusive totality or polymorphous whole (or, in a critical perspective, as a fuzzy, ambiguous, weakly defined entity) is not peculiar to Islamists, and it may be conceptually translated into the language of sociology or the history of religions. This normative inclusiveness of Islam qua religion and sociopolitical system may be compared to the ideal of the church in the nineteenth century and the normative project that it failed to achieve. In fact it has become commonplace to approach Islam by arguing, within categories understandable to a Western public, that it is both a religion (a belief system) and a civilization (a cultural system endowed with a history), or again that it is "at once a religion and a political system." (Rémy Leveau and Dominique Schnapper, "Religion et politique: juifs et musulmans maghrébins en France," in Rémy Leveau and Gilles Kepel, eds., *Les Musulmans dans la société française*, Paris: Presses de la Fondation nationale des sciences politiques, 1988, p. 99.) Hence the diversity of practices associated with Islam. Islam as a denomination—or, if one prefers, secularized Islam—involves *inter alia* two distinct aspects: the privatization or individualization of belief, and the identity function of belief combined with norms and rituals that frame and articulate the different ages of human life. See Jocelyne Cesari, *Musulmans et républicains: les jeunes, l'islam et la France*, Brussels: Complexe, 1998, pp. 42–45.

20. According to al-Banna, "armed struggle for God's cause" should be conducted by those in the "first armed phalanx" of the First Rank—that is, the special Secret Organization—whose task it is to fight in Palestine (initially against the British). (See Carré and Michaud, *Les Frères musulmans*.) On the topical importance of Hassan al-Banna's thought, as seen by his grandson, the reader may refer to Tariq Ramadan, *Aux sources du renouveau musulman. D'al Afghani à Hassan al Banna, un siècle de r éformsime islamique,*

Paris: Bayard-Centurion, 1998. On August 18, 1988, the Islamic Resistance Movement, more widely known by its name Hamas, published a charter or "covenant" in which it defined itself as "one of the wings of the Moslem Brotherhood in Palestine" (art. 2), and, more precisely, as a distinct "Palestinian movement, whose allegiance is to Allah, and whose way of life is Islam. It strives to raise the banner of Allah over every inch of Palestine" (art. 6). In the preamble, moreover, we read the following quotation from Hassan al-Banna: "Israel will exist and will continue to exist until Islam obliterates it, just as it obliterated others before it." MidEast Web Historical Documents, *The Covenant of the Islamic Resistance Movement (Hamas) 18 August 1988*, http://www.mideastweb.org.

21. For an overview, see Jean-Philippe Conrad, "Origines et réalité de l'islamisme activiste," *Stratégique*, 1997/2–3, pp. 13–63.

22. Leon Trotsky, "Moralists and Sycophants Against Marxism," in *Their Morals and Ours*, London: New Park Publications, 1968, p. 51.

23. See Joseph Maïla, "Les 'héros' d'une antimondialisation frénétique," *Le Monde*, October 4, 2001, p. 19.

24. "Message to the Tricontinental" (April 1967), in Che Guevara, *Guerrilla Warfare*, Lincoln: University of Nebraska Press, 1985, p. 211.

25. Monique Canto-Sperber, "Injustifiable terreur," *Le Monde*, October 4, 2001, pp. 1, 19.

26. The Palestinian nationalist Abdul Wahhab Kayyali, who is attached to the PLO Research Center, ended his contribution to the thick (and fascinating) dossier of *Les Temps modernes* on the "Israeli-Arab conflict" with the following sentence: "In fact, the body and cancer cannot coexist with each other: the struggle between them is a struggle for existence" ("Sionisme et expansionnisme," *Les Temps Modernes* No. 253, 1967, p. 155).

27. Bat Ye'or, "L'antisionisme euro-arabe," in *[Nouveaux] visages de l'antisémitisme*, Paris: NM7, 2001, p. 32.

28. The term "eliminationist anti-Semitism" entered the specialist's vocabulary through the historical and ideological debates aroused by Daniel Jonah Goldhagen's highly controversial book *Hitler's Willing Executioners: Ordinary Germans and the Holocaust* (New York: Alfred A. Knopf, 1996)—see especially pp. 27–128.

29. Saul Friedländer uses this term to characterize Hitler's racist anti-Semitism: "It is this redemptive dimension, this synthesis of a murderous rage and an 'idealistic' goal, shared by the Nazi leader and the hard core of the party, that led to Hitler's ultimate decision to exterminate the Jews" (op. cit., p. 3). In my view, this redemptive dimension may be found in radical Islamist Judeophobia, which suggests that the Muslim world can be saved only through extermination of the Jews.

30. *Our Arab Language*, fifth grade, Palestinian National Authority, Ministry of National Education, 1996, pp. 64–66.

31. Ibid., p. 67.

32. *Islamic Education*, seventh grade, Palestinian Authority, Ministry of Education and Higher Education, 1996, p. 125. For other examples, see Yohanan Manor, André Marcus, et al., *The Palestinian Authority School Books*, report of the Center for Monitoring the Impact of Peace, New York, March 2001; "Les enfants palestiniens à l'école de la haine. L'image d'Israël et du Juif dans les manuels scolaires de l'Autorité palestinienne," dossier published in *L'Arche* No. 515, January 2001; and Yohanan Manor, "L'antisémitisme des manuels scolaires palestiniens," in *[Nouveaux] visages de l'antisémitisme*, op. cit., pp. 123–150.

33. The revival of anti-Jewish persuasions on the left has in fact been a periodic occurrence since the last third of the nineteenth century, and it may be interpreted as a perpetual return to its origins (the anti-capitalism of the socialist and anarchist milieux of the first two-thirds of the nineteenth century, illustrated by the names of Fourier, Toussenel, and Proudhon, who were all hostile to the Jews). See, especially, Léon Poliakov, *History of Anti-Semitism*, vol. 3, *From Voltaire to Wagner*, London: Routledge & Kegan Paul, 1975; Henri Arvon, *les Juifs et l'idéologie*, Paris: Presses universitaires de France, 1978; Paul Bénichou, "Sur quelques sources françaises de l'antisémitisme moderne," *Commentaire* No. 1, 1978, pp. 67–79; Antoine Leca, "Les themes idéologiques de l'antisémitisme chez les socialistes français (1845–1890)," *Revue de la recherché juridique. Droit prospectif*, XX-62, 1995, No. 3, pp. 983–1003; Marc Crapez, *La Gauche réactionnaire. Mythes de la plèbe et de la race dans le sillage des Lumi ères*, Paris: Berg International, 1997; Simon Epstein, *Les Dreyfusards sous l'Occupation*, Paris: Albin Michel, 2001.

34. Mounthir Anabtawi, "Le sionisme: un movement colonialiste, chauvin et militariste," *Les Temps modernes* No. 253, 1967, p. 126.

35. For a historical approach to Zionism, see Walter Laqueur, *A History of Zionism*, with a new preface by the author, New York: Schocken Books, 2003; Shlomo Avineri, *The Making of Modern Zionism: Intellectual Origins of the Jewish State*, New York: Basic Books, 1981; Élie Barnavi, *Israël au XXe siècle*, Paris: Presses universitaires de France, 1982; Mitchell Cohen, *Zion and State: Nation, Class, and the Shaping of Modern Israel*, New York: Basil Blackwell, 1987; Alain Dieckhoff, *Invention of a Nation: Zionist Thought and the Making of Modern Israel*, New York: Columbia University Press, 2003; Zeev Sternhell, *The Founding Myths of Israel: Nationalism, Socialism, and the Making of the Jewish State*, Princeton, N.J.: Princeton University Press, 1998; Ilan Greilsammer, *La Nouvelle Histoire d'Israël. Essai sur une identité nationale*, Paris: Gallimard, 1998. See also two illuminating works: Claude Klein, *Le Caractère juif de l'État d'Israël*, Paris: Éditions Cujas, 1977; and Catherine Kaminsky and Simon Kruk, *Le Nationalisme arabe et le nationalisme juif*, Paris: Presses universitaires de France, 1983.

36. It is not going too far to say that, after the creation of the State of Israel, anti-Zionism and/or anti-Israelism constituted—at least until 1967—the only structuring principle of Arab unity.

37. *Le Petit Robert*, Paris, 1977 ed.

38. It is true that some individuals of Jewish origin take part in the formation and propagation of the new Judeophobia, for many different reasons and in many different ways: self-hatred, conformism or anti-conformism, sincere compassion for other groups, selective xenophilia (unconditional pro-Palestinism, for example), personal strategies, revolutionary commitment, cowardice, feeble-mindedness, and so on. But this fact, though highly regrettable, is neither new nor surprising, and it cannot be used to deny the anti-Jewish content of certain attitudes or positions taken publicly by individuals of Jewish origin. Contrary to what common sense might suggest, it is not impossible for an individual who considers himself, or is considered by others, as Jewish to take part in anti-Jewish actions or demonstrations. There is no cause for astonishment in the fact that some individuals of Jewish origin can be naive, conformist

or anti-conformist, cynical, cowardly, corrupt, ashamed of their origins—or "anti-Zionist." To think otherwise would be to suppose that human passions are not universally distributed. Bernard Lewis tackled a few aspects of this question in his article "The Pro-Islamic Jews," *Judaism*, Fall 1968. Discussion of the case of Karl Marx—a thinker of Jewish origin, some of whose writings (*On the Jewish Question*, 1844) and statements (in his correspondence) may be formally recognized as anti-Jewish—is paradigmatic in this connection. Since Marx's specific article was written in reply to an essay of Bruno Bauer's that appeared in 1843, it is important to read the two texts together: Karl Marx, "On the Jewish Question," in *Early Writings*, London: New Left Review/Penguin Books, 1975, pp. 211–241; and Bruno Bauer, *Die Judenfrage*, Brunswick, 1843 [*La Question juive*, Paris: Union générale d'Éditions, 1968]. See Francis Kaplan, *Marx antisémite?*, Paris: Berg International/Éditions Imago, 1990. It might be argued that, among certain "left-wing" (but especially extreme left-wing) Jews, the old self-hatred is turning into hatred of the state, and especially the Jewish state, which has actually put an end to Jewish self-hatred.

39. In this chaotic international context, where Islamist propaganda exploits themes of resistance to uncontrolled globalization, it is important that the leaders of anti-globalization movements take a clear position against Islamism, even and especially when those leading the "holy war" justify it by claiming that it expresses the despair of the poverty-stricken masses in the South, and that they are defending the noble cause of the famished victims of capitalism or American imperialism. Although a certain imperial type of "Westernization of the world" should be rejected (the expression is borrowed from Serge Latouche), this makes it all the more necessary to combat those who seek to achieve the Islamization of the world through terror and propaganda. "No constraint in matters of religion!" as the Koran so rightly says. "Your duty is only to warn them: you are not their keeper" ("The Overwhelming Event", 88:21, 22). For a "nonconservative" commentary on such verses from (the French translation of) the Koran, see Mohamed Charfi, *Islam et liberté. Le malentendu historique*, Paris: Albin Michel, 1998, pp. 164–166.

40. See Georges Vajda, "Juifs et Musulmans selon le hadith," *Journal asiatique*, 1937, pp. 57–127, and "L'image du Juif dans la

tradition islamique," *Les Nouveaux Cahiers* Nos. 13–14, Spring–Summer 1968, pp. 3–7; Bat Ye'or, *The Dhimmi: Jews and Christians Under Islam*, London and Toronto: Associated University Presses, 1985; Bernard Lewis, *Jews of Islam*, Princeton, N.J.: Princeton University Press, 1984, and "Semites and Anti-Semites", op. cit., esp. pp. 146–176. See also David F. Green, ed., *Les Juifs et Israël vus par les théologiens arabes*, selected records of the 4th conference of the Academy of Islamic Research, Cairo, Al-Azhar, September 1968, compiled and introduced by David F. Green, with a preface by Léon Poliakov, Geneva: Éditions de l'Avenir, 2nd corrected ed., 1974.

41. We owe it to the anthropologist Clifford Geertz that, in his study of the development of "classical religious styles" in Morocco and Indonesia, he has well pointed up the diversity of Islam: see *Islam Observed: Religious Development in Morocco and Indonesia*, New Haven: Yale University Press, 1968.

42. Thus, since the beginning of the twentieth century, anti-Jewish forces have repeatedly presented a well-known forgery, the *Protocols of the Elders of Zion*, as proof of the existence of a worldwide Jewish or Jewish-Masonic conspiracy. On the "pedagogic" use of the "Protocols" by the neo-Muslim Brotherhood in Egypt, which describes it as "one of the books of the Jews," see Gilles Kepel, *Prophet and Pharaoh*, op. cit., pp. 111–113, where he analyzes the article "The Jews" that appeared in October 1980 in *Al Da'wa*, the monthly of the Muslim Brotherhood. For other examples, see my *Les Protocoles des Sages de Sion. Faux et usages d'un faux*, Paris: Berg International, 1992, vol. 1, pp. 274ff.

43. Fouad Benabdelhalim, "Les véritables ennemis de l'Algérie," *El Mounquid* ["The Savior"] No. 9, February 1990, quoted in Mustafa Al-Ahnaf, Bernard Botiveau and Franck Frégosi, *L'Algérie par ses islamistes*, Paris: Karthala, 1991, p. 277. The first number of *El Mounquid* [*Al Munqidh*], bimonthly organ of the FIS (founded on March 21, 1989), appeared on October 5, 1989. Its last issue (No. 75) was dated February 2, 1992 (after six months of censorship, between June 26 and December 1, 1991). See Gilles Kepel, *Allah in the West: Islamic Movements in America and Europe*, Stanford, Calif.: Stanford University Press, 1997, pp. 156–173.

44. Ritual denunciations of Islamophobia, or polemical amalgams of Islam and Islamism, Islamic fundamentalism and terrorism,

etc., may in certain contexts function as self-protective rhetoric—
a kind of safety belt or immune system that effectively blocks any
criticism of Islam or the behavior of Muslims. This form of intellectual terrorism, though based on legitimate and necessary warn-
ings against contempt, rejection, and confusion, ends up with a
definition of "Islamic correctness." Human nature being what it is,
nothing is clear or straightforward when the invocation of fine sentiments and ideas is overdetermined by legitimacy conflicts. See the
remarks of Gérard Donnadieu in "Islam, islamisme et violence,"
Futuribles No. 269, November 2001, pp. 74–83, as well as Paul
Fenton's clarification of his position, "L'intégrisme musulman fait
bien partie de l'islam," *L'Arche* No. 524–525, October–November
2001, p. 55.

45. This basic position of the Algerian Islamists was presented
as follows by Fayçal Tlilani: "Anyone who thinks that our problems
with French colonialism ended with Algeria's independence in 1962
is mistaken. Indeed, this strong and ancient colonialism is more
concerned than ever to strengthen its presence on our soil in various ways, the most important being its cultural presence. It hopes
to achieve through a poisonous cultural invasion that which it was
unable to do through iron and fire, by taking over hearts and minds
in order to see its illusory dream of French Algeria come true"
("Permanence de la lutte contre le colonialisme," *El Mounquid* No.
3, November 1989, quoted in Mustafa Al-Ahnaf, et al., *L'Algérie
par ses islamistes*, op. cit., p. 273).

46. Fouad Benabdelhalim, "Les véritables ennemis de l'Algérie,"
pp. 277–278.

47. Fayçal Tlilani, "Permanence de la lutte contre le colonialisme," p. 274.

48. Ibid., p. 273. On the theme of the "war against the West,"
see especially Jean-Pierre Péroncel-Hugoz, *Le Radeau de Mahomet*, Paris: Lieu commun, 1983; V. S. Naipaul, *Among the Believers: An Islamic Journey*, London: André Deutsch, 1981; Olivier
Carré and Claire Brière, *Islam: guerre à l'Occident?*, Paris: Éditions Autrement, 1983; Bruno Étienne, *L'islamisme radical*, pp.
209ff.; Gilles Kepel, *Allah in the West*, op. cit.; Roland Jacquard,
Fatwa contre l'Occident, Paris: Albin Michel, 1998; Ibn Warraq,
Pourquoi je ne suis pas musulman, Lausanne: L'Âge d'Homme,
1999; Gilles Kepel, *Jihad: The Trail of Political Islam*, Cambridge,

Mass.: Harvard University Press, 2002; Florent Blanc, *Ben Laden et l'Amérique*, Paris: Bayard, 2001.

49. Ali Belhadj (b. 1956), who is considered the "most charismatic leader of the FIS," is a disciple of Moustapha Bouyali, founder in July 1982 of the first Islamist guerrilla force in independent Algeria, the Armed Islamic Movement or MIA. Ali Belhadj became "the brightest and most eloquent spokesman" for the "Salafists," an Islamist current that took shape in the early 1980s. The term *"salafiyyun"* refers to the "pure" tradition of the "devout ancestors" of early Islam *(salaf)*. Gilles Kepel, *Allah in the West*, op. cit., p. 166.

50. On the fundamental term the "Umma" (community), see Louis Massignon's brief but illuminating account in "L'Umma et ses synonymes: notion de communauté sociale en Islam," (1946) reprinted in *Sur l'Islam*, Paris: Éditions de l'Herne, 1995, pp. 17–30.

51. See Mustafa Al-Ahnaf, et al., *L'Algérie par ses islamistes*. p. 86.

52. Ali Belhadj, "Un coup de massue porté au dogme démocratique," *El Mounquid* No. 23, September 1990 (quoted in Al-Ahnaf et al., op. cit., pp. 87–90).

53. Dominique Sigaud, *La Fracture algérienne, 1990: carnets de route*, Paris: Calmann-Lévy, 1991, p. 127.

54. As the terms "Zionist" and "Jewish" count as insults with the same referent, they sometimes appear together in the same sequence. On June 25, 1991, for example, in Algiers, groups of young Islamists taunted soldiers with shouts of "dogs, Jews, Zionists, pharaohs, bastards" (reported in *Le Monde*, June 26, 1991, p. 24).

55. For a more detailed account of events on August 17, 1990, see Sigaud, *La Fracture algérienne*, pp. 128–133.

56. Ibid., p. 133.

57. Interview in *Politique internationale*, September 1989 (quoted in Alexandre del Valle, *Islamisme et États-Unis: une alliance contre l'Europe*, enlarged ed., Lausanne: L'Âge d'Homme, 2001, p. 329).

58. Ali Belhadj, in Al-Ahnaf, op. cit., pp. 91–92.

59. Ibid., pp. 90, 93, 96–97. See A. El-Difraoui, "La critique du système démocratique par le FIS," in Gilles Kepel, ed., *Exils et Roy-*

aumes. Les appartenances au monde arabo-musulman aujourd'hui, Paris: Presses de la Fondation nationale des sciences politiques, 1994, pp. 105ff. On the way in which the themes of the Jewish or Zionist plot were banalized in Algeria in 1990–1991 under the ideological-political influence of the FIS, see my *Les Protocoles des Sages de Sion,* op. cit., vol. 1, pp. 344–354. It was in the midst of this Islamist mobilization, in November and December 1991, that the weekly *Le Jeune Indépendant* serialized a version of the *Protocols.* In 1990 in Tunisia, the Islamists of the PLI (Islamic Liberation Party) published and widely distributed a book under the author's pseudonym Abdelkadim Zalloum: *La Démocratie, régime d'athéisme.* The subtitle, "It is a sin to adopt or apply it or to call for its introduction" (quoted from Mohamed Charfi, *Islam et liberté,* op. cit., p. 53), leaves no room for ambiguity. Similarly, for Ali Belhadj, democracy is a "sin" since it is "an invention of the heathen West" (ibid.).

60. Fouad Zakariya, *Laïcité ou islamisme. Les Arabes à l'heure du choix,* Paris: La Découverte and Cairo: Al-Fikr, 1991, p. 37.

61. For Anwar Al-Jindi, for example, "secularism is a pure product of Talmudic Judaism, which has had an extreme influence on Western thought" (quoted in Zakariya, ibid., p. 28). Muhammad Yahya adds the following clarification: "The secular idea is one axis of the vast plane we have called Westernization and cultural colonization. . . . It is therefore not surprising that secularism is the secular arm of Crusader proselytism" (*Refutations of the Secularists* [in Arabic], Cairo, 1988, p. 12; quoted in Zakariya, op. cit., 29). On secularism as a "plot," see ibid., pp. 27–30.

62. Ibid., pp. 63–64.

63. As Bruno Étienne has pointed out, "the pressure for Unity, a consequence of the Oneness of God, lies at the origin of Islam, even though Islam is socially, historically, and geographically plural" (*L'Islamisme radical,* op. cit., p. 21).

64. Zakariya, op. cit., p. 64.

65. In addition to the previously quoted works by Fouad Zakariya and Mohamed Charfi, see Muhammad Saïd Al-Ashmawy, *L'Islamisme contre l'islam,* Paris: La Découverte and Cairo: Al-Fikr, 1989. For a contextualization of the currents favorable to a "secular Islam," see Olivier Carré, *Le Nationalisme arabe,* Paris: Fayard, 1993, pp. 216ff.

66. Quoted in Gilles Kepel, "Un ramadan lourd de menaces" (an interview with Alain Louyot), *L'Express* No. 2627, November 8–14, 2001, p. 83.

67. In an interview conducted by Peter Arnett in Afghanistan in 1997, Osama bin Laden declared: "It is said in the Hadith: 'I swear to Allah, I wish to fight for Allah's cause and be killed.' ... Being killed for Allah's cause is a great honor achieved only by those who are the elite of the nation. We love this kind of death for Allah's cause as much as you like to live. We have nothing to fear for." Transcript of Osama bin Laden [television] interview by Peter Arnett, March 1997, http://www.anusha.com/osamaint.htm. Concerning the Islamist Arab volunteers who went to fight alongside the Taliban in Afghanistan, an Afghan witness who wished to remain anonymous said in early November 2001: "They waited so many years for this confrontation, which they present as a battle between believers and infidels. They have come here for that and trained themselves for that. Each morning they wake up and proclaim: we love death more than you love life." Quoted by François Chipaux, special correspondent in Islamabad, *Le Monde*, November 3, 2001, p. 4.

68. Quoted from Roland Jacquard, *Au nom d'Oussama Ben Laden . . . Dossier secret sur le terroriste le plus recherché du monde*, Paris: Jean Picollec, 2001, p. 358. See Gilles Kepel, *Jihad: The Trail of Political Islam*, op. cit., pp. 289, 317–322; and Antoine Basbous, *L'Islamisme, une revolution avortée?*, Paris: Hachette Littératures, 2000, pp. 197–198, 220–224. We should remember that on April 18, 1996, Egyptian Islamists killed eighteen Greek tourists in the vicinity of the Pyramids, having "mistaken" them for Jews. Ibid., p. 221.

69. See Gilles Kepel, in "Entretien croisé avec Gilles Kepel et Farhad Khosrokhavar: 'La quête du martyre s'est propagée,'" *Libération*, November 19, 2001, p. 12.

70. Quoted in Jacquard, *Au nom d'Oussama Ben Laden*, p. 324 (text 11, n.d., dating from the 1990s, signed by Emir Abu Abdullah al Sharif). This communiqué is organized around the aim of "giving the land back to the people of Morocco despoiled by the West." The division of the Maghreb into different nations (Morocco, Algeria, Mauritania, Sahara, etc.) is denounced as a classical conspiracy (ibid.): "This division is a plot for which the colonialist

infidels are responsible: the French, the Spanish and Portuguese, the Jews, and the international corporations. The plot was hatched by world Judaism. . . ."

71. Ibid.

72. *Jihad Against Crusaders and Jews: World Islamic Front Statement*, February 23, 1998, http://www.atour.com/news/international/20010928b.html. See Gilles Kepel, *Jihad* . . ., op. cit., pp. 319–320; and Bernard Lewis, "Licence to Kill: Usama bin Ladin's Declaration of Jihad," *Foreign Affairs*, vol. 87/6, November–December 1998, pp. 14–19.

73. *Jihad Against Crusaders and Jews*, 23 February 1998; Kepel, ibid. See also *L'Arche*, ibid., p. 51. The corollary necessarily follows: "We [therefore] call on Muslim ulema, leaders, youths, and soldiers to launch the raid on Satan's U.S. troops and the devil's supporters allying with them" (ibid.).

74. See the communiqué of the World Islamic Front for Jihad against Jews and Crusaders, dated August 12, 1998, which mentions the "two huge explosions" of August 7 and puts forward a number of arguments to justify them (Roland Jacquard, op. cit., p. 354).

75. Written in November 2001.

76. On bin Laden's plan to use chemical and bacteriological weapons, see Basbous, op. cit., p. 56, and Jacquard, op. cit., pp. 237–261. It is known that Saddam Hussein's Iraq produced huge stocks of chemical and bacteriological weapons, with a view to their military use. But the same can also be said of Russia, China, and North Korea—as well as the United States, of course. The new traffic in weapons means that attention needs to be paid to Mafia connections (especially in the case of Russia) as much as to Islamist networks. See Jean-Luc Marret, ed., *Violence transnationale et sécurité intérieure*, Paris: Paris II/LGDJ, 1999; Walter Laqueur, *The New Terrorism: Fanaticism and the Arms of Mass Destruction*, New York: Oxford University Press, 1999; Jean-Luc Marret, *Techniques du terrorisme*, Paris: Presses universitaires de France, 2000, esp. pp. 13–24; Olivier Lepick and Patrice Binder, *Les armes biologiques*, Paris: Presses universitaires de France, 2001.

77. From a work by Mohamed Abdul Salam Faraj, published by the Egyptian Islamic Movement in February 1995, p. 35 (quoted in Jacquard, op. cit., document 12, p. 328).

78. Within a historical and anthropological perspective, however, it should be remembered that violent behavior and criminal acts of the kind visible among Islamists are to be found everywhere in the field of religion. See, for instance, the impressive work by Denis Crouzet: *Les Guerriers de Dieu. La violence au temps des troubles de religion (vers 1525–vers 1610)*, Seyssel: Champ Vallon, 1990, 2 vols. See also David C. Rapoport, "Why Does Religious Messianism Produce Terror?," in Paul Wilkinson and Alasdair M. Stewart, eds., *Contemporary Research on Terrorism*, Aberdeen: Aberdeen University Press, 1989; and Magnus Ranstorp, "Le terrorisme au nom de la religion," *Stratégique* 66–67, 1997, pp. 89–114.

79. Michèle Tribalat rigorously demonstrates this in her reference article "Sortir des amalgames," *Le Figaro*, September 21, 2001, p. 16.

80. Hani Ramadan is the brother of the Islamist orator Tariq Ramadan, grandson of Hassan al-Banna (founder of the Muslim Brotherhood) and son of Sa'id Ramadan who lives in Geneva. His public interventions are less inclined to euphemism than those of his brother Tariq, an Islamist with a human face and telegenic looks who skillfully plays the card of "dialogue." Hani Ramadan happily says of his brother and himself: "We are two sides of the same coin." On the doctrinaire Islamist lecturer Tariq Ramadan, who is supported by neo–Third Worldist circles, including many Communists or ex-Communists, see Gilles Kepel, *Jihad . . .*, op. cit., pp. 369, 428 (n. 15).

81. Hani Ramadan, site of the Islamic Center in Geneva (quoted by Michèle Tribalat, op. cit.).

82. Ibid. On Jacques-Yakoub Roty, first president of the National Muslim Federation of France (founded in 1985), see Gilles Kepel, *Les Banlieues de l'Islam*, Paris: Le Seuil, 1987, pp. 364–366, 372–373; and idem, *Allah in the West*, op. cit., p. 193. In the fundamentalist literature, Europe is denounced as the "world of impiety" or the "land of impiety" (*dar el-kufr*), the incarnation of the "Crusader West." According to Islamist theoretician Abul A'la Mawdudi (an Indo-Pakistani Sunni), the whole being of the Infidel or Unbeliever (*kafir*) is "impure": "Each organ of his body . . . will complain of the injustice and cruelty that he imposes on it. Each part of his being will denounce him before God, who, being the fount of justice, will reward him with the greatest punishment that

he deserves. Such is the wretched outcome of the *kufr*" (quoted in Bat Ye'or, *Juifs et Chrétiens sous l'Islam. Les Dhimmis face au défi intégriste*, Paris: Berg International, 1994, p. 291). See also Alexandre del Valle, *Islamisme et États-Unis*, op. cit., p. 72.

83. Meryem Djamila, "Caractéristiques et conséquences du modernisme," *El Mounquid* No. 12 (in French in the original), reprinted in Al-Ahnaf, et al., *L'Algérie par ses islamistes*, op. cit., pp. 270–272.

84. Al-Ahnaf, et al., p. 269. The polemical expression "*l'occidentose*" (here translated as "Westitis") probably derives from the neologism that gave its name to a famous pamphlet by the Iranian essayist Jalal Al-e Ahmad, *Gharbzadegi* Tehran, 1962 and 1978. (For an English translation, by John Green and Ahmad Alizadeh, see *Weststruckness*, Costa Mesa, Calif.: Mazda Publishers, 1997.) In Persian the neologism suggests the image of a deplorable infatuation with things Western. See Yann Richard, "Clercs et intellectuels dans la République islamique d'Iran," in G. Kepel and Y. Richard, eds., *Intellectuels et militants . . .*, op. cit., pp. 50, 69 (n. 46).

85. Abdelkadim Zalloum, *La Démocratie, régime d'athéisme*, op. cit., pp. 22, 23, 25, 28 (quoted in Mohamed Charfi, op. cit., p. 54).

86. Ibid., p. 46.

87. See Gilles Kepel, *The Revenge of God: The Resurgence of Islam, Christianity, and Judaism in the Modern World*, University Park, Pa.: Pennsylvania State University Press, 1994, pp. 7–8.

88. Roger Garaudy, quoted in Kepel, *Les Banlieues de l'Islam*, op. cit., pp. 340–341.

89. Rémy Leveau and Dominique Schnapper, "Religion et politique: juifs et musulmans maghrébins en France," in Rémy Leveau and Gilles Kepel, eds., *Les Musulmans dans la société française*, op. cit., p. 111.

90. Ibid.

91. Quoted in ibid., pp. 111–112.

92. For numerous examples of statements, attitudes, and practices affirming inequality or discrimination, see Jean-Pierre Péroncel-Hugoz, *LeRadeau de Mahomet*, op. cit., esp. pp. 67ff. Following the Islamic expert Bernard Lewis, this *Le Monde* journalist identifies and illustrates three categories of inequality: between men and women, between Muslims and non-Muslims, and between masters

and slaves. His candid analyses have earned him, as they did Lewis, denunciations as an "enemy of Islam" or "enemy of the Arabs." See also Olivier Carré, *L'Islam laïque* . . ., op. cit., pp. 108–124; Ibn Warraq, *Pourquoi je ne suis pas musulman*, op. cit., pp. 207–295, 346–388; Juliette Minces, *Le Coran et les femmes*, Paris: Hachette Littératures, 2001.

93. Message supporting the *mujahedeen*, sent to the forum (Islamic Center in Geneva) from a scout unit in Belgium (quoted in Michèle Tribalat, ibid.).

94. Michel Renard, an ex-Communist convert to Islam and director of the journal *Islam de France*, used this evasive formula in an interview with Daniel Licht ("Le ramadan n'est pas une fête," *Libération*, November 16, 2001, p. 20). As an ideological entrepreneur and self-styled spokesman, Renard is a good example of the sociological category of "professional Muslims" (Alexandre del Valle, *Islamisme et États-Unis*, op. cit., pp. 52–53, and p. 52, n. 32).

95. See Jean-Paul Charnay, *La Charia et l'Occident*, Paris: Éditions de l'Herne, 2001, pp. 100ff.

96. For a historical approach and a definition of the problem, see Bernard Lewis, *Race and Color in Islam*, New York: Harper & Row, 1971.

97. It is also necessary to consider the "re-Islamization from below" advocated and pursued by certain "pietist" Islamist movements, in contrast to the "revolutionary" activists or radical Islamists who advocate the use of violence for the conquest of power ("re-Islamization from above"). See, among others, Gilles Kepel's summary account "Les mouvements de 'réislamisation' de la société," (1990) in Pierre-André Taguieff, ed., *Face au racisme*, Paris: La Découverte, 1991, vol. 2, pp. 208–215. See also Gilles Kepel, *Prophet and Pharaoh*, op. cit.; and Kepel and Richard, eds., *Intellectuels et militants de l'islam contemporain*, op. cit. It is possible to argue that the terminological uncertainty here reflects the indeterminacy of the observable political and religious realities.

98. See especially Jean Baudrillard, "L'esprit du terrorisme," *Le Monde*, November 3, 2001, and *The Spirit of Terrorism*, London: Verso Books, 2002. For a critical reaction, see Jacques Juillard, "Misère de l'antiaméricanisme," *Libération*, November 13, 2001.

99. René Girard, *Celui par qui le scandale arrive*, Paris: Desclée de Brouwer, 2001, p. 151. Cf. Martin Heidegger, "Anaximander's

Saying" (1946), in M. Heidegger, *Off the Beaten Track (Holzwege)*, Cambridge: Cambridge University Press, 2002.

100. On the reformulation of racism in "culturalist" or "civilizational" terms, see my books: *La Force du préjugé. Essai sur le racisme et ses doubles*, Paris: La Découverte, 1988; *Les Fins de l'antiracisme*, Paris: Michalon, 1995; and *Le Racisme*, Paris: Flammarion, 1997.

101. Quoted in Roland Jacquard, *Au nom d'Oussama Ben Laden . . .*, op. cit., p. 352 (document 23).

102. Carlos, interview published on October 21, 2001, by the Venezuelan daily *El Universal* (quoted from Alain Abellard, "L'hommage de Carlos à Oussama Ben Laden," *Le Monde*, October 26, 2001, p. 35). Carlos, who was captured in Sudan on August 15, 1994, by the French secret services, is serving a life sentence at La Santé prison for the murder of two policemen and their Lebanese informer in 1975. Wadi Haddad, considered "one of the PLO hardliners at the time of Black September," is the man who recruited Carlos (Roland Jacquard, op. cit., p. 157, n. 10). For a detailed study, see Roland Jacquard and Dominique Nasplèzes, *Carlos, le dossier secret*, Paris: Jean Picollec, 1997.

103. Quoted in Neil MacFarquhar, "Anti-Western and Extremist Views Pervade Saudi Schools," *New York Times*, October 19, 2001.

104. Samuel P. Huntington, "The Clash of Civilizations?", *Foreign Affairs* 72/3, Summer 1993, pp. 22–49. Significantly, Huntington's book-length version (*The Clash of Civilizations and the Remaking of World Order*, New York: Simon & Schuster, 1996) has recently become a best-seller in Arabic translation.

105. Interview conducted by Farraj Ismaïl with Mullah Omar: "Notre pays est un cimetière pour les envahisseurs," *Marianne* No. 237, November 5–11, 2001, p. 23. Originally published in Arabic, in the London-based Saudi weekly *Al-Majalla*.

106. Official statement broadcast by Al Jazeera television, translated by the BBC Monitoring Service, Caversham, UK: news.bbc.co.uk/hi/english/world/monitoring/ media_reports/ newsid_1636000/1636782.

107. She recalled this formulation in an interview she gave to Victor Malka in October 1983—reprinted in Annie Kriegel, *Réflexion sur les questions juives*, Paris: Hachette, 1984, p. 631.

108. Text composed by Emir Abu Abdullah al-Sharif, quoted in Roland Jacquard, *Au nom d'Oussama Ben Laden . . .*, op. cit., p. 324 (document 11).

109. Interminable repentance implies a special kind of brooding that can be put down to what Tzvetan Todorov so lucidly analyzed in *Les Abus de la mémoire* (Paris: Arléa, 1995). It fuels resentment, which itself becomes infinite or insatiable—witness the profuse demands on the West to make reparations for all the ills of non-Western humanity.

110. Since 1999 or 2000 this expression has become commonplace in France, where it refers to the so-called radical antiglobalization movements (that is, those which seek not to regulate processes of globalization but to transform them root and branch or to destroy them). Such movements have drawn attention to themselves through more or less violent mass demonstrations (Seattle, Nice, Gothenburg, Genoa), which have brought together nearly all the neoleftist groups, from libertarians to Trotskyists, as well as anti-establishment movements of the "have-nots" in which young people form a large part of the activists. For a well-informed but overly sympathetic approach, see Isabelle Sommier, *Les Nouveaux mouvements contestataires à l'heure de la mondialisation*, Paris: Flammarion, 2001. More critical analysis may be found in "La gauche, l'extrême gauche, les intellectuels," *Le Débat* No. 103, January–February 1999, pp. 28–99 (Roland Hureaux, Bernard Poulet, Christophe Bourseiller, Jean-François Sirinelli, Pierre Grémion); and in Philippe Raynaud, "Les nouvelles radicalités. De l'extrême gauche en philosophie," *Le Débat* No. 105, May–August 1999, pp. 90–116.

111. One sign of this is the way in which the French Trotskyist ideologue Daniel Bensaid has redefined revolution as the "regulative horizon" of political action (*Le Pari mélancolique*, Paris: Fayard, 1997). It is a rather shamefaced rallying to the reformist perspective, or, in more elegant language, to a "possibilist" political practice. See his "Sous la révolution, le réformisme?" (an interview with Christophe Bourseiller), *Le Débat* No. 103, January–February 1999, pp. 60–66.

112. Sophie Bessis, "Les belles paroles de l'Occident," *Libération*, October 24, 2001, p. 9. For a general indictment of the West, see a recent book by this historian-journalist: *L'Occident et les*

autres: Histoire d'une suprématie, Paris: La Découverte, 2001 [*Western Supremacy: Triumph of an Idea?*, London: Zed Books, 2003]. The declared enemies of "the West" reject it as "accidental" (therefore neither necessary nor essential), and as given to crime and decadence. Two books by Roger Garaudy—as we can already see from their titles—illustrate the first two charges: *Pour un dialogue des civilisations: l'Occident est un accident* (Paris: Denoël, 1977), and *Les États-Unis avant-garde de la décadence* (Paris: Éditions Vent du Large, 1997). In 1981 this Islamist–cum–Third Worldist ideologue summed up his view of the world as follows: "The West is an accident. Its culture is an anomaly, mutilated by primordial dimensions. . . . The first renaissance of the West began to emerge in Muslim Spain, four centuries before the Italian Renaissance. . . . The deadly adventure of hegemony would lead the West, and with it the world that it dominated, towards a suicidal model of growth and civilization. . . . In a perspective of millennia, the West is the greatest criminal in history." Roger Garaudy, *Promesses de l'Islam*, Paris: Le Seuil, 1981, pp. 17, 19–20.

113. Quoted in Jean-Pierre Langellier, "De nouveaux éléments sur l'implication d'Al-Qaida dans les attentats du 11 septembre," *Le Monde*, November 17, 2001, p. 6.

Chapter 2. Israelophobia and Palestinophilia

1. See the annual report on the work of the National Consultative Commission on Human Rights: 2000. *La lutte contre le racisme et la xénophobie*, Paris: La Documentation française, 2001, pp. 398–400 ("Données chiffrées comparatives concernant l'antisémitisme" [comparative figures on anti-Semitism]).

2. On October 12, 2000, Palestinian police arrested two Israeli reservists and took them to a police station in Ramallah, where they were savagely beaten and murdered by a large crowd. An Italian television crew photographed the scene, and despite Palestinian Authority censorship some of their pictures were eventually broadcast. The most horrifying was an image of one of the lynchers, a young Palestinian, proudly displaying at a window his bloodstained hands. (Some color photos were reproduced on the front page of *Libération*, October 13, 2000; cf. *L'Arche* Nos. 524–525, October–November

2001, p. 47.) See the articles in *Le Monde*, October 14, 2000, pp. 1–3 ("Israël-Palestine: la tentation du pire") and *Libération*, October 14–15, 2000, pp. 1–4 ("Proche-Orient, L'attente après l'horreur"), as well as the report by Guy Sitbon, "Palestine: la révolte arabe," *Marianne* No. 182, October 16–22, 2000, pp. 14–16.

3. On October 10, 2000, three Molotov cocktails were thrown at the synagogue in Les Ulis: two exploded and wrecked the ground floor, so that the rabbi had to climb to the first floor to escape the flames. On the same day an arson attack destroyed the synagogue at Trappes. On the night of October 12–13, one or more firebombs were hurled at the synagogue in Bondy, devastating a room of a little more than thirty square yards; and that same night a synagogue door at rue Julien Lacroix (in the 20th arrondissement of Paris) was set on fire while people were asleep in the building. See the testimony of Rabbi Philippe Haddad (for Les Ulis), *Durban. Hourban*, Safed Éditions (n.p.), 2001, pp. 19–33. (*Hourban* or *hurban* is a Hebrew word meaning "devastation.")

4. See the investigation by François Dufay, "Juifs de France: le chagrin et la colère," *Le Point* No. 1466, October 20, 2000, pp. 59–62.

5. For an initial inventory of the anti-Jewish acts and threats in France between the fall of 2000 and the fall of 2001, see "Une atmosphere d'insécurité," *Observatoire du monde juif*, bulletin no. 1, November 2001, pp. 2–9 (whose figures need to be revised upward, since the victims are sometimes too intimidated or terrorized by the use or threat of violence to make the incident known). See also Marc Knobel, "Les agressions antijuives," ibid., pp. 17–21.

6. The establishment in question, Le Gan Pardess, located in the Frais Vallon district in the north of the city, can take approximately one hundred children in its nursery and primary schools. Daniel Sperling, the deputy mayor and head of the Jewish radio in Marseilles, stated: "This is an anti-Semitic but in no way a terrorist attack. The kindergarten is in a sensitive area in the north of the city, surrounded by large housing projects with a high North African component" (quoted from José d'Arrigo, "École juive incendiée: Marseille tente de se rassurer," *Le Figaro*, October 30, 2001, p. 12). Significantly, the subtitle of the article is: "Anti-Semitism: The Shocked City Would Like to Think It Is a Mere 'Provocation.'" Clément Yana, head of the Marseilles council of Jewish organizations

(CRIF), did indeed try to downplay the attack as an "isolated action" or an "insignificant provocation" (ibid.), justifying this with a call for dialogue with all the local "communities": "We mustn't fall into paranoia; we must resist the temptation to withdraw into ourselves." But he admitted: "I feel uneasy when I see how complacently people talk about the Palestinian attacks" (quoted from Claude Askolovitch, "Le grand désarroi des Juifs de France. Le ghetto dans la tête," *Le Nouvel Observateur* No. 1931, November 8–14, 2001, p. 30).

7. "Incendie criminel d'une école juive" (subhead: "Marseille. Des inscriptions antisémites ont été retrouvées"), *Le Figaro*, October 29, 2001, p. 13; José d'Arrago, art. cit. Investigators also found "holes dug in the ground to conceal nails capable of wounding children during recreation" (José d'Arrago, ibid.).

8. List compiled by Claude Askolovitch, art. cit., p. 28.

9. Heinrich Heine, quoted by Maurice Blanchot in *The Infinite Conversation*, Minneapolis: University of Minnesota Press, 1993, p. 124 (translation slightly modified).

10. See Nonna Mayer and Guy Michelat, "Sondages, mode d'emploi: xénophobie, racisme et antiracisme en France: attitudes et perceptions," in 2000. *La lutte contre le racisme et la xénophobie*, op. cit., pp. 96–100. Variations in the percentage of "don't knows" on this issue is highly revealing: whereas some 30 percent fell into the category in 1988 and 1991 (a very high figure, perhaps reflecting the postwar taboo on expressions of anti-Semitism), the figure was down around 12 percent in 1999 and 2000 (ibid., p. 98).

11. On the model of "symbolic racism," see especially my *Les Fins de l'antiracisme*, op. cit., pp. 304ff., 635 (n. 98–, where I mention a number of English works on the question).

12. The arguments used by Malek Boutih to justify this kind of "testing" do not seem to me convincing. See his *La France aux Français? Chiche!*, Paris: Mille et une nuits, 2001, pp. 92–97.

13. Michèle Tribalat showed, in the early 1990s, that 31 percent of young Frenchmen of Algerian origin aged between twenty and twenty-nine were unemployed, compared with 15 percent for all young men in this age group; and that 34 percent of boys of Algerian origin with baccalaureate qualifications or higher were without a job, compared with 9 percent in France as a whole. This study, which used criteria of "ethnic affiliation" (based on mother tongue)

as well as "ethnic origin" (defined by parental birthplace), made it possible to demonstrate and measure the scale of job discrimination against young people of Algerian descent. Such is the first act of genuine anti-racism: the acquisition of knowledge. See Michèle Tribalat, ed., *Cent ans d'immigration. Étrangers d'hier, Français d'aujourd'hui*, Paris: INED/PUF, 1991; and Michèle Tribalat, *Faire France. Une enquête sur les immigrés et leurs enfants*, Paris: La Découverte, 1995, and *De l'immigration à l'assimilation. Enquête sur les populations d'origine étrangère en France*, Paris: La Découverte, 1996. Those who helped prevent further studies of this kind, on the pretext that the republic officially recognizes only full French nationals "irrespective of race, origin, or religion," should be classified among the new obscurantists. Political correctness, linked to a fantasy anti-racism, thereby excludes precisely the research that is necessary for the struggle against ethnically based discrimination to be effective. Suspicion on grounds of ethnicity has unfortunately grown more intense since the attacks in the United States on September 11, 2001, so that it is now more difficult than ever for young people of North African origin to gain access to the labor market. See Francine Aizicovici, "Les galères des diplômés maghrébins depuis le 11 septembre," *Le Monde Campus*, supplement to *Le Monde*, November 20, 2001, pp. 21–23.

14. Even such a well-informed political scientist as Catherine Withol de Wenden does not escape a certain airiness on this issue, as we may see from her highly synthetic article "Les 'jeunes issus de l'immigration,' entre intégration culturelle et exclusion sociale," in Philippe Dewitte, ed., *Immigration et intégration. L'état des savoirs*, Paris: La Découverte, 1999, pp. 232–237. In her view, the obstacles to integration of "young people" mainly come down to unemployment and xenophobia toward North Africans: "Chronic unemployment is often the cradle of an instrumental communalism that turns its back on integration. Another obstacle to integration lies in a very powerful image that stigmatizes people of North African descent, especially when they are young, from poor backgrounds, and unemployed" (ibid., p. 236). Thus, if many "young people" sink into Islamism, drugs, or delinquency, it is not their fault: it is because "French society" does not give them work and rejects, stigmatizes, and humiliates them. This set of images and judgments has become a new common creed among sociologists.

15. The Socialist party deputy Julien Dray, co-founder of SOS Racisme, wrote in his report on youth violence in the suburbs: "Many young people involved in acts of urban violence are blacks or of North African descent. This fact is surrounded with a false sense of propriety in the circumlocution 'suburban youth.' . . . Their demand is for an identity rebuilt on the basis of Islam, skin color, and ethnic origin. Racism then responds to racism. Car-burning, extortion rackets, rapes." (*État de violence*, Paris: Éditions 1, 1999; quoted in Jean-Paul Gourévitch, *La France africaine. Islam, Intégration, Insécurité: Infos et Intox*, Paris: Le Pré aux Clercs, 2000, p. 15.) For an approach to the question of "urban violence," see Christian Bachmann and Nicole Le Guennec, *Autopsie d'une émeute. Histoire exemplaire d'un quartier nord de Melun*, Paris: Albin Michel, 1997; and Sophie Body-Gendrot, *Les Villes face à l'insécurité. Des ghettos américains aux banlieux françaises*, Paris: Bayard, 1998.

16. See Christian Jelen's illuminating and courageous *La Guerre des rues. La violence et les "jeunes,"* Paris: Plon, 1999, one of the few works of investigative journalism on "young people" that departs from the usual "political correctness." Of course it has come under attack from a number of sociologists who, having imperceptibly turned into ideologists of "youthism," justify petty delinquency and sing the praises of "salvation through immigration"— a kind of inverted racism in which "others" are supposed to be better than "us." By championing multiculturalism and setting themselves against any "French-style republican system" (which they see as "archaic" or "out of date"), these sociologists have masked the Islamization of "young people" in the suburbs and, in the name of a perverted "egalitarian" ideal, helped to destroy the republican educational system by orienting it to pupils "with difficulties" (a pious euphemism) or violent tendencies, or even to petty criminals. Thus, as part of the "struggle against exclusion," they denounce any "return to the past that involves excluding a large number of pupils" (François Dubet, *Pourquoi changer l'école?*, Paris: Textuel, 1999, p. 34). The implication is that, if nothing can be passed on to very many pupils, then nothing should be passed on. Hence the rule formulated by the educational "reformer" Philippe Meirieu: "The teacher should change from someone who hands things down to someone who coaches"—a rule he illustrates by a comparison with

a football coach. (Philippe Meirieu and Marc Guiraud, *L'École ou la guerre civile*, Paris: Plon, 1997, p. 102; quoted in Christian Jelen, ibid., p. 166). As the educational system becomes less archaic, the future is supposed to belong to coaches! For a lucid view of the disastrous consequences, see Liliane Lurçat, *La Destruction de l'enseignement élementaire et ses penseurs*, Paris: François-Xavier de Guibert, 1998; and idem, *Vers une école totalitaire?*, Paris: François-Xavier de Guibert, 1999. A reader who rejects this abdication of responsibility, dressed up in anti-exclusionist demagogy, may find useful material in Danièle Sallenave, *À quoi sert la littérature?*, Paris: Textuel, 1997; Charles Coutel, *Que vive l'école républicaine!*, Paris: Textuel, 1999; and *Sauver les lettres. Des professeurs accusent*, Paris: Textuel, 2001.

17. This kind of resurgence was analyzed in the case of Le Pen's supporters in the 1980s and 1990s. See my two studies: "Mobilisation national-populiste en France. Vote xénophobe et nouvel antisémitisme politique," *Lignes* No. 9, March 1990, pp. 91–136; and "Antisémitisme politique et national-populisme en France dans les années 1980," in Pierre Birnbaum, eds., *Histoire politique des Juifs de France. Entre universalisme et particularisme*, Paris: Presses de la Fondation nationale des sciences politiques, 1990, pp. 125–150. See also Nonna Mayer, "Racisme et antisémitisme dans l'opinion publique française," in Pierre-André Taguieff, ed., *Face au racisme*, ed., op. cit., vol. 2, pp. 64–72; idem, *Ces Français qui votent FN*, Paris: Flammarion, 1999, esp. pp. 47–74; Olivier Guland, *Le Pen, Mégret et les Juifs. L'obsession du "complot mondialiste,"* Paris: La Découverte, 2000.

18. This argumentative framework, based on a series of combinations, does not occur as such in ordinary speech, where only some of the equated terms appear. It is a formal model, then, which illustrates the strong version of the accusatory vision. A weaker version might be derived through various modifications: for example, the equation "Zionism = colonialism, imperialism, and racism" might be replaced with "Zionism = colonialism and imperialism" or "Zionism = colonialism." In anti-Zionist rhetoric, however, the accusation of "colonialism" is most often connected with imperialism and racism.

19. I have extensively used this category of critical thought (the present formulation being borrowed from Leo Strauss) in my two

previously cited works: *Les Fins de l'antiracisme* (esp. chs. 7 and 9), and *Résister au bougisme*, pp. 86–108.

20. The comparison between Nazi atrocities and the massacres at Sabra and Shatila (from September 16 to 18, 1982), perhaps even more than the one at Deir Yassin (April 9, 1948), has become paradigmatic in the kind of propaganda that depicts Israelis as engaged in "genocide" against the Palestinians. The demonization of Sharon is a necessary premise for the false accusation that he was responsible for, and guilty of, the massacres at Sabra and Shatila. Some have even drawn from this the practical political conclusion that the current prime minister of Israel should be tried for "crimes against humanity." Palestinian propaganda immediately began to exploit this attempt to criminalize Israel through Sharon. See the document "La plainte contre Ariel Sharon avec constitution de partie civile" (Brussels, June 18, 2001; signed by Chibli Mallat, Luc Walleyn, and Michaël Verhaeghe), *Revue d'études palestiniennes* No. 81, Fall 2001, pp. 12–41; Sophie Claudet, "Sabra et Chatila: fin de l'impunité des criminels?", ibid., pp. 42–47. Suheil Natour, a Beirut-based member of the Democratic Front for the Liberation of Palestine, does not conceal his satisfaction: "For Palestinians from the territories, it is a political card to play against Israel in the present context of the Intifada. . . . Whatever our motives, it is an unexpected opportunity that Belgium is able to accept such an accusation against Sharon" (quoted by Claudet, ibid., p. 46). Indeed, what a heavenly surprise for a DFLP-style "democrat!" Poor Belgium! On the media treatment of the massacre at Sabra and Shatila, see Gilles William Goldnadel, *Le Nouveau Bréviaire de la haine. Antisémitisme et antisionisme*, Paris: Ramsay, 2001, pp. 117–118.

21. Israeli military leaders can be blamed for allowing the Lebanese militias a free hand: it is well known, in fact, that the massacre was committed by the Christian Phalange, on the authority of Elias Hobeika. Let us forget the propaganda clichés and "political correctness." Claude Lanzmann has given a firm clarification about what happened at Sabra and Shatila: "It was Arabs who killed Arabs. . . . Christian Arabs killed Muslim Arabs. One is entitled to blame Sharon for the fact that, as the Palestinians had just been disarmed, he had a duty to protect the camps. That is clear. . . . There was a commission of enquiry, and he was blamed and punished for

the precise thing for which he was responsible." ("Sur le courage," an interview given to Patrice Blouin, Frank Nouchi, and Charles Tesson, in *Cahiers du cinema* No. 561, October 2001, p. 57.) Éliane Amado Lévy-Valensi rightly noted: "The identity confusion reached its height in relation to the massacres at Sabra and Shatila. A Palestinian camp fell victim to the Christian Phalangists while the Israelis were there. . . . When someone kills, there may be shared responsibilities. But the guilty party remains the one that does the killing." *À la gauche du seigneur ou l'illusion idéologique*, Paris: Éditions Bibliophane, 1987, p. 163.

22. Fayez A. Sayegh, *Le Colonialisme sioniste en Palestine*, reprint, Nancy: Éditions Taranis, n.d. [1992], pp. 24–25, emphasis in the original. Sayegh is one of the main founders of the PLO's Research Center and architect of the 1975 UN resolution equating Zionism and racism. He is also the author of a propaganda tract with the significant title: *Zionism: A Form of Racism and Racial Discrimination*, Geneva: Office of the Permanent Observer of the PLO to the United Nations, 1976. The Taranis publishing house, which published his book on Zionist colonialism, was founded by a regional group of the (now defunct) French neofascist organization Troisième Voie [Third Way].

23. See Marwan Bishara, *Palestine/Israel: Peace or Apartheid*, London and New York: Zed Books, 2001, p. 22: "The policy of separation . . . has transformed a twenty-six-year occupation into a system of Apartheid." See also ibid., ch. 8: "The West Bank Settlements: Apartheid in Practice," pp. 114–125.

24. See "Oslo Institutionalizes Apartheid," ibid., pp. 121–124.

25. "An informal, state-sponsored neo-Apartheid has separated Israeli Jews from Palestinians ever since the establishment of the Jewish state in 1948" (ibid., p. 6). Carried along by the polemic, the same author denounces the Palestinian "bantustans" that Israel is supposed to have created (ibid., p. 115).

26. The rhetoric of allusion is especially developed in comparisons such as: "Just as South Africa . . ., so Israel . . ." (e.g., ibid., p. 4); "Again, as in South Africa, . . ." (ibid.); or "Like the Afrikaners, . . ." (p. 5). On October 17, 2001, when Marwan Bishara was invited to speak on the issue of "Jews between the Shoah and Israel" for Radio France 3's "Culture and Dependency" program, he conducted himself as a perfect propagandist, calmly and diligently

repeating the lessons he had learned from Palestinian manuals: "Zionism is a form of racism" or "a racist ideology"; the Palestinians are victims of an "apartheid system of segregation" (to which he opposed, of course, a "system of peace and justice"); "I am your Jew" (addressed to round-table participants including Claude Lanzmann and Serge Klarsfeld); "I am against the fact that three-fourths of Palestinians are not at home" (a reference to the "right of return" for all Palestinians, which in practice would mean the disappearance of the State of Israel).

27. Sulaiman Abu Ghaith, born in Kuwait in 1965, was the imam of a large mosque before going to fight in Bosnia, in 1994, alongside the Muslim International Brigade (formed by members of bin Laden's network).

28. *Le Péché originel d'Israël. L'expulsion des Palestiniens revisitée par les "nouveaux historiens" israéliens*, Paris: Les Éditions de l'Atelier/Les Éditions Ouvrières, 1998. We should make it clear that Dominique Vidal is a journalist for *Le Monde diplomatique*. This apologetic work, designed to propagate in France the "theses" of the Israeli "new historians," demonstrates that the group in question exists as much by its pro-Palestinian political commitment as by its historiographical activity, which is largely a matter of searching through new archival material to confirm the Palestinian positions on the history of Israel. Moreover, as one might have expected, most of these "new historians" are on the far left and may be considered Communist militants (with a Trotskyist inspiration recognizable here and there). Ilan Pappé, a member of the Communistic Hadash Front for Peace and Equality, does not conceal his real sources of inspiration (converted into working hypotheses): "It is from them [Palestinian intellectuals] that I learned the Palestinian version of the events of 1948. Afterwards, I looked in the archives for proof of their grievances. And this work of mine did establish the legitimacy of some of their grievances" (quoted in ibid., p. 195). It therefore comes as no surprise that the French translation of his *The Making of the Arab-Israeli Conflict 1947–51* (London: I. B. Tauris, 1992) has been brought out by a pro-Trotskyist publishing house: *La Guerre de 1948 en Palestine aux origines du conflit israélo-arabe*, Paris: La Fabrique, 2000. For an illuminating critical survey of the Israeli debates and controversies connected with the "new historians," see Ilan Greilsammer, *La Nouvelle Histoire d'Israël*, op. cit., esp. pp. 7–212, 493–519.

29. Gérard, a Socialist party member for thirty years, at Charité-sur-Loire, in the Nièvre region (quoted in Renaud Dély, "Les socialistes malmenés par leur base. L'antiaméricanisme perdure chez les militants," *Libération*, October 16, 2001, p. 10). This cliché about Islam functions as a favorable prejudice in the discourse of the European and American left. Islam—the chief editor of *Le Monde diplomatique* notes in passing—"is the religion of people who mostly suffer from exclusion" ("Les enjeux d'un dialogue. Entretien avec Alain Gresh," *Regards* [a Communist monthly] No. 73, November 2001, p. 20).

30. Vincent "Mansour" Monteil, quoted in Lisbeth Rocher and Fatima Cherqaoui, *D'une foi à l'autre. Les conversions à l'islam en Occident*, Paris: Le Seuil, 1986, p. 125. In 1982, referring to the regime of Ayatollah Khomeini, Monteil said: "The Islamic Revolution and the Islamic Republic respond to a centuries-old aspiration to justice; they think of themselves as the party of the underprivileged" (in Marc Kravetz, *Magazine littéraire* No. 181, February 1982; quoted in Rocher/Cherqaoui, op. cit.). On Monteil's conversion, see ibid., p. 29, n. 11. The author of numerous works on the Arab and Muslim world, Monteil has also published a thick volume of "anti-Zionist" propaganda: *Dossier secret sur Israël. Le terrorisme* (Paris: Éditions Guy Authier, 1978), whose fourth and last part, entitled "Zionism Is a Form of Racism" (pp. 329–410), seeks to justify the accusatory slogan adopted by the UN General Assembly in its resolution of November 10, 1975 (later abrogated in 1991). It is scarcely surprising to see his name among the contributors to a collection of papers defending the freedom of expression and (in some cases) the actual "theses" of Holocaust revisionists: Jean-Gabriel Cohn-Bendit, Éric Delcroix, Claude Karnoouh, Vincent Monteil, and Jean-Louis Tristani, *Intolérable intolerance*, Paris: Éditions de la Différence, 1981—a collection that takes the form of a petition to the magistrates of the Paris Court of Appeal. With regard to Monteil's contribution ("Le prêt-à-porter au tribunal de l'Histoire," pp. 139–160), it will be sufficient to quote the first sentence and a few lines from the conclusion: "Is the trial of Robert Faurisson more despicable than absurd? . . . I do not wish to let myself be 'carried away' by the tireless propaganda in favor of the Zionist entity known as the State of Israel. Besides, the too brief (but so instructive) time I spent in Jerusalem in 1948, as a United Nations observer, convinced me of the more and more racist, terrorist,

and Nazi-type character of the Jewish State (that is its official name). . . . To return to Robert Faurisson, I tend to believe witnesses who have everything to lose—and he has already lost a great deal. His unjust and unacceptable conviction, if upheld on appeal, would spell the victory of cowardice over courage" (pp. 139, 160).

31. Roger Garaudy, *Promesses de l'Islam*, Paris: Le Seuil, 1981, pp. 150–151. On the figure of Mahmud Darwish and the mythical-political uses to which it has been put, see Olivier Carré, *Le Nationalisme arabe*, op. cit., pp. 155–175 (ch. 6: "Le grand mythe palestinien: Darwish").

32. Shlomo Ben-Ami, *Quel avenir pour Israël?*, interviews with Yves Charles Zarka, Jeffrey Andrew Barash, and Elhanan Yakira, with a preface by Yves Charles Zarka, Paris: Presses universitaires de France, 2001, pp. 336–337.

33. See Élisabeth Schemla, *"Ton rêve est mon cauchemar."* Les *six mois qui ont tué la paix*, Paris: Flammarion, 2001. This is a good context in which to reread Emmanuel Lévinas's fine article "Politique après!", *Les Temps modernes* No. 398, September 1979, pp. 521–528.

34. See Raymond Aron's seminal article "L'avenir des religions séculières," in Aron, *L'Âge des empires et l'avenir de la France*, Paris: Défense de la France, 1945; "The Future of Secular Religions," in Raymond Aron, *The Dawn of Universal History: Selected Essays from a Witness of the Twentieth Century*, New York: Basic Books, 2002, pp. 177–202.

35. On "simplification of the single enemy" as the first rule of the discourse of propaganda, see Jean-Marie Domenach, *La Propagande politique*, 2nd ed., Paris: Presses Universitaires de France, 1955, pp. 49–53. In polemical discourse, this principle operates especially through Manichean amalgam and recourse to a synthetic designation of the adversary. See Marc Angenot, *La Parole pamphlétaire. Contribution à la typologie des discours modernes*, Paris: Payot, 1982, pp. 92, 126–130.

36. Text signed by Ahmed Sahnoun, Abdellatif Soltani, and Abbassi Madani; quoted from Mustafa Al-Ahnaf, et al., op. cit., p. 45.

37. See Gilles Kepel, *Jihad: The Trail of Political Islam*, op. cit., pp. 150–158; and Alexandre del Valle, "Intifada ou guerre sainte?" *Politique internationale* No. 92, Summer 2001, pp. 31ff. The first Intifada ("uprising," "war of stones") was launched in December

1987, and the second began immediately after Ariel Sharon's visit to the Mosque Esplanade (Temple Mount, for Jews) on September 28, 2000, which sparked violent demonstrations that were put down with great firmness. But *post hoc* is not the same as *propter hoc*: the temporal sequence of events does not indicate a causal relationship. Sharon's visit to the Mosque Esplanade did not provoke the second Intifada but was only an occasion for the Palestinian Authority to launch a wave of spectacular violence that had already been "prepared, organized, and planned" by its strategists (Ilan Greilsammer, art. cit., p. 14). One year later this new uprising seemed to have resulted in a "total impasse." See Gilles Paris, "Le premier anniversaire de la deuxième Intifadah célébré dans la morosité," *Le Monde*, September 29, 2001, p. 8.

38. See Antoine Basbous, *L'Islamisme . . .*, op. cit., p. 37; Alain Chevalérias, "Le Hezbollah libanais, une force politique," *Stratégique*, 1997/2–3, pp. 145–159. For a (generally pro-Palestinian) attempt to place Palestinian Islamism in historical perspective, see Jean-François Legrain, "Islamistes et lutte nationale palestinienne dans les territoires occupés par Israël," *Revue française de science politique* 36/2, April 1986, pp. 227–247; idem, "Les islamistes palestiniens à l'épreuve du soulèvement," *Maghreb-Machrek* 121, July 1988, pp. 4–42; idem, "Mobilisation islamiste et soulèvement palestinien, 1987–1988," in Gilles Kepel and Yann Richard, eds., *Intellectuels et militants de l'Islam contemporain*, Paris: le Seuil, 1990, pp. 131–166. See also the not unsympathetic study by Agnès Pavlowsky, *Hamas ou le miroir des frustrations palestiniennes*, Paris: L'Harmattan, 2000.

39. See Ehud Ya'ari, "Hamas Attempts to Take Control," *Jerusalem Report*, August 27, 2001.

40. Joseph Maïla highlights this extremely important symptom in "Israël et la Palestine sous tension. Entretien avec Daniel Lindenberg et Joseph Maïla," *Esprit* No. 277, August–September 2001, pp. 11–12.

41. In the Islamist view of the Middle East, the four major enemies of Islam are Marxism, freemasonry, secularism, and Judaism (the last being the common origin of the first three). See Gilles Kepel, *Prophet and Pharaoh*, op. cit., pp. 110–124; idem, *Allah in the West*, op. cit., p. 170 and n. 1. For the Algerian Islamists, France and especially French influence (France "in the mind") are an additional figure of the absolute enemy.

42. See Jean-Michel Foulquier, *Arabie séoudite: la dictature protégée*, Paris: Albin Michel, 1995; Richard Labévière, *Les Dollars de la terreur. Les États-Unis et les islamistes*, Paris: Grasset, 1999; Alexandre del Valle, *Islamisme et États-Unis*, op. cit; Jean-Charles Brisard and Guillaume Dasquié, *Ben Laden, la vérité interdite*, Paris: Denoël, 2001; Arundhati Roy, "The Algebra of Infinite Justice," *The Guardian* [London], September 29, 2001; Noam Chomsky, *9-11*, New York: Seven Stories Press, 2002. See also the fine article by Fethi Benslama, "Islam: quelle humiliation?" *Le Monde*, November 28, 2001, p. 16, which subjects the Saudi regime to a rightly pitiless critique and exposes the scandal that the Western countries (beginning with the United States) support it for strictly commercial reasons.

43. See Joseph Maïla's stimulating reflections in "L'attentat vu par l'islam," *Esprit* No. 278, October 2001, pp. 64–73.

44. Bin Laden, quoted by Antoine Basbous, *L'Islamisme*, op. cit., pp. 44–45. For other examples of calls for *jihad* against Christians (Westerners or Americans) and Jews, see ibid., pp. 44–47.

45. This book, written in French and published in Algiers in 1992 by Salama Editions, has been on sale in a number of Muslim bookshops in Paris as well as at the Institut du Monde arabe (Michel Gurfinkiel, *Israël. Géopolitique d'une paix*, op. cit., p. 95).

46. Mohammed Yacine Kassab, op. cit., p. 75.

47. Ibid., p. 96.

48. Ibid., p. 87.

49. "Believers, do not enter into relations of protection with either Jews or Christians. Let them do that with one another! Whoever of you enters into such relations with them shall become one of theirs" (translated from *Le Koran, essai de traduction de l'arabe annoté et suivi d'une étude exégétique par Jacques Berque*, revised and corrected ed., Paris: Albin Michel, 1995, p. 129).

50. Mohammed Yacine Kassab, op. cit., p. 97.

51. On the organizational background, see Gilles Kepel, *Jihad . . .*, op. cit., pp. 282, 412 (n. 4).

52. Quoted in Antoine Basbous, ibid., p. 221. These zoomorphic metaphors are commonplace in Islamic anti-Jewish discourse. The previously mentioned communiqué of the Islamic Jamaa Mujahedeen, for example, asks: "What would the presence of 20,000 apes and pigs mean in Morocco" (quoted in Jacquard, *Au nom*

d'Oussama Ben Laden . . ., op. cit., p. 326). Similarly, an imam's sermon from Mecca, broadcast live on Radio-Orient on October 27, 2000, contained these words: "Yesterday's Jews are a bad legacy and . . . today's are even worse; ungrateful toward their benefactors, worshipers of the calf, killers of prophets, . . . dross of humanity. They were execrated and banished by God, who made them into apes, pigs, and idolaters straying off the right path." Quoted from *L'Observateur du monde juif,* bulletin no. 1, November 2001, pp. 49–50.

53. Quoted from ibid., pp. 50–51.

54. On this Qatar-based television channel, which largely serves Islamist propaganda, see Safa Haeri, "Al-Jazira, la CNN des islamistes," *Marianne* No. 234, October 15–21, 2001, p. 25; and Ouda Ibrahim, "Al-Jazira, nouvel oeil médiatique," *Regards* No. 73, November 2001, pp. 16–17.

55. Translation by Associated Press, quoted from *The Guardian* [London], October 7, 2001.

56. "CNN March 1997 Interview with Osama bin Laden," news.findlaw.com/cnn/docs/binladen/binladenintvw-cnn.pdf

57. Olivier Roy, quoted in Vincent Hugeux, et al., "Ce que pense vraiment le monde musulman," *L'Express* No. 2627, November 8–14, 2001, p. 82.

58. France Inter broadcast, October 11, 2001, 8:45 a.m. In his previously mentioned live sermon of October 27, 2000, the Imam of Mecca was more straightforward: "Our conflict with the Jews is not over an event, a land, or certain frontiers; . . . it is a conflict involving beliefs, identity, and existence." Quoted from *L'Observatoire du monde juif,* op. cit., p. 49.

59. The Armed Islamic Group (or Groups) consists of a cluster of small informal groups. On the ideological and political origins and the murderous activity of the Islamist groups in Algeria, see Rémy Leveau, ed., *L'Algérie dans la guerre,* Brussels: Complexe, 1995; Luis Martinez, *La Guerre civile en Algérie,* Paris: Karthala, 1998; Gilles Kepel, *Jihad* . . ., op. cit., pp. 176–184, 276–278; Antoine Basbous, *L'Islamisme* . . ., op. cit., pp. 109–195; Antoine Sfeir, *Les Réseaux d'Allah,* Paris: Plon, 2001, pp. 118–131. I shall not discuss here those writers on the Muslim world who, in persistently denying the existence of the Islamist phenomenon or Islamic terrorism (which they present as a fabrication of the Algerian secret

services), or in interpreting it as a good old "democratic" reaction to a barely disguised military dictatorship, may be considered accomplices or new-style "deniers" of the massacres in question. The fact that special forces may have manipulated Islamist groups does not mean that Islamism can be reduced to one huge manipulation, nor that the massacres can be blamed only on the Algerian state. (See Rachid Boudjedra's lucid essay *FIS de la haine*, Paris: Gallimard, 2nd enlarged ed., 1992.) Since the early 1990s a number of freethinkers have actually specialized in ironic denials of the "Islamist peril," arguing that, like the "yellow peril" of the late nineteenth century, it is a fantasy or mirage maintained by "headquarters." In the same spirit, certain "anti-racist" circles have ritually and indignantly denounced "anti-Islamism" on the grounds that there is no "Islamist threat" in the real world. To be credible, however, this line of argument has to involve the surreptitious replacement of hostility to Islamism (which is my position in this book) with hostility to Islam (which I condemn), and therefore a positive identification of Islam and Islamism. See, for example, Fred Halliday, "Les fondements de l'hostilité à l'islam," in Alain Gresh, ed., *Un péril islamiste?*, Brussels: Complexe, 1994, pp. 61–79. Justifiable denunciations of Islamophobia may then degenerate into the mere construction of a protective belt around all the totalitarian and terrorist spin-offs of Muslim fundamentalism, so that anything invoking Islam, even falsely, becomes immune from criticism. A fine example of intellectual terrorism.

   60. Sermon published in part in *L'Arche* No. 524–525, October–November 2001, p. 43. See the analysis by Farhad Khosrokhavar, "Les nouveaux martyrs d'Allah," *Le Monde*, October 2, 2001, p. 19.

   61. "Bin Laden's 'Letter to Muslims,'" http://news.bbc.co.uk/1/hi/world/monitoring/media_reports/1633204.stm

   62. See Antoine Basbous, *L'Islamisme* . . ., op. cit., pp. 40–57.

Chapter 3. Construction, Content, Functioning, and Metamorphoses of the "New Anti-Semitism"

   1. See Jacques Givet, *La Gauche contre Israël? Essai sur le néo-antisémitisme*, Paris: Jean-Jacques Pauvert, 1968; idem, "Contre une

certaine gauche," *Les Nouveaux Cahiers* No. 13–14, Spring–Summer 1968, pp. 116–119; Léon Poliakov, *De l'antisionisme à l'antisémitisme*, Paris: Calmann-Lévy, 1969; Shmuel Ettinger, "Le caractère de l'antisémitisme contemporain," *Dispersion et Unité* No. 14, 1975, pp. 141–157; and Michael Curtis, ed., *Antisemitism in the Modern World*, Boulder: Westview Press, 1986.

2. See my critical study: "L'antisionisme arabo-islamophile. Éléments d'une analyse froide de la forme dominante de l'antisémitisme contemporain," *Sens* No. 11, November 1982, pp. 253–266. I focus there especially on an article published in *Le Monde* on June 17, 1982, in the form of a publicity announcement: "Le sens de l'agression israélienne," signed by Roger Garaudy, Father Michel Lelong, and Pastor Étienne Mathiot, and reprinted in Roger Garaudy, *Mes Témoins*, Paris: Éditions "À Contre-Nuit," 1997, pp. 108–116. For a critical analysis, see also Alain Dieckhoff, "Le sionisme, 'diable' des Palestiniens," *Les Nouveaux Cahiers* No. 79, Winter 1984–1985, pp. 17–22.

3. See Yohanan Manor, "L'antisionisme," *Revue française de science politique* 34/2, April 1984, pp. 295–323; and Bernard Lewis, *Semites and Anti-Semites*, op. cit.

4. See Salomon Reinach, *L'Accusation du meurtre ritual*, Paris: Librairie Léopold Cerf, 1893. On the accusation that Jews are inherently cruel and dominating, see my *Les Protocoles des Sages de Sion. Faux et usages d'un faux*, op. cit., vol. 1, pp. 354–357.

5. Many examples of press articles expressing this standard Judeophobia may be found in the report of the Simon Wiesenthal Center: *Egypt: Israel's Peace Partner: A Survey of Antisemitism in the Egyptian Press, 1986–1987*, Los Angeles: Simon Wiesenthal Center Publications, 1988; and in Rivka Yadlin, *An Arrogant Oppressive Spirit: Anti-Zionism as Anti-Judaism in Egypt*, New York: Pergamon Press, 1989.

6. See Pierre Vidal-Naquet, *Assassins of Memory: Essays on the Denial of the Holocaust*, New York: Columbia University Press, 1992 (a collection of essays published in France between 1980 and 1987); Alain Finkielkraut, *The Future of a Negation: Reflections on the Question of Genocide*, Lincoln: University of Nebraska Press, 1998; Florent Brayard, *Comment l'idée vint à M. Rassinier. Naissance du révisionnisme*, with a preface by Pierre Vidal-Naquet, Paris: Fayard, 1996.

7. See my study "La nouvelle judéophobie. Antisionisme, antiracisme, anti-impérialisme," *Les Temps modernes* No. 520, November 1989, pp. 1–80.

8. Adolf Hitler, *Mein Kampf*, London: Hurst & Blackett, 1939, vol. 1, ch. X.

9. Interview with Robert Faurisson conducted by Antonio Pitamitz, *Storia illustrata* No. 261, August 1979, reprinted in Serge Thion, *Vérité historique ou vérité politique? Le dossier de l'affaire Faurisson. La question des chambres à gaz*, Paris: La Vieille Taupe, 1980, p. 187; and as "The Gas Chambers: Truth or Lie?" *Journal of Historical Review* 2/4, Winter 1981, p. 319.

10. Robert Faurisson, duplicated "supplement" (dated June 16, 1978), sent by Faurisson together with his article "Défense de l'Occident," to "various public figures;" reproduced in Thion, op. cit., p. 89 [translated and quoted in Nadine Fresco, "The Denial of the Dead: On the Faurisson Affair," *Dissent*, Fall 1981].

11. Roger Garaudy's commitment to the campaign to demonize Israel was already evident in a book he published in 1983: *L'Affaire Israël*, Paris: S.P.A.G.-Papyrus, 1983 [translated as *The Case of Israel: A Study of Political Zionism*, London: Shorouk International, 1983]. In his conclusion, the enthusiastic Stalinist who had already converted to absolute anti-Zionism (in the name of a Marxist-Christian-Islamic hodgepodge) began by asserting: "In the areas where it has been implanted, the Zionist State has no historical, biblical, or juridical legitimacy" (p. 195).

12. Roger Garaudy, *Les Mythes fondateurs de la politique israélienne*, Paris: La Vieille Taupe, 1996; subsequently Paris: Samiszdat, 1996. (English translation: *The Mythical Foundations of Israeli Policy*, London: Studies Forum International, 1997.) No time was lost in translating the book into Arabic, Turkish and Persian, and it was republished in French in Lebanon (Beirut: Al Fihrist) in May 1998, with a new preface ("Pourquoi ce livre?", pp. 7–15) and several appendices (pp. 389–418), the first of which was devoted to the "new historians in Israel" (pp. 391–401). In *The Holocaust in American Life* (Boston: Houghton Mifflin, 1999), a highly interesting scholarly work that sparked considerable controversy when it appeared in 1999, the historian Peter Novick has critically analyzed the centrality and religiosity of "Holocaust remembrance" in "American Jewish consciousness." But he tends to underestimate

the impact of Holocaust denial and fails to understand the force with which it has spread around the world (see esp. pp. 270–272), while also somewhat naively assuming the common thesis that anti-Semitism is in the course of disappearing (esp. pp. 175f.). In relation to contemporary Judeophobia, a certain America-centrism linked to a—in itself justifiable—critique of "Judeocentrism" may cloud the best of minds. It is true, however, that Novick wrote his book in the late 1990s, before the second Intifada and especially before the anti-American (and symbolically anti-Jewish) attacks of September 11, 2001.

13. Article in the Palestinian journal *Al Manar*, May 3, 1999 (quoted in Meïr Waintrater, "La montée de l'antisémitisme dans le monde arabe," *L'Arche* No. 523, September 2001, p. 89). Garaudy's "anti-Zionist" tract was very well received by anti-Jewish circles in Romania, where a mixture of conspiracy fantasies and Holocaust denial serves as a kind of post-Communist vulgate for many intellectuals. See George Voicu, "L'honneur national roumain en question," *Les Temps modernes* No. 606, November–December 1999, pp. 142–152; and idem, "L'imaginaire du complot dans la Roumanie postcommuniste," *Les Temps modernes* No. 613, March–April–May 2001, pp. 173–203. On Holocaust denial Romanian-style, see Randolph L. Braham, "Offensive contre l'Histoire. Les nationalistes hongrois et le Shoah," *Les Temps modernes* No. 606, November–December 1999, pp. 123–141; and idem, "The Exculpatory History of Romanian Nationalists: The Exploitation of the Holocaust for Political Ends," in Randolph L. Braham, ed., *The Destruction of Romanian and Ukrainian Jews During the Antonescu Era*, Social Science Monographs; East European Monographs, no. 483. Boulder, New York: Columbia University Press, 1997.

14. See my *Les Protocoles des Sages de Sion. Faux et usages d'un faux*, op. cit., vol. 1, pp. 251–363.

15. "Égorge, égorge, égorge et sois sans pitié./ Égorge, égorge, égorge et jette leur tête dans le désert./ Égorge, égorge, égorge tout ce que tu voudras." Quoted in Jacques Givet, *La Gauche contre Israël?*, op. cit., p. 164.

16. Olivier Carré, *L'Orient arabe aujourd'hui*, Brussels: Complexe, 1991, p. 194.

17. On the context of this anti-Zionist "relaunch," see Annie Kriegel, *Israël est-il coupable?*, Paris: Laffont, 1982, and *Réflexion*

sur les questions juives, op. cit., pp. 538–617; and Alain Finkielkraut, *La Réprobation d'Israël,* Paris: Denoël/Gonthier, 1983.

18. See, for example, Sophie Claudet, "Mourir en martyr," *Revue d'études palestiniennes,* new series, No. 28, Summer 2001, pp. 96–102. In this propaganda article, which is designed to arouse pity, compassion, and action-inducing indignation, several interesting notes lift the veil on the cynical strategy of using a religious pretext to send children or young people to their death: "The *shuhada* [plural of *shahid*: martyr] are honored, whether they die in combat or as a result of bombing or stray bullets. A *shahid*'s death is the most beautiful there is; it assures you of a place in paradise," explains Fatin al-Masari, director of a UNWRA women's center at Beit Hanun, in the northern part of the Gaza Strip. A hit song from the period of the first Intifada, now revived in line with more recent tastes, orders mothers to rejoice: "Begin your whooping, shahid's mother, begin your whooping, for today is your martyr's wedding day. Begin your whooping . . ." (ibid., p. 97). The "wedding," we are told, does not here have "a religious connotation, but represents the most important and joyful day for a boy and his family" (p. 97, n. 3). After the death of Fares Odeh on November 8, 2000, shortly before his fifteenth birthday, his mother stated: "He used to watch the Hezbollah television channel. He wanted to join them and used to wear their headband. . . . My son was a leader and even carried older people along with him." To the question: "So did Fares die a hero?" she replied: "Yes, and I'm proud of it" (p. 99). We also learn that "the Intifada has a ludic side for young people." "It is one of the few distractions they have access to," said Doctor al-Sarraj. "Children feel invincible and do not realize the danger they are in" (p. 99). One cannot help wondering what their parents and teachers do. Are they happy just to witness the mass production of "martyrs," later saying they are proud of them? The Islamization of the Palestinian cause also manifests itself in this kind of support for the culture of death.

19. Article 32 of "Allah's Charter," http://www.mideastweb.org/hamas.htm. See Renée Neher-Bernheim, "Le best-seller actuel de la literature antisémite: les *Protocoles des Sages de Sion,*" in P.-A. Taguieff, ed., *Les Protocoles . . .,* op. cit., vol. 2, p. 415.

20. Quoted in Michèle Tribalat, "Sortir des amalgames," art. cit.

21. Ibid.

22. Ibid. From a contribution to the stcom.net chat room.

23. Quoted in Gidéon Kouts, "Choses vues au Pakistan," *L'Arche* No. 524–525, October–November 2001, p. 44.

24. Quoted in *L'Arche* No. 523, September 2001, p. 65. See Frédéric Encel, "Assad à Paris: une faute morale, une erreur géopolitique," *Libération*, June 29, 2001, p. 6.

25. See Jean-Claude Buhrer, "Nombreux conflits en vue à la Conférence mondiale contre le racisme," *Le Monde*, August 31, 2001, p. 2; idem, "La Conférence de Durban s'est ouverte dans un climat de disaccord à propos d'Israël," *Le Monde*, September 2–3, 2001, p. 2; idem, "Américains et Israéliens quittent la conference de Durban sur le racisme," *Le Monde*, September 5, 2001, p. 2; idem, "La Conférence de l'ONU contre le racisme s'achève à Durban dans le désarroi," *Le Monde*, September 9–10, 2001, p. 4; idem, "La querelle sur le Proche-Orient a desservi la lutte contre le racisme à Durban," *Le Monde*, September 11, 2001, p. 5; Sabine Cessou, "Le Proche-Orient rattrape Durban," *Libération*, September 1–2, 2001, p. 6; idem, "Durban: l'échec du fourre-tout," *Libération*, September 8–9, 2001, p. 5.

26. In 1982–1983 I suggested that the "new anti-Semitism," carried along and legitimated by absolute anti-Zionism, might be speeding up the use of a certain kind of anti-racism (on the left and far left), and therefore leading to the emergence of an "anti-Jewish anti-racism." See, for example, my "L'antijudaïsme contemporain. Rupture de tradition et nouvelle naissance," *Cahiers Bernard Lazare* No. 101–103, May–July 1983, pp. 27–30.

27. The resolution passed by 72 votes to 35, with 32 abstentions, and was rescinded by the General Assembly only on December 16, 1991. See my book *Les Fins de l'antiracisme*, op. cit., pp. 216–217, 435–436, as well as the analyses in Bernard Lewis's *Semites and Anti-Semites: an Enquiry into Conflict and Prejudice*, op. cit. From July 24 to 28, 1976, an international symposium on Zionism and racism was held in Tripoli, Libya; see *Zionism and Racism: Proceedings of an International Symposium*, Tripoli: International Organization for the Elimination of All Forms of Racial Discrimination, 1977.

28. This may be illustrated by Norman G. Finkelstein's tract *The Holocaust Industry: Reflection on the Exploitation of Jewish*

Suffering, New York: Verso, 2000; *L'Industrie de l'Holocauste. Réflexions sur l'exploitation de la souffrance des Juifs*, Paris: La Fabrique, 2001. It will come as no surprise that this wretched essay was translated and published in French by Trotskyist circles that have replaced their project of permanent world revolution with this mixture of Israelophobia and Palestinophilia, which leads certain individuals (some of Jewish origin) into a logic of Judeophobia. This is far from being a historical novelty in Europe: since the mid-nineteenth century, self-hatred, shame, identification with the dominant party, and submission to hegemonic beliefs have repeatedly coalesced and plunged into Judeophobia certain individuals of Jewish origin. Reputed to be credible authorities on the "Jewish" or "Zionist" question, they are feted for their "courage" or "lucidity," their determination to "seek out the truth," or their salutary function of "demystification." The responsibility of these Jews who have agreed to speak or write against the Jews is therefore immense. See above, Chapter 1, note 38. Let us here simply recall a few of the works by authors of Jewish origin that helped to fuel anti-Jewish passions in the last third of the nineteenth century: Jacob Brafman, *Livre du Kahal. Matériaux pour étudier le judaïsme en Russie et son influence sur les populations parmi lesquelles il existe*, Odessa: Imprimerie L. Nitzsche (translation of a work first published in Russian in 1869); Joseph Lémann, *L'Entrée des israélites dans la société française et les États chrétiens d'après des documents nouveaux*, Paris: Victor Lecoffre, 1886; idem, *La Prépondérance juive*, Part One, *Ses origines (1789–1791)*, Paris: Victor Lecoffre, 1889, and Part Two, *Son organisation*, Paris: Lecoffre, 1894; Osman-Bey, *La Conquête du monde par les Juifs*, Paris: H. Gautier, 1887 (translated from the 7th German edition of 1875). Jacob Brafmann (1825–1879) was a Russian-Jewish convert to Orthodoxy and a police informer; Joseph Lémann (1836–1915) was a French Jew who converted to Catholicism and became a priest; Osman-Bey was one of the pseudonyms used by a Jew of Serb origin named Millinger (?–1898?), a low-level international swindler who specialized in the production and sale of anti-Jewish writings. See F. Lovsky, *Antisémitisme et mystère d'Israël*, Paris: Albin Michel, 1955, pp. 337–338, 346; Walter Laqueur, *Russia and Germany: A Century of Conflict*, London: Weidenfeld and Nicolson, 1965, p. 96; Norman Cohn,

Warrant for Genocide: The Myth of the Jewish World Conspiracy
and the Protocols of the Elders of Zion, Chico, Ca.: Scholars Press,
1981; Jeannine Verdès-Leroux, Scandale financier et antisémitisme
catholique. Le krach de l'Union Générale, Paris: Le Centurion,
1969, pp. 127–128; Léon Poliakov, History of Anti-Semitism, vol.
4, Suicidal Europe 1870–1933, London: Routledge & Kegan Paul,
1985, p. 85. For a more extensive set of references, see Theodor
Lessing, Der jüdische Selbsthaß, Berlin: Jüdischer Verlag, 1930
(French translation: La Haine de soi. Le refus d'être juif, Paris:
Berg International, 2nd enlarged ed., 2001); Sander L. Gilman,
Jewish Self-Hatred: Antisemitism and the Hidden Language of the
Jews, Baltimore: Johns Hopkins University Press, 1986. A special
study should be made of individuals of Jewish origin who have involved themselves in Holocaust-denial propaganda in France
(around Robert Faurisson) and the United States. The case of the
anarchist agitator Jean-Gabriel Cohn-Bendit, a specialist in "alternative" pedagogy and political mentor of his famous younger
brother Daniel, is particularly interesting. We come across him in
the far-left group that supported Faurisson in 1979–1980: Serge
Thion's book Vérité historique ou vérité politique? (1980) is described as "published under the trade name La Vieille Taupe and
on the responsibility of Jacob Assous, Denis Authier, Jean-Gabriel
Cohn-Bendit . . ." (op. cit., p. 4, with the information repeated on
p. 7). On January 22, 1979, "Gaby" signed with Pierre Guillaume
(among others) an article defending the French pioneer of Holocaust denial, Paul Rassinier ("Connaissez-vous Paul Rassinier?",
reprinted in Thion, op. cit., pp. 128–130). And on March 4, 1979,
the elder brother of "Dany" (who himself stayed out of these
stormy debates) published a letter in the daily Libération under the
title "Question de principe," after it had been turned down by Le
Monde. In this letter he defended people such as Rassinier or Faurisson and slipped in: "The millions of dead Jews are constantly
used as a counterargument against any criticism of the policy of the
State of Israel, for example" (in Thion, op. cit., p. 133; reprinted
in Jean-Gabriel Cohn-Bendit, Éric Delcroix, et al., Intolérable in-
tolérance, Paris: Éditions de la Différence, 1981, p. 29). In the latter collective work, where he rubs shoulders with the far-right
lawyer Éric Delcroix and the frenzied anti-Zionist Vincent Monteil, "Gaby" published a contribution (also under the title "Ques-

tion de principle") based on extracts from an article in a far-left journal that had gone over to Holocaust revisionism: "Génocide, chambres à gaz. Des procès au débat," *L'Anti-Mythes* No. 25. While recognizing that Hitler "ordered that Jews should . . . die purely because they were Jewish," (p. 27) he immediately follows this up with the statement that "all this [was] without gas chambers, without an order for extermination."

29. In an interview published on March 29, 1991, in the French Catholic weekly *La Vie*, Abbé Pierre echoed Palestinian propaganda: "I note that, after the establishment of their state, the Jews turned from victims into butchers." See my book *Les Protocoles des Sages de Sion*, op. cit., pp. 283–284.

30. For an objective approach to the Zionist type of "regroupment nationalism," see Alain Dieckhoff, "Nationalisme d'État et intégrisme nationaliste: le cas d'Israël," in Gil Delannoi and Pierre-André Taguieff, eds., *Nationalismes en perspective*, Paris: Berg International, 2001, pp. 29–44.

31. Edward W. Said, "Intellectual Origins of Imperialism and Zionism," in *Zionism and Racism*, op. cit., pp. 125–130. The thesis of the celebrated American Palestinian professor is as follows: "Zionism and imperialism draw on each other. . . . The struggle against modern European imperialism and racism is a civilizational struggle, and we cannot wage it successfully unless we understand its system of ideas and where they originate. . . . In theory and practice then, Zionism is a degraded repetition of European imperialism" (pp. 125, 129).

32. *Zionism and Racism*, op. cit., p. 3.

33. Abdullah Sharafuddin explicitly focuses on the "ramifications" of Zionism, which "threaten to destroy the human race" (ibid., p. 4). In the same volume we find an article by Alfred M. Lilienthal, "Zionist Manipulations to Induce Immigration to Israel" (pp. 47–58). Since the 1950s this American Jewish lawyer has made a profession out of denunciations of "Zionism" and the State of Israel and a view of "Zionism" as nothing other than "manipulation," "Mafia connections," "conspiracy," and so on). See especially his book *The Zionist Connection: What Price Peace?*, New York: Dodd, Mead, 1978. It is not surprising that this "anti-Zionist" and explicitly pro-Palestinian polemicist is seen in the United States as an "anti-Semitic Jew."

34. Amalgams, prejudices, and negative stereotypes directed against Islam jostle with others directed against the Muslim world and the Arab world: Islamophobia is often indistinguishable from Arabophobia (see especially Louis Gardet, *Les Hommes d'Israël. Approche des mentalités*, Paris: Hachette, 1997, pp. 316ff.; Maxime Rodinson, *Europe and the Mystique of Islam*, op. cit., pp. 23–82; Paul Balta, "Stéréotypes et réalités," in Abderrahim Lamchichi, ed., *Islam-Occident, la confrontation?*, Paris: Les Cahiers de Confluences, 2001, pp. 49–54). The principle that they should be vigorously rejected and denounced is largely accepted in the world of the intellectual elites as well as among the political leaders of Western/democratic countries. The norm of struggle against all forms of ethnocentrism and sociocentrism is now part of the *doxa* of pluralist democratic societies. But the declared ideal should never be confused with the social and political reality: pluralism and positive tolerance are regulative ideas, destined to be realized only in the realm of infinity.

35. Quoted in Michèle Tribalat, art. cit.

36. Ibid. This "passionate message from Sheikh Osama bin Laden to the Muslim world" may be found online on the site of the Islamic Center in Geneva (stcom.net).

37. On this "moderate" Islamism, sponsored especially by the current around *Le Monde diplomatique* in the name of dialogue with the representatives of "moderate political Islam," see Jocelyne Cesari, *Être musulman en France d'aujourd'hui*, Paris: Hachette, 1987; and idem, *Musulmans et républicains: les jeunes, l'islam et la France*, Brussels: Complexe, 1998, esp. pp. 131–148.

38. Tariq Ramadan, in Alain Gresh and Tariq Ramadan, *L'Islam en questions*, Arles: Actes du Sud, 2000, p. 213. See, for example, Robert Miles, *Racism*, London/New York: Routledge, 1989, pp. 17–19 (and the works listed therein). This may be a good place to mention AGRIF, a French far-right association founded on October 30, 1984 (by traditionalist Catholics belonging to or close to the Front National), which has specialized in the denunciation of "anti-Christian racism," "anti-Catholic racism," and "anti-French racism." See my study "Les métamorphoses idéologiques du racisme et la crise de l'antiracisme," in P.-A. Taguieff, ed., *Face au racisme*, op. cit., vol. 2, pp. 54–60.

39. See Christophe Boltanski, "Londres, base arrière de l'islamisme," *Libération*, September 18, 2001, p. 19; and "À 'Londonistan,' l'islamisme a droit de cité," *Libération*, October 18, 2001, pp. 15–16. According to a number of sources, Imam Abu Qatada (real name: Omar Mahmud Othman), a Palestinian with Jordanian citizenship who has had political refugee status in London since 1993, trained a number of Islamic terrorists there in the 1990s: for example, Djamel Beghal, Nazir Trabelsi, and Zacharias Moussaoui (the latter a Frenchman of Algerian origin suspected of being intended as the twentieth plane hijacker but taken in for questioning at his flying school in Minnesota three weeks before 9/11). London is also the base for Islamist preachers such as Abu Hamza al-Masri (a former *mujahed* in Afghanistan) and Sheikh Omar Bakri Mohammed, a Syrian dissident who has lived in the British capital since 1986 and is head of the Al Muhajirun ("Exiles") movement. Having immediately approved of the September 2001 attacks, in the name of "legitimate self-defense," Abu Hamza went on to denounce repeatedly a "Zionist plot to unleash a third world war" (quoted in Boltanski, *Libération*, October 18, 2001).

40. See Fabienne Pompey, "Sans violences, manifestants et 'contre-sommet' ont fait entendre leur voix," *Le Monde*, September 2–3, 2001, p. 2; "À Durban, le 'contre-sommet' des ONG accuse Israël de génocide," *Le Monde*, September 4, 2001, p. 3; and "Durban: de nombreuses ONG se désolidarisent des mouvements qui assimilent sionisme et racisme," *Le Monde*, September 6, 2001, p. 4; "L'échec de Durban" (editorial), *Le Monde*, September 5, 2001; Sabine Cessou, "À Durban, les ONG qualifient Israël d 'État raciste,' *Libération*, September 3, 2001, p. 10; Caroline Dumay, "Les ONG stigmatisent le 'racisme d'Israël,'" *Le Figaro*, September 3, 2001, p. 2.

41. *World Conference against Racism: NGO Forum Declaration*, http://www.racism.org.za/index.html

42. This kind of argument may be found in numerous publications of the Nation of Islam, the black American organization led by Louis Farrakhan. See especially a work published by its "Historical Studies Department": *The Secret Relationship Between Blacks and Jews*, Chicago: Latimer Associates, 1991, vol. 1, which describes the involvement and crucial responsibility of Jews in the African slave trade, on the supposition that it was the real

"holocaust," the main genocide, in the history of the world (with an estimated 100 million victims). We read, for example: "The Jews have undeniably been linked to the biggest criminal operation ever undertaken against an entire race; the holocaust of the Blacks of Africa. They took part in the capture and forced export of millions of citizens of Black Africa into a life of inhuman and degrading servitude, all for the financial benefit of Jews" (p. vii); "The Jews, as key operatives in the enterprise, have carved out for themselves a monumental culpability in slavery—and the holocaust" (p. 178). See Gilles Kepel, *Allah in the West*, op. cit., pp. 10, 59–62, 67–68; Henry Louis Gates, Jr., "The Uses of Anti-Semitism" (July 1992), in Paul Berman, ed., *Blacks and Jews: Alliances and Arguments*, New York: Delta Books, 1994, pp. 217–223; Harold Brackman, *Ministry of Lies: The Truth behind the Nation of Islam's "The Secret Relationship Between Blacks and Jews,"* New York/London: Four Walls Eight Windows, 1994; Arthur J. Magida, *Prophet of Rage: A Life of Louis Farrakhan and His Nation*, New York: Basic Books, 1996, pp. 173–202. Significantly, a publishing house close to the Nation of Islam has brought out an American translation of an anti-Jewish, anti-Masonic book by Léon de Poncins, *Freemasonry and Judaism: Secret Powers Behind Revolution*, New York: A & B Book Publishers, 1994. For an overview of American Islam since the late 1960s, see Steven Barboza, *American Jihad: Islam After Malcolm X*, New York: Doubleday, 1994.

43. Arab Lawyers Union, *That Is the Fact . . . Racism of Zionism and Israel*, Durban 2001 (retranslated from the French). It is not surprising that we find among these Arab lawyers a Moroccan "socialist," Khalid Alsufyani, who in January 1998 supported Roger Garaudy at a time when he and his publisher, Holocaust-denier Pierre Guillaume, were in court being defended with understandable conviction by Jacques Vergès and Éric Delcroix. See the account of the court proceedings (January 8, 15, and 16, 1998) in the far-right "anti-Zionist" and "anti-globalist" journal *Résistance!* (Françoise Puech, "Procès de Roger Garaudy. Ambiance au Palais de Justice," *Résistance!* No. 3, March 1998, pp. 4–5). It should be made clear that this journal presents itself as the "bi-monthly of the Resistance Fighters against the New World Order and Single-Model Thought [*la Pensée Unique*]." The anti-globalization label can take in anything. . . .

44. George Orwell, quoted in Jean-Claude Michéa, *Orwell, anarchiste tory*, suivi de *À propos de 1984*, Castelnau-le-Lez: Climats, 2000, p. 132.

45. Caroline Fourest, "Journal de bord sur la Conférence de Durban contre le racisme," *ProChoix* No. 19, October 2001 (web site: Durban2001.com). See also Henri Pasternak, "Le pogrom de Durban," *L'Arche* No. 524–525, October–November 2001, pp. 78–80.

46. Yasser Arafat, as quoted by *Libération*, September 1–2, 2001, p. 6. One anti-Israeli slogan on demonstrators' boards in Durban used the wordplay "Apartheid isreal" (reproduced in *Libération*, ibid.). T-shirts sporting the slogan "Israel-Zionism = Racism" were handed out to the people of Durban. Some pamphlets contained the formula: "One Jew, one bullet." "Anti-Zionist" militants in the streets of Durban offered "licenses to kill Jews" on which there was space for the bearer's photograph to be attached. And all this was in an officially "anti-racist" context, as one could tell from a T-shirt worn by most of the young people there: "One race, the human race." For other examples, see the reports by the president of the European Center for Public Action (who was present in Durban): David Lévy-Bentolila, *Pendant Durban*, Brussels: B'nai B'rith Europe, October 2001, 5 pp., and by Rabbi Philippe Haddad, op. cit., pp. 35–84.

47. Farouk Kaddoumi, statement of August 29, 2001 (quoted by Jean-Christophe Ploquin, "Des discriminations bien partagées," *La Croix*, August 31, 2001, p. 5. On the same day this Palestinian leader, who headed the political (foreign affairs) department of the PLO, denounced Israel as a "racist state" (Yann Mens, "La réunion de Durban risque le détournement," *La Croix*, ibid., p. 4). In a self-justificatory text published as a supplement to *Le Monde* on September 15, 2001 (*Afrique du Sud. Un bilan globalement positif*), we come across an astonishing article entitled "Durban, World Capital of Tolerance" (p. 1). Understandably enough, the Paris daily felt it necessary to add a prominent notice: "This report has been written and edited by INTERFRANCE MEDIA, which alone is responsible for its content. The editorial team at *Le Monde* did not play any role in its production" (ibid.). On the events and significance of the Durban Conference, see Jacques Tarnero, "De Jérusalem à Durban, les jouisseurs de haine," *Le Monde*, September 11, 2001, p. 18; Roger

Cukierman, "Durban prémonitoire?" *Le Figaro*, September 18, 2001, p. 15; Elie Wiesel, "Pour nous, Juifs, Durban est un avertissement," *L'Arche* No. 524–525, October–November 2001, p. 81.

48. Louis-Ferdinand Céline, especially in the first of his three tracts (*Bagatelles pour un massacre*, Paris: Denoël, December 1937), placed his huge talent at the service of this major theme of anti-Jewish propaganda: "The war was already fine manure for the bourgeoisie—but war now for the Jews! . . . A war for the delectation of the Jews! . . . I can imagine no worse humiliation than to get yourself killed for the yids" (p. 86). For an impartial analysis (a rare thing in these times of unconditional Celinophilia), see Annick Duraffour, "Céline, un antijuif fanatique," in Pierre-André Taguieff, ed., *L'Antisémitisme de plume 1940–1944*, Paris: Berg International, 1999, pp. 147–197.

49. Paul Rassinier, *Les responsables de la deuxième guerre mondiale*, Paris: Nouvelles Éditions latines, 1967.

50. See, for example, the delirious book by Bernard Granotier, *Israël. Cause de la Troisième Guerre mondiale?*, Paris: L'Harmattan, 1982. In his days as a leftist / Third Worldist sociologist, Granotier published a book that is still cited as a pioneering study: *Les Travailleurs immigrés en France* (Paris: Maspero, 1970; reprinted, 1979). See my article "La nouvelle judéophobie . . ." (1989), art. cit., p. 61, n. 32.

51. A strict fundamentalist movement has no other political project than "the sharia, all the sharia, nothing but the sharia," (Olivier Roy, epilogue to Ahmed Rashid, *L'Ombre des taliban*, Paris: Éditions Autrement, 2001, p. 268; cf. Rashid, *Taliban: Islam, Oil, and the New Great Game in Central Asia*, London: I. B. Tauris, 2000).

52. See Bernard Botiveau and Jocelyne Cesari, *Géopolitique des islams*, op. cit.

53. According to Paul Balta, the number of Muslims in 2001 could be calculated at between 1.3 and 1.5 billion (*L'Islam*, Paris: Le Cavalier Bleu, 2001, p. 119).

54. The work of these scholars has demonstrated the wealth of the mysticism, spirituality, and philosophy of the Muslim world. Other writers in French who might be mentioned in connection with this high cultural tradition are Roger Arnaldez, Mohammed Arkoun, Henri Laoust, Régis Blachère, Marc Bergé, André Miquel, Eva de Vitray-Meyerovitch, and Christian Jambet. See Mohammed

Arkoun, *L'Islam. Approche critique*, 3rd revised and enlarged ed., Paris: Jacques Grancher, 1998; and "L'Islam et ses philosophies. Entretien avec Christian Jambet," *Esprit* No. 277, August–September 2001, pp. 186–201.

55. This is actually the title of a book written in the 1930s by the Druze figure Shakib Arslam. See Emmanuel Sivan, *Mythes politiques arabes* (translated from the Hebrew), Paris: Fayard, p. 182.

56. The title of a book by the Egyptian Islamist Muhammad Qutb (brother of the famous theorist Sayyid Qutb), which appeared in 1964 (ibid.). It is probable that Osama bin Laden followed the course at Jeddah University given by the brother of Sayyid Qutb (Gilles Kepel, *Jihad* . . ., p. 314).

57. Emmanuel Sivan, op. cit., p. 183.

58. Sayyid Qutb, *Milestones*, Delhi: Markazi Maktaba Islami, 1981 (translated from the Arabic original: Cairo 1964), quoted (and retranslated) from Sivan, op. cit., p. 183. To understand the Islamist argument, one should really read the remarkable work by Olivier Carré, *Mystique et politique. Lecture révolutionnaire du Coran par Sayyid Qutb, Frère musulman radical*, Paris: Les Éditions du Cerf/Presses de la Fondation nationale des sciences politiques, 1984. On the struggle against Jews and Christians, see pp. 117–119. Jews should be considered "as traitors, as people who do not respect treaties, as hypocrites, as friends of bad Muslims" (p. 118)—so it is hardly surprising that "all offensives against the 'Islamic resurrection' come from the Jews" (p. 119). See also Gilles Kepel, *Prophet and Pharaoh*, op. cit., pp. 36–69.

59. Sayyid Qutb, quoted by Raphaël Israéli, "La conspiration judéo-chrétienne contre l'Islam," *L'Arche* No. 524–525, October–November 2001, p. 69.

60. Farhad Khosrokhavar, "Marginalisation de la jeunesse, marginalisation des élites," in Alain Gresh, ed., *Un péril islamiste?*, op. cit., p. 129.

61. In 1989, the year of his own death, Ayatollah Khomeini issued his *fatwa* against the writer, condemning him to death for his publication of *The Satanic Verses*.

62. See Antoine Basbous, *L'Islamisme*, op. cit., pp. 234, 246, 265.

63. This has nothing to do with the fact that Islam, like most religions, has a number of dogmas. See Mohammed Arkoun, *L'Islam* . . ., op. cit., pp. 113–116.

64. Nassira.net—a website on which the wearing of the Islamic scarf is glorified (quoted from Michèle Tribalat, art. cit.).

65. Hani Ramadan, "Le Coran et la Sunna," *Bulletin du Centre islamique de Genève*, October 2000, internet site (quoted in Tribalat, ibid.).

66. Aslim-Taslam web site, quoted in Tribalat, op. cit.

67. Lecture delivered at the Alliance régionale du Nord, in Amiens, on October 9, 1997 (quoted by Tribalat, ibid.).

68. On Sudan, and sub-Saharan Africa in general, see René Otayek, ed., *Le Radicalisme islamique au sud du Sahara*, Paris: Karthala, 1993; Bernard Botiveau and Jocelyne Cesari, *Géopolitique des islams*, op. cit., pp. 41–50; Abderrahim Lamchichi, *Géopolitique de l'islamisme*, Paris: L'Harmattan, 2001, pp. 139–158. The situation of Nigeria, the most populous country in Africa with 120 million inhabitants, is more and more comparable to that of Sudan: in the year 2000, ten or more states in the north of the country (Sokoto, Katsina, Borno, Kaduna, etc.) introduced the *sharia* against opposition from non-Muslims. Violent clashes between Muslims (who are the majority in the North) and Christians (mainly concentrated in the South) have since become more frequent, causing several thousand victims (2,000 just in the city of Kaduna in February 2000). In the Northern states, Islamic courts order amputation of the hands of thieves, public flogging, and even death by stoning for women found guilty of adultery. Since 9/11, anti-American demonstrations have degenerated into rioting and murderous violence. Thus, on the night of October 13–14, a demonstration organized by the Muslim Youth Congress in Kano (the largest city in the North) and punctuated with posters of bin Laden, led to scenes of Christian-hunting and ended in dozens of deaths. See Isabelle Lasserre, "Le Nigeria gagné par la haine de l'Amérique," *Libération*, October 15, 2001, p. 5.

69. Abdullahi A. An-Na'im, "L'islam politique dans les contextes nationaux et les relations internationales," in Peter L. Berger, ed., *Le Réenchantement du monde*, Paris: Bayard, 2001, p. 154; cf. idem, *The Desecularization of the World. Resurgent Religion and World Politics*, Washington, D.C.: Ethics and Public Policy Center, 1999.

70. An-Na'im, ibid., pp. 154–155.

71. The term came into use in France after the publication of Bruno Étienne's *L'Islamisme radical* (Paris: Hachette, 1987). See

also Emmanuel Sivan, *Radical Islam: Medieval Theology and Modern Politics*, New Haven and London: Yale University Press, 1985; R. Hrair Dekmejian, *Islam in Revolution: Fundamentalism in the Arab World*, Syracuse: Syracuse University Press, 1985; Olivier Roy, *L'Afghanistan, Islam et modernité politique*, Paris: Le Seuil, 1985; idem, *Islam and Resistance in Afghanistan*, 2nd ed., New York: Cambridge University Press, 1990; Olivier Carré and Paul Dumont, eds., *Radicalismes islamiques*, Paris: L'Harmattan, 1985–1986, 2 vols. On the problem of these terms and the imagery associated with them, see François Burgat and William Dowell, *The Islamic Movement in North Africa*, Austin, Tex.: Center for Middle Eastern Studies, 1997; Olivier Roy, *The Failure of Political Islam*, Cambridge, Mass.: Harvard University Press, 1994; Alain Gresh, ed., *Un péril islamiste?*, op. cit.; Olivier Carré, *L'Islam laïque . . .*, op. cit.; Lahouari Addi, et al., *L'Islamisme*, Paris: La Découverte, 1994; François Burgat, *Face to Face with Political Islam*, London: I. B. Tauris, 1997 (new ed. 2003); Olivier Roy, *Généalogie de l'islamisme*, Paris: Hachette, 1995. The principal competing terms are "Islamism," "radical Islam," "political Islam," "radical Islamism," "Islamic fundamentalism," "Islamic integrism." See, for example, Joel Benin and Joe Stork, *Political Islam*, Berkeley and Los Angeles: University of California Press, 1997; and Lawrence Davidson, *Islamic Fundamentalism*, Westport, Conn.: Greenwood Press, 1998.

72. See Olivier Roy, "Les islamologues ont-ils inventé l'islamisme?", *Esprit* No. 277, August–September 2001, pp. 132–135; idem, "Le postislamisme," ibid., p. 137.

73. See Olivier Carré, *L'Islam laïque . . .*, op. cit., pp. 108–124; Mohamed Charfi, *Islam et liberté*, op. cit., pp. 68f.; Antoine Basbous, *L'Islamisme . . .*, op. cit., pp. 70f.; Juliette Minces, "La solitude glacée des Afghanes," interview material collected by Joseph Macé-Scaron, *Le Figaro*, October 17, 2001, p. 15.

74. On the Islamic doctrine of "dhimmitude," see Bat Ye'or, *The Dhimmi: Jews and Christians Under Islam*, op. cit.

75. On wahhabism, especially "wahhabi salafism" (or the "salafist *jihad*" currently represented by bin Laden), see Olivier Carré, *L'Utopie islamique dans l'Orient arabe*, Paris: Presses de la FNSP, 1991, pp. 87–118; Olivier Roy, *Généalogie de l'islamisme*, op. cit., pp. 30f.; Gilles Kepel, *Jihad . . .*, op. cit., 219–236, 313–322; Antoine Sfeir, *Les Réseaux d'Allah*, op. cit., pp. 76–82, 209–215; Abdelwahab Meddeb (interview), "La maladie de

l'islam," *Esprit* No. 278, October 2001, pp. 80f.; Gilles Kepel, "Clés pour le 'salafisme djihadiste'," *Le Nouvel Observateur*, October 18–24, 2001, p. 18.

76. Olivier Roy, "Les islamologues . . .," art. cit., p. 105. See also the remarks of Thérèse Delpech in "Bâtir des relations d'un autre type," *Libération*, October 11, 2001, p. 13. We should add that Saudi Arabia holds our critical attention because of its lack of any freedom of religious worship, which implies a complete exclusion of other religions. See Agnès Levallois, "Arabie saoudite," in Jean-Marc Balencie and Arnaud de La Grange, eds., *Mondes rebelles. Acteurs, conflits et violences politiques*, Paris: Michalon, 1996, vol. 2, pp. 529–538; Gilles Kepel, *Jihad . . .*, op. cit., pp. 205–226; Abderrahim Lamchichi, *Géopolitique de l'islamisme*, op. cit., pp. 159–175.

77. Bin Baz, in a work published in Saudi Arabia by the Department for Scientific Research, "Fatwa and Proselytism," Riyadh, 1982 (quoted from Antoine Basbous, *L'Islamisme . . .*, op. cit., p. 69).

78. Bin Baz, quoted in Basbous, ibid. On the role of bin Baz, see Gilles Kepel, *Jihad . . .*, op. cit., pp. 210ff.

79. Mohammed Arkoun, "L'impensé religieux," *L'Humanité*, November 16, 2001, p. 12. See the same author's *Pour une critique de la raison islamique*, Paris: Maisonneuve et Larose, 1984; *Ouvertures sur l'islam*, Paris: Jacques Grancher, 1989; *L'Islam . . .*, op. cit., esp. pp. v–xxxii, 187–245; and "Clarifier le passé pour construire le futur?", in Abderrahim Lamchichi, ed., *Islam-Occident, la confrontation?*, Paris: Les Cahiers de Confluences, 2001, pp. 17–30.

80. See the analyses of Rachel Mimouni on the economic and psychosocial preconditions of the FIS's hold in Algeria: *De la barbarie en général et de l'intégrisme en particulier*, Paris: Belfond-Le Pré aux Clercs, 1992.

81. The reader will forgive this personal contribution to the Islamization of Latin.

82. Friedrich Nietzsche, *Thus Spoke Zarathustra*, translated by R. J. Hollingdale, Harmondsworth: Penguin Books, 1961, pp. 44–45 (§§ 4 and 5).

83. See Gilles Kepel, *Jihad . . .*, op. cit., pp. 313–322; Antoine Sfeir, op. cit., pp. 209ff.

84. Bat Ye'or, "L'antisionisme euro-arabe," in *[Nouveaux] visages de l'antisémitisme*, op. cit., p. 33. See also Jean-Paul Charnay, *La Charia et l'Occident*, op. cit.

85. See Samuel P. Huntington, *The Clash of Civilizations and the Remaking of World Order*, London: Simon & Schuster UK, 2002, pp. 81–101, 112–113.

86. See *Guerres contre l'Europe*, updated ed., Paris: Éditions des Syrtes, 2000, p. 36.

87. In France, apart from the always illuminating interventions of the philosopher and historian Mohammed Arkoun, special mention should be made of the anthropologist-psychoanalyst Malek Chebel and the imam of the Marseilles mosque, Soheib Bencheikh (who, it should be stressed, enjoys far from unanimous support in Muslim circles). Since September–October 2001 both these men have spoken out in public to condemn Islamist terrorism and provided the necessary bearings in relation to the Islamic religion. See Martine Gozlan, *L'Islam et la République*, Paris: Belfond, 1994; Soheib Bencheikh, *Marianne et le Prophète. L'Islam dans la France laïque*, Paris: Grasset, 1998. At an important conference in Cairo on November 26–27, 2001, Mohammed Arkoun declared: "It is important for Islam to engage in self-criticism [it being understood that 'criticism does not mean an attack']. . . . The Arab world has a vital need for an independent and critical voice. The presence of intellectuals in the life of society remains precarious and exceptional. They express themselves little, and when they do [they] expound the point of view of the street, or, more rarely, that of the authorities." (Quoted in Claude Guibal, "Les intellectuels arabes se mobilisent," *Libération*, November 28, 2001, p. 7.)

88. Mohamed Charfi, *Islam et liberté*, op. cit., quoted by Michèle Tribalat, who in her previously mentioned article endorses this picture of the continuum between peaceful Islam and Islamism. It remains the case, however, that the "moderate" and "extremist" poles are distinct, as they are in Judaism and Christianity.

89. See Fouad Zakariya, *Laïcité ou islamisme. Les Arabes à l'heure du choix*, Paris: La Découverte, and Cairo: Al-Fikr, 1991, esp. pp. 13–46. The Egyptian philosopher argues in favor of a "reformist" or modernizing position, illustrated by the "secular option." See also Olivier Carré, *L'Islam laïque . . .*, op. cit., pp. 85–91, 136–141.

90. A brief comparative side-glance should remind us here that at the time of the war between the "two Frances" over the principle of secularization, and perhaps even until 1984, Catholics and

agnostic Republicans accused each other of seeking to indoctrinate the country's youth.

91. See the stimulating reflections in Danièle Hervieu-Léger, *Le Pèlerin et le converti. La religion en mouvement*, Paris: Flammarion, 1999.

92. I am here appropriating the definition of a "decent society" used by philosopher Avishai Margalit: that is, "a society in which institutions do not humiliate people"—as distinct from a "civilized society," or "a society whose members do not humiliate one another." (*The Decent Society*, Cambridge, Mass.: Harvard University Press, 1996, p. 1.) As to the ideal of a just or equitable society, it encompasses the normative idea of a balance between liberty and equality. It is postulated that "any equitable society must be a decent society," but the reverse does not hold (p. 3).

93. See Cornelius Castoriadis, "Notations sur le racisme," *Connexions* No. 48, 1987, pp. 117–118; and my book *Les Fins de l'antiracisme*, op. cit., pp. 530–534.

94. See the interesting but somewhat irenic article in the journal *Esprit* (No. 239, January 1998, pp. 5–136): "L'islam d'Europe."

95. Emmanuel Sivan, *Mythes politiques arabes* [1988], op. cit., p. 243.

96. Quoted in Paul Balta, *L'Islam*, op. cit, p. 43.

97. Mohamed Charfi, *Islam et liberté*, op. cit., pp. 56–57. See the fine study by Bernard Lewis: "Islam and Liberal Democracy," *Atlantic Monthly*, February 1993.

98. Between 1992 and the Dayton accords of November 21, 1995, the highest Arab estimates speak of four thousand *mujahedeen* (Muslim volunteers fighting under tested "Afghans"), who helped to convert into a *jihad* the ethnic-nationalist war of the Bosnian Muslims against the Serbs. See Roland Jacquard, *Au nom d'Oussama Ben Laden . . .*, op. cit., pp. 126–127.

99. Isabelle Lasserre, "Les brigades islamistes de Bosnie ont essaimé en Europe," *Le Figaro*, October 12, 2001, p. 5. For a geopolitical approach to this set of conflicts, see Alexandre del Valle, *Guerres contre l'Europe*, op. cit., pp. 110–160.

100. Among the Islamists who fought in Bosnia was "Commander" Abu Abdel Aziz, nicknamed Barbarossa (for his long henna-colored beard), who in Afghanistan had worked from 1984 as an instructor for the special commandos of Palestinian Abdallah Azzam,

an Islamist activist killed in Peshawar in the fall of 1989 (Jacquard, op. cit., pp. 113, 127). Funded by bin Laden to recruit *mujahedeen*, Abu Abdel Aziz was noted in Bosnia for his cruelty and extreme savagery; he did not hesitate to display the severed heads of Serbs (ibid., pp. 127–128; and see, on page 11 of the photo section, a picture of this fighter for Allah holding a Serb's severed head by the hair in his two hands—which did not stop Abderrahim from presenting him as "a highly colorful figure" in *Géopolitique de l'islamisme*, Paris: L'Harmattan, 2001, p. 290, n. 405). On the funding of the UCK by bin Laden and the drug trade, see Jacquard, ibid., pp. 132–133.

101. Quoted in Wladimir Rabi, "L'Establishment juif, structures et idéologie," *Recherches* No. 38, September 1979, p. 21.

102. The proceedings of a distinctly pro-Palestinian conference on "the right of return" (Boston, April 8, 2000) have been published through the good offices of Naseer Aruri as *Palestinian Refugees: The Right of Return*, London and Sterling: VA, 2001. Among the list of mainly academic contributors, there are naturally Palestinians and Americans of Palestinian or Middle Eastern origin, but also Americans of Jewish origin on the far left (Noam Chomsky, Norman G. Finkelstein); one of the leaders of the Israeli "new history" school, Ilan Pappé; the chief editor of *Le Monde diplomatique*, Alain Gresh (son of Third World activist Henri Curiel); and Michael Prior, an academic in the sphere of biblical studies whose recent work has been on the Bible and colonialism in their relationship to Zionism and the State of Israel.

103. See the critical remarks of Christian Delacampagne in "À un ami palestinien," *Commentaire* No. 95, Fall 2001, pp. 569–570.

104. It is a dictatorship involving an efficient system of corruption, based particularly on the diversion of funds. See the severe article by the American Palestinian intellectual Edward Said, "Are There No Limits to Corruption?" (July 2, 1997), reprinted in his *The End of the Peace Process*, London: Granta Books, 2002, pp. 177–181.

105. See the extracts from Palestinian schoolbooks in Yohanan Manor, André Marcus, et al., op. cit., pp. 18–22.

106. *Islamic Education*, fifth grade, p. 143 (quoted in ibid., p. 13).

107. *Some Outstanding Examples of Our Civilization*, eleventh grade, p. 16 (quoted in ibid., p. 17).

108. *Islamic Education*, twelfth grade, p. 284 (quoted in ibid., p. 24).

109. For example: "Kill them wherever you find them" (2:191). See Rivka Yadlin, "Théologie et idéologie antisémites dans le monde arabe," in Léon Poliakov, ed., *Histoire de l'antisémitisme 1945–1993*, Paris: Le Seuil, 1994, p. 377 (other examples quoted). For a contextualization in which things appear less clear-cut, see Olivier Carré, *L'Islam laïque* . . ., op. cit., p. 132.

110. Vladimir Illich Ramirez Sanchez, alias Carlos, interview published on October 21, 2001, by the Venezuelan daily *El Universal* (quoted from Alain Abellard, "L'hommage de Carlos à Oussama Ben Laden," *Le Monde*, October 26, 2001, p. 35). In Carlos's view, the Taliban were "defending the world revolution," and Yasser Arafat had dissociated himself from bin Laden only because he had "officially placed the security and destiny of the Palestinian people in the hands of the CIA" (ibid.).

111. See Rivka Yadin, "Théologie et idéologie . . .," art. cit., pp. 375, 378. In 1986 a collective Arabic work appeared in Paris in French translation: *L'Invasion israélienne du Liban* (the publisher being given as "J. A. Conseil," and its authors as "a group of Syrian researchers under the authority of General Mustapha Tlass, with a preface by General Mustapha Tlass.") The valiant general concluded his preface with a solemn oath to Allah: "We swear before God and before History always to fight the Israeli aggressor and Zionism, until they recover their senses and withdraw from our beautiful land. . . . And God leads to victory those who have faith in Him. God is strong and great" (op. cit., p. 11). In the main body of the text, the accusation of genocide does not fail to appear: "The extermination of a whole people is being carried out in systematic fashion, and the Zionist state remains indifferent to condemnation by the international community" (p. 238).

112. Quoted in Meïr Waintrater, "La montée de l'antisémitisme dans le monde arabe," *L'Arche* No. 523, September 2001, p. 82. To give some idea of the murderous frenzy of the enemies that Israel has to face, we might mention a speech to Parliament by the Syrian defense minister (according to the official Syrian daily *Algerida Rasmiya*, July 11, 1974). Tlass "congratulated a soldier who was said to have killed twenty-eight Israeli prisoners with an ax and to have engaged in cannibalism with several others" (Frédéric Encel, *Le*

Moyen-Orient entre guerre et paix. Une géopolitique du Golan,
Paris: Flammarion, 1999, p. 81, n. 28). Such savagery is unfortunately all too common among Israel's absolute enemies in the Middle East, as well as among the Islamist terrorists (especially in
Algeria, where throat-slitting, decapitation, skinning alive, and dis-
memberment have been practiced since the early 1990s). Mohamed
Charfi has rightly said in connection with the GIA massacres in Algeria: "They have been convinced that they have a mission to
cleanse the earth of everything 'stinking,' and that in this way they
will guarantee a place for themselves in paradise" (*Islam et liberté*,
op. cit., p. 55).

Chapter 4. Silence in the Face of the New Judeophobia

   1. See the fine and disturbing investigation of Michèle Tribalat:
Dreux, voyage au coeur du malaise français, Paris: La Découverte
& Syros, 1999. For a sociological approach to the question, see es-
pecially Dominique Schnapper, *La France et l'intégration. Sociolo-
gie de la nation en 1990*, Paris: Gallimard, 1991, esp. pp. 193ff;
Henri Rey, *La Peur des banlieues*, Paris: Presses de la Fondation nationale des sciences politiques, 1996; Christian Bachmann and
Nicole Le Guennec, *Violences urbaines*, Paris: Albin Michel, 1996;
Véronique Le Goaziou and Charles Rojzman, *Les Banlieues*, Paris:
Le Cavalier Bleu, 2001.
   2. An involuntary caricature of this image of Épinal's is provided in a book by Dounia Bouzar, a youth worker since 1991 at
the French "Protection judiciaire de la jeunesse": *L'Islam des banlieues. Les prédicateurs musulmans: nouveaux travailleurs sociaux?*
(Paris: La Découverte & Syros, 2001). The author describes as follows the purpose of her apologetic essay: "To understand what at-
tracts to Islam certain young people who are the responsibility of
our educational and judicial services" (p. 22); accordingly, "the behavior described is restricted to cases of young people in great difficulty, or in trouble with the courts" (ibid.). She presents Islam as an
effective cure for marginalization and delinquency, and the preacher
as a youth worker who gets success. Hence her conclusion: "Muslim preachers . . . carry out effective social work among young people. Their success seems largely due to the fact that they give young

people a means to orient themselves in the present-day world" (p. 171). The path to salvation is therefore a "plural" path—as one would expect in the age of the "plural left" and "plural France," magic formulas that idealize the state of conflictual fragmentation in which French society finds itself today. "The fundamental debate with regard to the future of young people in trouble lies in an awareness of the plural dimension of the new French identity, which can no longer be set out in accordance with a single model. . . . To the plural dimension of young people's identity corresponds a need for plural intervention on the part of all who can contribute to the harmonious construction of their future" (pp. 173, 175). Many social workers and sociologists do no more than convert into a result of scientific investigation a widely used slogan of Islamist propaganda: "Islam is important. It's the only way to stop everything going haywire" (Lamine, aged twenty-four years, in Asnières, quoted by Bertrand Bissuel, "Les interrogations des banlieues," *Le Monde*, November 7, 2001, p. 14). This is echoed by another ready-made idea: "If fewer young people [children of immigrants] believed in the Muslim religion, there would be civil war" (Issa, twenty-five years old, Asnières, quoted in Bissuel, ibid.). But, in certain suburbs, is intermittent civil war not what we are already witnessing?

3. Quoted in Isabelle de Gaulmyn, "Lyon craint un islam plus radical," *La Croix*, November 16, 2001, p. 7. See also Hanifa Chérifi's severe and lucid analysis of the Islamist drift in France: "Les beurs face à leur identité," *L'Humanité*, November 2001, p. 13. Most press reports pass over in silence these negative aspects of re-Islamization. See, for instance, "L'islam apaisé des musulmans de France" [The Calmed Islam of France's Muslims], *Le Monde*, October 5, 2001, pp. 1, 10–11, which is certainly an appeasing [*apaisant*] article, or at least one designed to appease. But why this desire to appease at all costs? Why this choice of minimum vigilance concerning the growing hold of the Islamists in certain suburbs?

4. Nathaniel Herzberg and Cécile Prieur, "Enquête sur le pouvoir méconnu du prosélytisme islamiste en milieu carcéral," *Le Monde*, October 31, 2001, p. 10. See the testimony that this prisoner, a Frenchman of Algerian origin, wrote up on a daily basis between 1996 and 1998: "Un détenu témoigne du prosélytisme islamiste dans les prisons françaises," *Le Monde*, October 31, 2001, pp. 14–15.

5. Statements quoted from Jacques Tarnero, "Les territoires occupés de l'imaginaire beur," *Observatoire du monde juif*, Bulletin
No. 1, November 2001, pp. 39–40.
6. See Gilles Kepel, *Jihad . . .*, op. cit., pp. 309–311, 418 (n. 28
and 32).
7. An Armed Islamic Group (GIA) communiqué denounced the
"martyrdom of brother Kelkal at the hands of an army of Christian
soldiers" (quoted in Jean-Paul Gourévitch, op. cit., p. 199). In this
"anti-racist," victim-centered interpretation, "Khaled Kelkal was
not given a chance, either at school or in life. They killed him like a
dog. Why?" "It is always young Arabs who get a bullet in the
back—why?" (statements quoted from Ternero, art. cit., p. 39).
8. See my book *La République menacée*, Paris: Textuel, 1996,
pp. 25–27. Kelkal did not conceal his intention to establish an Islamist regime "by all means, that is, having children or waging jihad by taking seven-digit sums of money in one swoop" (quoted in
Gourévitch, op. cit., p. 198). Let us recall the context: between July
25 and October 17, 1995, Kelkal was involved in eight attacks that
caused ten deaths and more than 175 injuries. The process of heroization was made easier by the publication in *Le Monde* (October
7, 1995) of a long and sympathetic interview that German sociologist Dietmar Loch had conducted with Kelkal in 1992, in the course
of an investigation into the children of immigrants in the Lyons suburbs. The young Islamist terrorist appeared there as a victim of republican France, which had not known how to integrate him and,
by excluding him, had driven him to despair and revolt. This is the
main point: we are not supposed to hold the terrorist responsible
for his actions but should rather blame French society for the exclusion and discrimination that led a fine boy of North African origin to become a terrorist and to commit attacks and murders. See
also Gilles Kepel's remarks in "Réislamisation et passage au terrorisme: quelques hypothèses de réflexion," in Rémy Leveau, ed., *Is-
lam(s) en Europe. Approches d'un nouveau pluralisme culturel
européen*, Berlin, *Les Travaux du Centre Marc-Bloch* No. 13, 1998,
pp. 108–109.
9. In his "Revolutionary Catechism," Nechaev laid down certain standards for revolutionaries: "The revolutionary must be hard
on himself as well as on others. All the potentially softening sympathies and feelings, which stem from the family, friendship, love,

or gratitude, must be stifled in him through the single cold passion for revolutionary work" (*Catéchisme révolutionnaire*, reprint, Paris: Éditions Spartacus, 1971, p. 62). In the circles of revolutionary "anti-imperialist" Islam, now represented by bin Laden after a long embodiment in Khomeini's Iran, we find the same glorification of this type of fanatical combatant trained for "suicide attacks."

10. See Cécilia Gabizon, "À Aulnay, 'Oussama, il est trop fort!'", *Le Figaro*, October 9, 2001, p. 9.

11. See Dan Galli, "Pourquoi le monde n'a pas vu les manifestations de joie des Palestiniens," *L'Arche* No. 524–525, October–November 2001, pp. 70–73. The Palestinian police put a lot of pressure on journalists, even going so far as to confiscate film and cassettes. See the Agence France-Presse dispatch of September 14, 2001, from the Musseirat camp in the Gaza Strip, as well as the communiqué issued the same day by Reporters sans Frontières (RSF).

12. Article quoted by Philippe Val: "Comment n'aimer ni le jambon ni la démocratie" (editorial), No. 491, November, 2001, p. 3.

13. Ibid.

14. For an informed and measured account of juvenile delinquency in this section of the population, which eschews the usual political correctness, see Sebastian Roché, *La Délinquance des jeunes. Les 13–19 ans racontent leurs délits*, Paris: Le Seuil, 2001, pp. 199–229.

15. See, for example, Bernard Stasi, "Y croire encore," *Libération*, October 9, 2001, p. 18.

16. Zidane, for his part, in no way cultivates ambiguity.

17. See Alain Auffray and Emmanuel Davidenkoff, "Lycéens et Palestiniens, l'identification joue à fond," *Libération*, October 18, 2000, p. 27. It is worth noting the use of the euphemism *"lycéens"* [schoolchildren]: the *lycéens* in question, who identify with the Palestinians as "victims," are "young people," and—as the article makes clear—young people "stemming from the North African immigration." The communalist withdrawal of "young people" is a solution favored by the victim-centered demagogy of the *bien-pensant* left, as Malek Boutih, president of the SOS Racisme movement, recognizes and deplores (op. cit., pp. 43f.).

18. See, for example, Alain Bauer and Xavier Raufer, *Violences et insécurité urbaines*, 3rd corrected ed., Paris: Presses universitaires

de France, 1999, p. 31. See also the sometimes justified criticisms of this work in Laurent Mucchielli, *Violences et insécurité. Fantasmes et réalités dans le débat français*, Paris: La Découverte, 2001, pp. 32f. But themes of insecurity continue to be ideologized in approaches that simply invert the catastrophism, ending in an angelic vision that legitimates the indulgence of the *bien-pensant* left and far left. Deconstructive critique of categories cannot replace serious investigative work, and an ironic, scornful tone is not the same as a demonstration. It is all too easy to show that any object of academic or semi-academic discourse ("urban riots," "urban violence," etc.) is a construction, and to insist that a correct reading of statistics is required to avoid current labels (always attributed to the "far right" or those who follow its lead). "Political correctness" in the social sciences consists in always sticking to this ritualistic and intellectually comforting labor, illustrated by all the articles on "media constructs" or "political and journalistic construction" of anything one cares to name. The truism is indefinitely shown to be correct: everything is constructed. But what then? Should we conclude with a satisfaction that "all is well," in the tone of someone delivering a lesson? That is one of the quirks of French-style sociology and political science, whose deconstructive pretensions and endless chatter about methodology are less and less able to conceal a basic sterility. It is not surprising that, for all their foibles and inadequacies, more information and empirical material is to be found in studies signed by professionals: Richard Bousquet, *Insécurité: nouveaux risques. Les quartiers de tous les dangers*, Paris: L'Harmattan, 1998; Lucienne Bui Trong, *Violences urbaines. Des vérités qui dérangent*, Paris: Bayard, 2000.

19. A sociological study of these forms of gangster terrorism remains to be written. The "Roubaix gang," several of whom had fought in Bosnia in 1994 and 1995, distinguished themselves in 1996 through a number of armed attacks. On October 19, 2001, the Douai assizes sentenced three of its members (Omar Zemmiri, Mouloud Bouguelane, and Hocine Bendaoui) to long terms of imprisonment ("Gang de Roubaix: entre 18 et 28 ans," *Libération*, October 20–21, 2001, p. 16). In Béziers, on the night of September 1–2, 2001, a local petty criminal, twenty-five-year-old Safir Bghioua, attacked a police patrol with a rocket-launcher, made a number of provocative telephone calls (he told the police he wanted

to "become a cop" or "kill a cop"), opened fire in the street leading to the city police headquarters, killed Jean Farret, the mayor's private secretary, with a burst of machine-gun fire, and was finally killed while wearing a white headband in the early hours, after he had threatened a GIPN special policeman and called himself "Allah's son." Police found an impressive stock of military weapons in his car and in the studio flat he had been renting in Béziers. See Catherine Bernard, "À Béziers, coup de sang au lance-roquettes," *Libération*, September 3, 2001, p. 13; Philippe Motta, "Fusillade meurtrière à Béziers," *Le Figaro*, September 3, 2001, p. 9; and Richard Benguigui, "À Béziers, les policiers tentent de cerner la personnalité de Safir Bghioua," *Le Monde*, September 7, 2001, p. 10.

20. Malek Boutih, op. cit., p. 45.

21. On the outburst of Judeophobia in October 2000, see "Antisémitisme. Le signal d'alarme" (dossier), *Libération*, October 12, 2000, pp. 1–4; "Des synagogues prises pour cibles en France" (dossier), *Le Figaro*, October 12, 2000, pp. 1, 4–5; Henri Tincq, "Série d'agressions antisémites en France," *Le Monde*, October 13, 2000, p. 3; "Une synagogue a brûlé" (editorial), *Le Monde*, October 13, 2000, p. 17; Christian Duplan, "Musulmans de France, les mots qui dérangent," *Marianne* No. 182, October 16–22, 2000, pp. 20–22; Bénédicte Charles, "Les Juifs, ils ont voulu niquer notre religion," ibid., pp. 22–24.

22. Akram B. Ellyas, "Ces voyous font honte à l'Algérie," *Libération*, October 9, 2001. See also the same author's *À la découverte du Maghreb*, Paris: La Découverte, 2001.

23. See the telling remarks in Jean-Claude Maurice, "Oussama, le héros!", *Le Journal de Dimanche*, October 14, 2001, pp. 1–2. Many "young people" from the Cité des Indes housing project in the Paris suburbs see bin Laden as "a tiger, the only man capable of deposing American imperialism." These same "young people" told a *Journal du Dimanche* reporter: "Now September 11 is our national holiday" (Elsa Guiol, "Cité des Indes, Ben Laden, ce héros," ibid., p. 9).

24. The Movement Against Racism and for Friendship Among Nations (MRAP) had a public presence at the demonstration. A few days later, after protests from Jewish community leaders, the MRAP finally condemned the anti-Jewish insults and the calls for hatred of the Jews. Martine Gozlan, "L'immense désarroi des Juifs de

France," *Marianne* No. 182, October 16–22, 2000, pp. 24–26. See also Mouloud Aounit (MRAP general secretary) and Michel Tubiana (president of the League of Human Rights), "Le racisme n'est pas divisible," *Libération*, October 20, 2000, p. 5.

25. Jean-Claude Amara, spokesman for the "Droits devant!" association, claims to be defending the most disadvantaged sections of the population—that is, "prisoners, asylum-seekers, illegal immigrants" (Dominique Simonnot and Yann Walter, "Droits devant!! Contre le coût de la vie en prison," *Libération*, October 20–21, 2001, p. 18). Not surprisingly, Albert Jacquard, an "all-is-woe" demagogue seeking to take over where Abbé Pierre left off, is joint chairman of this association. As to the "radicals" of the MIB (Immigration and Suburbs Movement), the main focus of their struggle is what they call the "dual punishment" (a jail sentence plus deportation for non-national offenders). In the minds of these new *gauchistes*, the undifferentiated ethnic-national entity of "the Palestinians" forms part of the category of the "most underprivileged" (a fine example of essentialism), together with "prisoners" and non-national offenders subject to the "dual punishment." The preference for marginal or "excluded" groups, which has been a feature of far-left milieux since the working class and the "proletariat" receded from view, is here transformed into the defense of lawbreakers as supervictims. Noble hearts tend to concern themselves with the offender purely as a "potential victim"—a fact that (former Socialist minister) Jean-Pierre Chevènement has often pointed out and deplored.

26. Edward N. Luttwak, *Turbo-Capitalism: Winners and Losers in the Global Economy*, London: Weidenfeld and Nicolson, 1998.

27. Benjamin R. Barber, *Jihad versus McWorld*, New York: Times Books, 1995.

28. Arundhati Roy, "The Algebra of Infinite Justice," *The Guardian* [London], September 29, 2001.

29. One year after his anti-Zionist tract that came close to Holocaust denial, Roger Garaudy published an anti-American broadside: *Les États-Unis avant-garde de la décadence*, Paris: Éditions Vent du Large, 1997. The pairing of the two enemy-figures was thus complete.

30. See my "L'abbé Pierre et Roger Garaudy. Négationnisme, antijudaïsme, antisionisme," *Esprit* No. 224, August–September

1996, pp. 206–216; and the investigative report by Éric Conan and
Sylviane Stein, "Ce qui a fait chuter l'abbé Pierre," *L'Express*, May
2–8, 1996, pp. 30–36.

31. Let us quote here from an authoritative chronology:
"Around October 20, 1970, after the events of 'Black September,'
Jean Genet was invited to Jordan to visit the Palestinian camps. Instead of the expected eight days, he would remain there for six
months, having obtained a permit from Yasser Arafat to travel
wherever he wished. At Irbid he got to know Hamza and his
mother, the emblematic couple in *Prisoner of Love* [London: Pica-
dor, 1989]. At the end of his fourth stay in the Middle East, Genet
was arrested by the Jordanian authorities and expelled on November 23, 1972. In 1973 he began writing a book about the times he
had spent in the Palestinian camps and with the Black Panthers."
(*Genet à Chatila*, texts collected by Jérôme Hankins, Arles and
Paris: Éditions Solin, 1992, p. 177.) See also Jean Genet, "Four
Hours in Shatila," *Journal of Palestinian Studies*, 12/3, Spring
1983, pp. 3–22. On the Judeophobia of the "committed" writer, see
Samuel Blumenfeld, "Le racisme de la lettre. Antisionisme et anti-
sémitisme de Jean Genet: analyse critique d'*Un Captif amoureux*,"
Pardès No. 6, 1987, pp. 117–125.

32. Jean Genet, "Four Hours in Chatila," art. cit.

33. Abbé Pierre, quoted in *Le Monde*, June 2–3, 1996.

34. Abbé Pierre, interview published in the Swiss daily *Le
Matin*, June 17, 1996 (quoted in *Le Monde*, June 19, 1996: "L'abbé
Pierre met en cause le 'mouvement sioniste'").

35. Abbé Pierre, "Lettre ouverte," printed in facsimile in Roger
Garaudy, *Mes Témoins*, Paris: Éditions "À Contre-Nuit," 1997,
p. 105, and reproduced in part in Roger Garaudy, *Le Procès du
sionisme israélien*, Paris: Éditions Vent du Large, 1998, p. 12.

36. Ahmed Rami is an Islamist militant who has made a profession out of Holocaust denial and support for the Palestinian cause.
In a work for which he wrote a preface, he is presented as "One of
the leaders of the Islamic Movement in Morocco. A Member of the
Free Officers Corps of the Skhirat Revolt (1971) and the 16th of August Movement (1972). Condemned to death in absentia in Morocco. A political refugee in Sweden, where he currently directs
Radio Islam. Author of four books on the Palestinian question."
(Moumen Diouri, *À qui appartient le Maroc?*, Paris: L'Harmattan,

1992, preface by M. Ahmed Rami, p. 5, note.) When Moroccan oppositionist Moumen Diouri was threatened with permanent expulsion from France (under the emergency procedure introduced on June 20, 1991) but returned soon afterward quite legally (on July 16), Ahmed Rami expressed outrage at the "racism" in France and defended the unfortunate "victim": "In these times of xenophobia and galloping racism, the cancellation of the emergency procedure for M. Diouri's expulsion, followed today by the publication of his book, marks a victory for human rights and a proof, for French democracy, of its vitality. M. Diouri and his book almost fell victim to what is adorned with the name 'new world order' . . . which they are seeking to ground on the submission of the Arab-Muslim world" (ibid., p. 7).

37. In its issue dated November 15, 1990, *El-Mounquid* (the official organ of the Islamic Salvation Front—FIS) devoted an article to Rami with the headings: "Longest Trial in Swedish History / Six Months for Moroccan Islamist Rami / Struggle and Defiance Against Jewish and Zionist Plot." In the text we read: "Through the Radio Islam programs broadcast in Swedish from Sweden, Rami has succeeded in making known the Jewish falsifications of the history of the Second World War, designed to terrorize Western Europe, and to force it into blindly supporting Jewish positions and the Jewish occupation of Palestine and into lining up with everything anti-Islamic in Jewish propaganda." Quoted in *Revue d'histoire révisionniste* [directed by Henri Roques], No. 3, November–December 1990/January 1991, p. 222.

38. See Marine Gozlan, "France: enquête sur la montée de l'antisémitisme," *Marianne* No. 230, September 17–23, 2001, p. 31 (photographic reproduction of placard).

39. This cliché has been constantly repeated since 1983–1984 in France, where it functions as an ideological and rhetorical marker of the radical opposition to Le Pen. On the grounds that the Front National has prioritized "anti-Arab racism," a simple negation leads to the conclusion that the struggle against "anti-Arab racism" should head the anti-racist agenda, or even be seen as the only urgent struggle.

40. See, in this connection, the "Note" submitted to the Socialist party (PS) leadership in the spring of 2001 by Pascal Boniface, director of the Institute for International and Strategic

Relations (IRIS). The document ends with some suggestions for a new policy on the part of the (then-governing) left toward the Israeli-Palestinian conflict: "I am struck by the number of young *beurs*, and Muslim French of all ages, who say they are on the left but who, with reference to the situation in the Middle East, say they do not want to vote Jospin in the presidential elections. . . . The situation in the Middle East, and the timidity of the Socialists' condemnations of Israeli repression, reinforce a tendency for the Muslims of France to withdraw into an identity of their own, which no one can be happy about. . . . It is certainly better to lose an election than to lose our soul. But by placing the Israeli government and the Palestinians on the same level, we risk simply losing both. Is it worth losing in 2002 for the sake of supporting Sharon? It is high time that the PS ended its position of trying to strike a balance between the Israeli government and the Palestinians—a position which, because of the realities on the ground, is becoming more and more unjust, and is more and more seen to be so." See also Pascal Boniface, "Lettre à un ami israélien," *Le Monde*, August 4, 2001, p. 11; the firm reply by Élie Barnavi, "À propos d'un 'ami' français," *Le Monde*, August 8, 2001, pp. 1, 9; and the comment by Meïr Weintrater, "Docteur Pascal et Mister Boniface," *L'Arche* No. 524–525, October–November 2001, pp. 14–16.

41. Shmuel Trigano, "Questions sur un black out. Les Juifs de France visés par l'Intifada?", *Observatoire du monde juif*, Bulletin No. 1, November 2001, p. 1.

42. Notable exceptions, in the nonspecialist press, have been *Le Figaro* and *Marianne*. See especially the investigative reports in *Le Figaro*, November 30, 2001, pp. 1, 8–9 ("La nouvelle inquiétude des Juifs de France"); December 1–2, 2001, p. 10 ("Les Juifs dénoncent un regain d'antisémitisme"); and December 3, 2001, p. 12 ("Jospin tente d'apaiser l'inquiétude des Juifs de France"). See also Xavier Ternisien, "La communauté juive s'inquiète d'une recrudescence des agressions antisémites," *Le Monde*, December 2–3, 2001, p. 11; and idem, "M. Jospin se dit: 'déterminé à lutter contre l'antisémitisme'," *Le Monde*, December 4, 2001, p. 10.

43. Marc Knobel has provided the following details: "In all cases, those involved were young people from the suburbs, some of whom had already been in trouble with the authorities. Six were due to answer for the arson attack on the Trappes synagogue, in the

department of Yvelines. Twelve were being prosecuted for arson attacks on stores belonging to Jewish owners, and four for acts of violence against individuals of Jewish origin" ("Trop de silence face à la flambée antisémite," *Libération*, November 12, 2001, p. 10; and idem, "Les agressions antijuives," art. cit., p. 18).

44. Quoted in Martine Gozlan, art. cit., p. 34. The sermon from which I have quoted was extensively transcribed in *Observatoire du monde juif*, Bulletin No. 1, November 2001, pp. 49–51.

45. See Martine Gozlan, art. cit., p. 35.

46. Renaud Camus, *La Campagne de France. Journal 1994*, Paris: Fayard, 2000. The campaign of denunciation was launched by Marc Weitzmann in the weekly *Les Inrockuptibles*, on April 18, 2000. Unless one detects in Camus deep anti-Jewish intentions that he was covering up, his "anti-Semitism" is hard to demonstrate on the basis of the fragments of text quoted by his accusers. What is certain is that some passages assume with surprising naiveté a number of prejudices and stereotypes belonging to the anti-Semitic tradition, but in a context where there is no appeal for hatred or violence. Although some readers of the *Journal* sincerely found in it a number of "offensive" or "hurtful" passages, how can we explain that one or another puffed-up high-society aesthete, who affects to look down on "mildewed France" and takes offense at ubiquitous traces of "Petainism" (including in his contemporary Renaud Camus), does not feel shocked by the anti-Jewish outbursts among certain "young people"? It is true that, though he may not read Céline's own priceless tracts, such a refined soul also in his way holds France and the French in contempt. Today the Célinophile aesthete, yesterday Céline himself. (See Louis-Ferdinand Céline, *Les Beaux Draps*, Paris: Nouvelles Éditions françaises, 1941. Let us briefly recall that in 1941–1942 Parisian collaborationists usually spoke of "Judaized" France as "rotten" or "degenerate," and that in 1944 Jean Drault violently denounced Vichy as "Jérusalem-sur-Allier" (the river flowing through the town of Vichy). Céline, a genuinely anti-Pétain figure! And, of course, anti-Gaullist. But also a genuine pro-Hitlerite, a supporter of the Germanic-Nordic "New Europe." In short, the founder of a tradition. . . .

47. Quoted in Antoine Sfeir, *Les Réseaux d'Allah*, op. cit., p. 16.

48. Estimates range from four to six million, although it is not possible to obtain scientifically reliable statistics. See the critical

remarks in Michèle Tribalat, "Aucune donnée fiable sur l'islam," *Libération*, October 23, 2001, p. 19.

49. Quoted in Antoine Sfeir, op. cit., p. 16.

50. This was the reaction of the (Communist) youth and sports minister, Marie-George Buffet, following the disturbances of October 6, 2001, that halted the France-Algeria soccer match, which the left had hoped would be a "major festival." After a bottle hit her on one cheek, Marie-George Buffet simply turned the other: "It's nothing serious," she said. "Of course it's not really serious: they are invading the pitch to express something. . . . You've got to understand these young people." Neocommunism is a kind of distorted Christianity for the use of cowardly politicians, people sick with "youthism," and all-is-woe demagogues. Unfortunately (or fortunately), I have not had the opportunity to hear from Madame Guigou (former minister of social affairs and solidarity) the Socialist interpretation of another flying bottle that hit her on the head the same day. Did she too open a dialogue? Anyway, here were two ministers of the plural left who showed that they knew how to cash in on what happened to them. Is that a vice or a virtue in politics?

51. See Patrick Klugman, "Les 'antifeuj,'" *Le Monde*, November 22, 2001, p. 17. See also Nathalie Guilbert, "Dans un lycée: on a bien le droit d'être antisémite," *Le Monde*, December 2001, p. 10; Éric Conan, in *L'Express*, December 6, 2001, pp. 8–12.

52. Jacky Durand and Françoise-Marie Santucci, "Cette guerre n'est pas notre problème," *Libération*, November 5, 2001, p. 13.

53. See, in particular, the work of Sebastian Roché (op. cit.) as well as Hugues Lagrange, *De l'affrontement à l'esquive. Violences, délinquances et usages de drogues*, Paris: La Découverte & Syros, 2001.

54. Jean-Pierre Chevènement, *Discours de Vincennes, 9 septembre 2001*, Paris: Chevènement 2001, October 2001, pp. 19–20.

55. See, for instance, the caricatural example of two youthist demagogues, Azouz Begag (lately a professional spokesman for his community of origin) and Christian Delorme (a priest and leftist agitator in the Lyons region). In their "Énergumènes ou énerg-humains?" (*Le Monde*, October 13, 2001, p. 17), indulgence becomes actual acceptance of "dual identities" ("Franco-Algerian" rather than simply "French") while explanation turns into justification, to the point of glorifying the proud "noble savage": "They

brought the festivities to an early end, those wild children, those suspicious characters, those *calleras*. So here were the suburbs inviting themselves to the social debate, to the center of the arena, without giving advance notice, without bothering themselves about the extreme delicacy of the international context or the pressures on the Arab-Muslim world [why indeed?]. They trampled on the green grass, breached the rules of the sport, jeered at the elementary values of hospitality in the host society. . . . And yet. And yet . . . on this October 6, they were no longer afraid to assert their Algerian origin, no longer ashamed to utter the word 'Algerian'; they waved in the middle of the pitch the standard of their regained pride. . . . So, the match a failure? That is not so clear. Inside, no one was crushed against the wire netting as at [the Brussels stadium of] Heysel. Outside, the double-identity fans went on their way, once again misunderstood, and there were no reports of violent clashes with the forces of order. All is well that ends well." The "young people," then, were "super" in every sense. Nothing more to be said. To listen to their admirers, all they did was express themselves, make public "their suffering at having been so long crushed between their two identity-fragments." More precisely, with greater empathy: "At the seventy-sixth minute, all these identity frustrations came to the surface, just above the skin, and impelled them to stage themselves as a spectacle for the authorities and the cameras." A fine piece of amatory discourse, amid the sweltering heat of identity and the vapors of communalism, where the wise "Beurocrate" rubs shoulders with the fascinated "Beurophile." If we are to believe these demagogues, the essence of the "young person" (always a "victim of exclusion") is to express himself, and this self-expression, whatever its forms, is supposed to be always good: it amounts to a quest for dignity and self-esteem. This is a hangover from '68, spiced up with myths about identity and victimhood. For a critical analysis of this apologetic angelism, see Alain-Gérard Slama, "L'idéologie sauvageonne," *Le Figaro*, October 15, p. 17.

56. See Christian Jelen, *Ils feront de bons Français. Enquête sur l'assimilation des Maghrébins*, Paris: Robert Laffont, 1991.

57. Quoted in Jacky Durand and Françoise-Marie Santucci, art. cit., *Libération*, November 5, 2001, p. 13.

58. The caricatural "Beurophobia" that one finds in publications of the far right is inverted in the "Beurophilia" of periodicals

with a left-wing readership, where most reports involve an attempt to absolve "young people" of responsibility for acts of violence or for criminal offenses of which they have been found guilty. The quasi-sociological sophistry consists in dissolving responsibility into situational factors or socioeconomic determination. Journalistic investigation then turns surreptitiously into special pleading, on the principle that every "young person" who is hit by discrimination, lives in a "poor area," or suffers unemployment (or job insecurity) has, if not every right, then at least every excuse to do what he does. His "built-up rancor" and "humiliation" are supposed to explain and justify his "acts of incivility" and criminal offenses. It is necessary to "understand" them, say the beautiful souls. One "youthist" sociologist, showing the requisite empathy with the alleged victims of the "racism" of "racist France," made the following comment on the "young people's" behavior on October 6, 2001, at the Stade de France: "Huge space in the media was given to a minority of young people. These profited from what I call the logic of the occasion to say: I'm becoming what you want me to be, and dumping your beautiful display of friendship; we're not completely French, and that's what you wanted. You think we're dirty Arabs? Well, that's what we're becoming!" (Philippe Bataille, sociologist attached to Cadis-EHESS, quoted in Gilles Anquetil, et al., "L'avertissement du 6 octobre. Où vont les beurs?", *Le Nouvel Observateur*, November 1–7, 2001, p. 16.) Responsibility for the violent interruption of the France-Algeria match was thus placed on "French society," which had been unable and even unwilling to integrate the "young people" in question.

59. I have collected several reports from teachers and French-Jewish parents in the Paris suburbs stating that it has become difficult in many schools, especially for history teachers, to speak of World War II (and therefore to mention the Nazi genocide of the Jews) in front of children coming from the North African immigration. It is as if any talk of the Shoah were a glorification or defense of Israel. So, either the children ostentatiously block their ears, or they make a racket to stop the teacher from speaking. This is the result of media conditioning and all variants of anti-Israeli propaganda, from the neoleftists through the Communists to the Islamists.

60. See, for example, François Burgat, *L'Islamisme au Maghreb. La voix du Sud*, revised and enlarged ed., Paris: Payot,

1995. Drawing the final consequences of radical cultural relativism, certain specialists in Islamic studies end up arguing that "Islamism," far from being a "return to the past," actually expresses the legitimate quest of Muslim societies for a road of their own into modernity. "Realistic" experts recognize, of course, that it is a road paved with massacres, but the Leninist formula that "You can't make an omelette without breaking eggs" seems to keep coming back to them. As it slides toward apologetics, Islamic studies thus becomes the subsidized sector of Islamophilia. In Burgat's view, for example, we should simply accept that what we call "Islamism" involves "tensions inherent in the (painful, conflictual, and contradictory) phase through which these [Muslim] societies are passing . . . to build their own modernity" ("Une volonté de 'retour au passé'?", in Laouari Addi, et al., *L'Islamisme*, op. cit., p. 83). The principle is simple: "To each their own modernity." Any interference in the internal affairs of each "modernity," including the Islamist modernity currently under construction, would be inappropriate and involve the interlinked sins of ethnocentrism and imperialism. We should not judge but simply observe and understand, with the required methodological empathy. Nevertheless this empathy often changes from methodological to political, so that the cool detachment of the scientist gives way to the passion of the accredited counsel for the defense or the authorized singer of praises. Hatred of Western modernity may thus lead to justification of the worst forms of savagery.

61. On this distinctively modern doubling of sociocentrism (where the concept of "positive" sociocentrism encompasses the classical anthropological concept of ethnocentrism), see Raymond Boudon, *L'Idéologie ou l'origine des idées reçues*, Paris: Fayard, 1986, pp. 286–287; as well as my own remarks in *Les Fins de l'antiracisme*, op. cit., pp. 31–32.

62. Quoted in Gilles William Goldnagel, *Le Nouveau bréviaire de la haine*, op. cit., p. 59, note.

63. See François Heisbourg (director of the French Strategic Research Foundation—FRS), "Le basculement du monde" (interview with Thomas Hofnung), *Politique internationale* No. 93, Fall 2001, pp. 15–32.

64. See Denys de Béchillon and Michel Troper, "Légèreté," *Le Monde*, October 11, 2001, p. 18. In October 2001 some anti-racist

organizations even launched a campaign against the "Vigipirate Plan" (a series of measures introduced in 1995, and strengthened after 9/11, to ensure the security of sensitive state departments and of state offices where the public is received) by renaming it "Vichypirate" and equating it with Petainism! It was a comic but disturbing paradox. Here were professional "watchers" allowing themselves to be ironical or downright scornful about a set of measures justified by the extreme gravity of the situation. What stupidity and ideological blindness on the part of these "defenders of liberty"!

65. I am here repeating the diagnosis and prospects that I first outlined in my *Face au racisme*, vol. 1, *Les moyens d'agir*, op. cit., introduction: "La lutte contre le racisme, par-delà illusions et désillusions," pp. 11–43.

66. For a discussion of this tripartite model of racist or anti-Jewish configurations (attitude/ideology/behavior), see my *Les Fins de l'antiracisme*, op. cit., pp. 21–42.

67. When Jean-Pierre Chevènement was interior minister in the Socialist government (1997–2000), he worked hard to encourage the development of such a republicanized Islam. See the interview he gave to *Le Monde* on February 19, 2000: "L'islam à la française, selon Chevènement." A debt is owed to Jeanne-Hélène Kaltenbach and Pierre-Patrick Kaltenbach for their stimulating and groundbreaking essay *La France, une chance pour l'Islam*, Paris: Éditions du Félin, 1991. For a discussion of the problems involved in this orientation, see the issue of *Panoramiques* No. 29, 1997: "L'islam est-il soluble dans la République?"; the interview with Malik Chebel, "L'islam est-il victime de la République?", *Panoramiques* No. 35, 1998, pp. 188–193; and the issue of *Panoramiques* No. 50, 2001: "L'islam est-il rebelle à la libre critique?" (which includes the speech given by Jean-Pierre Chevènement on January 28, 2000). See also the article in *Esprit* No. 239, January 1998: "L'islam d'Europe"; the essays of Alain Boyer, *L'Islam en France* (Paris: Presses universitaires de France, 1998) and Olivier Roy, *Vers un islam européen* (Paris: Éditions Esprit, 1999); and the collective work edited by Felice Dassetto, Brigitte Maréchal, and Jørgen Nielsen, *Convergences musulmanes. Aspects contemporains de l'islam dans l'Europe élargie*, Louvain-la-Neuve: Bruylant-Academia, 2001.

68. Editorial in *Notre histoire*, special issue on Islam, November 1996 (quoted in Paul Balta, *L'Islam*, Paris: Le Cavalier Blanc,

2001, p. 121). Many difficulties stand in the way of establishing a Muslim representative body, however. See Alain Barluet and Élie Maréchal, "Les musulmans de France peinent à s'organiser," *Le Figaro*, October 18, 2001, p. 10; "Le mufti de Marseille juge la Constitution 'scandaleuse'" (statements of Soheib Bencheikh, collected by Daniel Licht), *Libération*, October 22, 2001, p. 19; and the article by Xavier Ternisien in *Le Monde*, November 30, 2001, p. 15.

69. *The Source of Our Evils* (St. Petersburg: December 1905), an unsigned pamphlet reproducing the full version of the *Protocols* that appeared as a supplement to the magazine *Znamya*, August 26–September 7, 1903. See my book *Les Protocoles . . .*, op. cit., p. 366.

70. "Non à la croisade impériale," appeal drafted on the initiative of Daniel Bensaïd (Ligue communiste révolutionnaire), Willy Pelletier (PCF—Parti communiste français), Jacques Bidet (PCF), Henri Maler (PCF), and others, and published on October 15, 2001. See *Le Monde*, October 21–22, 2001, p. 32: "113 intellectuels français lancent un appel contre la guerre en Afghanistan." The final list of signatories included Pierre Vidal-Naquet, Yves Benot, Elias Sanbar (chief editor of the *Revue d'études paléstiniennes*), and Aline Pailler (European deputy on the Communist list). See also, in the same neo-Communist spirit, the appeal that appeared under the title "Une guerre infinie?", signed by Christine Delphy (a leftist feminist), Jacques Bidet, Willy Pelletier, Jacques Texier, Danièle Kergoat, and Michel Husson (*L'Humanité*, October 23, 2001, p. 22). Trotskyists and neo-Stalinists (along with the inevitable mandarins in retirement) have learned to get along on the twin basis of global anti-Americanism and a dubious Israelophobia. Once again, against a backdrop of anti-globalization demonology, the Palestinian cause takes the place of the proletarian cause. A critique of technology-plus-market globalization here becomes mired in intellectualized hatred and a "cushy" pacifism of equidistance and the golden mean: the "neither one nor the other" dear to refined souls and Buridan's asses.

71. See, for example, Michel Warschawski, *Israël-Palestine, le défi binational*, with a postscript by Elias Sanbar, Paris: Textuel, coll. "La Discorde" (ed. by Daniel Bensaïd), 2001. Such a "two-state project," placed under the patronage of "the greatest Palestinian intellectual of the early 21st century," Edward Said (p. 18—and see his *The End of the Peace Process*, op. cit.), is the matrix for a

new and indefinite series of demands that would justify refusal to accept the legitimacy of the State of Israel even after the creation of a Palestinian state. Is it credible that, once such a binational state were created, the professional killers of Hamas and Islamic Jihad would turn into moderate Muslims, peaceful humanists, or pluralist democrats? We know that, after 1989, most of the Islamist volunteers in Afghanistan evolved into a corps of professional killers of non-Muslims or nonconformist Muslims and traveled the world looking for other conflicts in which they could serve (Sudan, Algeria, Bosnia, Chechnya, Kashmir, etc.). Like the demand for a "right of return" for all Palestinians, the "binational wager" is no more than a formidable symbolic weapon against the very principle of the existence of the State of Israel. Far from defining possible solutions to the Israeli-Palestinian conflict, these two kinds of demands are designed to block any exit from the conflict of legitimacies, except through Israel's abandonment of its right to exist. The refined souls offer Israel a single solution: its own suicide.

72. Dan Meridor, chairman of the Knesset foreign affairs and defense committee, who was part of Ehud Barak's delegation to Camp David (July 11–24, 2001), has lucidly posed the main geopolitical problem: "The Palestinian problem is not really what is essential. Although it is difficult to solve, a solution can be found to it. The great danger for our region comes from states such as Iran and Iraq, where the following three factors exist in combination: an advanced effort to obtain nuclear weapons and missiles to deliver them; direct and unprecedented involvement in terrorism, which is seen in the highest reaches of the state as a legitimate form of action; and a blunt recognition that the aim is the straightforward destruction of the State of Israel. Neither Egypt nor Syria nor the Palestinians use that kind of vocabulary, whereas Khamenei declares every week that Israel must be liquidated. Nor does Khatami, the "moderate reformist," say anything different." ("Vivre sans les Palestiniens?", an interview with Dan Meridor conducted by Emmanuel Halperin, *Politique internationale* No. 93, Fall 2001, p. 238.)

73. See François Géré, "Vers une victoire de façade," *Libération*, October 16, 2001, p. 11.

74. In this asymmetrical warfare, a state fights an enemy that is not another state but a transnational network enjoying varied support and resting on different forms of complicity.

75. After the Bolshevik Revolution, Max Weber said: "It is the Islam of modern times" (quoted by Hichem Djaït, *L'Europe et l'Islam*, Paris: Le Seuil, 1978, p. 138). See also the remarks of Bertrand Russell in 1921, in his book *The Theory and Practice of Bolshevism*, quoted by Ibn Warraq, op. cit., p. 207.

76. For many examples drawn from Leninist literature, see Dominique Colas, *Le Léninisme*, Paris: Presses universitaires de France, 1982, pp. 195–216. This takes us through the hellish regions of the Leninist landscape, where we find various "parasites," "vermin," "lice," "viruses," "bacilli," and "dregs of humanity." See also the editorial by Pierre Rigoulot in *Les Cahiers d'histoire sociale* No. 18, Fall/Winter 2001, pp. 3–7 ("D'un totalitarisme à l'autre").

77. On the appeal of the "113 intellectuals," Delfeil de Ton said what needed to be said, with the right touch of irony and gravitas: "What emerges from it is: '*This war is not our war.*' This war is not their war—but it is bin Laden who has declared war on the infidels, on all who do not believe in one God, on the Jews and Crusaders (that is, Christians of every persuasion), and on the hypocrites (that is, Muslims who do not share his fanaticism). In short, in whatever category he places them, bin Laden has declared war on our intellectuals. . . . Bin Laden's war is universal: you are in his camp or the camp of those he is fighting; bin Laden does not leave any other choice. . . . '*This war is not our war. The Western armada is administering its celestial justice in the name of the law and morality of the jungle.*' Is that humor, or what? 'Celestial justice'? Who talks of celestial justice if not the bin Laden crowd? He is ready to set the planet alight for his celestial justice. He says as much and is proud of it. He has made a start and says every day that he intends to continue. One feels sad to find certain names among the 113 intellectuals. One wishes they had had more common sense." ("Intellect," *Le Nouvel Observateur* No. 1929, October 25–31, 2001, p. 126.) See also the solidly argued text by a group of journalists, writers, and academics (Gérard Grunberg, Pascal Perrineau, Stéphane Courtois, Michel Taubmann, and others): "Cette guerre est la nôtre," *Le Monde*, November 8, 2001, p. 16; Robert Redeker, "Le discours de la cécité volontaire," *Le Monde*, November 22, 2001, supplement, p. iv, which hits the mark; and the fine article by Liliane Kandel, "Il ne s'est rien passé le 11 septembre?", *Libération*, November 5, 2001, p. 7, which ends with a

disturbing question: "This icy indifference, this haughty detachment, this insidious transformation of the victims into the guilty, this drastic (and vaunted) lack of compassion for them, this lack of a sense of horror (yes, horror) at the crime: is this the new politics promised us by the 'left of the left'?" Claude Lanzmann detected, behind the "old mechanical anti-imperialism" of the neoleftist circles, what he calls "their primal hatred of Israel, which considers it more guilty than bin Laden, guilty of having created him, alone guilty—why not?" ("The Disaster," *Les Temps modernes* No. 615–616, September–October–November 2001, pp. 1–3).

78. Max Weber, "Politics as a Vocation" (1918), in *From Max Weber: Essays in Sociology*, ed. by H. H. Gerth and C. Wright Mills, London: Routledge & Kegan Paul, 1948, pp. 125–126.

79. Quoted in Roland Jacquard, *Au nom d'Oussama Ben Laden . . .*, op. cit., p. 352.

80. Farhad Khosrokhavar, *L'Islamisme et la mort*, Paris: L'Harmattan, 1985, p. 14.

81. See Jean Daniel, "Pas d'indulgence pour les 'djihadistes,'" *Le Nouvel Observateur*, October 18–24, 2001, pp. 46–47. In the same spirit, Malek Boutih stated on October 21, 2001, on Canal+ television (Karl Zéro's program "Le vrai journal"): Bin Laden "is not a new Che Guevara, he is a fascist. He and his people have slit the throats of the largest number of Muslims anywhere in the world" (quoted by Christine Clerc, "Mon pays la France," *Le Figaro*, October 25, 2001, p. 32).

82. Soheib Bencheikh, "Le monde musulman est la première victime de l'intégrisme" (statements collected by Martine Gozlan), *Marianne* No. 236, October 29–November 4, 2001, p. 49. See also Soheib Bencheikh, "Ou l'islam marche avec son siècle, ou il reste à la marge de la société moderne" (statements collected by Henri Tincq), *Le Monde*, November 20, 2001, p. 16.

83. See the courageous positions taken by Soheib Bencheikh in *Le Matin* (an independent Algerian daily) on January 11, 1998, concerning the GIA Islamists and their attempts to offer a religious justification for their massacres: "I denounce the hypocrisy of the Muslim theologians who, while admittedly denouncing these actions and bloodbaths, do not challenge the theology underlying them. They should seize the opportunity to desanctify Muslim law, especially in areas that offer a pretext to these barbarians who clothe their criminal deeds with a kind of

canonization." Quoted in Alexandre del Valle, *Islamisme et États-Unis*, op. cit., p. 45.

84. Walter Laqueur, *Terrorism*, London: Weidenfeld and Nicolson, 1977, p. 234.

85. "Interview exclusif du mollah Omar," *Marianne* No. 237, November 5–11, 2001, p. 22. On the origin and dissemination of this rumor, see the dossier in *L'Arche* No. 524–525, October–November 2001, pp. 36–41. The kernel of the rumor is that the 9/11 attacks were "the work of Jewish-Israeli-American Zionism" or of the "top-level Jewish-Zionist 'brain' controlling the economy, the media, and politics throughout the world" (Ahmed Al-Mouslih, in the Jordanian paper *Al-Doustour*, September 13, 2001, quoted in ibid., p. 39). This framework for the interpretation of the anti-American attacks is directly inspired by the *Protocols of the Elders of Zion*: everything is to be explained by a "Zionist plot." See my book *Les Protocoles des Sages de Sion. Faux et usages d'un faux*, op. cit., vol. 1, pp. 159f., 251f.

86. See my *Les Protocoles . . .*, op. cit., pp. 341f.

87. This untitled text, distributed in academic circles over the signature of "Bruno Roy, associate professor (sociology) at the Paul Valéry University, Montpellier," is printed on the letterhead of the Paul Valéry University, Montpellier III.

88. George Orwell, *Collected Essays, Journalism and Letters*, London: Secker and Warburg, 1968, vol. 3, pp. 149–150; quoted in Simon Leys, *Orwell ou l'horreur de la politique*, Paris: Hermann, 1984, p. 70. See Robert Redeker's account of his virtual lynching during a lecture on Holocaust denial, because he mentioned Israel without denouncing its "colonialism," "imperialism," and "racism" ("De New York à Gaillac: trajet d'une épidémie logotoxique," *Les Temps modernes* No. 615–616, September–October–November 2001, pp. 4–9).

89. Orwell, op. cit., vol. 4, p. 70; quoted in Leys, ibid. See Raphaël Draï's analysis "Durban, le World Trade Center et le 'parti de la Mort,'" *L'Arche* No. 524–525, October–November 2001, pp. 46–49.

90. Primo Levi, 'Afterword: The Author's Answers to His Readers' Questions," in *If This Is a Man/The Truce*, combined ed., New York: Viking Penguin, 1979, p. 382.

91. Zygmunt Bauman, *Mortality, Immortality, and Other Life Strategies*, Cambridge: Polity Press, 1992, p. 209.

92. Ibn Warraq, op. cit., p. 423. In the same spirit, see Henri Pena-Ruiz, "Laïcité ou guerre des dieux: il faut choisir," *Marianne* No. 235, October 22–28, 2001, pp. 20–21.

93. See Jacques Tarnero, "Une maladie de l'âme," in *[Nouveaux] visages de l'antisémitisme*, op. cit., pp. 245–266.

94. Anatole Leroy-Beaulieu, *L'Antisémitisme*, Paris: Calmann-Lévy, 1897, p. 25.

95. But the Enlightenment itself had a darker other side: a special kind of intolerance that it introduced in the name of the "struggle against intolerance," and which should be subjected to the kind of critical examination that is precisely part of the Enlightenment tradition.

96. Friedrich Nietzsche, *The Anti-Christ*, trans. R. J. Hollingdale, Baltimore: Penguin Books, 1968, pp. 170–171 (§53).

97. André Breton, *Manifestes du surréalisme*, Paris: Gallimard ("Idées" series), 1963, p. 12.

Index

Abu Ghaith, Sulaiman, 48; and Muslim International Brigade, 154n. 27

Abu Qatada, Imam, 170n. 39

Afghanistan, 23, 35, 48, 60, 66, 76, 78, 92, 114, 116; air strikes in, 117, 119; professional killers in, 198–199n. 71

Africa, 26, 29, 65

AGRIF: and Front National, 169n. 38

Ahmad, Jalal Al-e, 142n. 84

Ahmad Taha, Rifa'i, 26

Albanian UCK (KLA), 83

Algeria, xv, 21, 24, 76, 198–199n. 71; and Armed Islamic Movement (MIA), 137n. 49; and French colonialism, 136n. 45; massacres in, 116, 181–182n. 112; and Palestine, 92; savagery in, 181–182n. 112

Algerian French: chronic unemployment of, 149n. 14; job discrimination against, 148–149n. 13; xenophobia toward, 149n. 14

Algerian Islamic Salvation Front, 56

Algerian Islamists, 56; and France, as enemy, 157n. 41

Algerian war, 91, 92

Algiers, 52

Algohri, Emile, 6

Al Jazeera, 57, 60

Al Jihad, 27, 56

Al-Qaeda, 39, 48, 93

Amara, Jean-Claude, 188n. 25

Anabtawi, Mounthir, 18

Anaximander, 33

Angelism, 95, 109, 113; and pacifism, 120; and sociologists, 96

An-Na'im, Abdullahi A., 76

Anti-Americanism, 5, 20, 114, 116; and 9/11, 58; and terrorism, 38

Anti-globalization, 20, 37, 38, 39, 96; and anti-Americanism, 114, 116; and Islamism, 134n. 39; and Judeophobia, 114, 121; radicalism of, 145n. 110; and the West, rejection of, 115

Anti-Muslims, 110

Anti-nationalism: and Judeophobia, 121

Anti-racism: and anti-Islamism, 159–160n. 59; and Judeophobia, 121; and political correctness, 109

Anti-Semitism, 7, 65, 100, 106, 109, 111; and anti-imperialists, 5; and anti-Zionism, 17; in Arab world, 5, 11, 62; in Austria, xiv; and conspiracy theory, 62; in Eastern Europe, xiii; and

Anti-Semitism (*cont.*)
eliminationist anti-Semitism,
131n. 28; and elites, 5;
etymological meaning of,
128–129n. 10; and far right, 5;
in France, xi, xii, xiii, 40, 43,
127–128n. 6; in Germany, xiv,
127n. 6; in Italy, xiv; and Jews,
as responsible for, 84; versus
Judeophobia, 11, 37; in
London, xiv; and Nazism, 37;
and neo-Christian movement, 5;
and radical Islam, 5; and
redemptive anti-Semitism, 132n.
29; and right, 101; semantic
usage, 128–129n. 10; and Six
Day War, 62; and Soviet empire,
62; struggle against, 121; usage
of, 11, 12; in Western Europe,
xiii, xiv
Anti-Westernism, 37; and militants,
31; and new radicalism, 37
Anti-Zionism, 19, 83, 87, 96; and
anti-Semitism, 17; and Arab
unity, 133n. 36; and colonialism,
15n. 18; and Communism, 18;
definition of, 17, 18; in France,
83; and Israel, destruction of, 17;
propaganda of, 50; and radical
anti-Zionism, 83; spread of, 17,
18; and Third World countries,
18; usage of, 19
Apartheid: and Israel, 47, 70, 71
Arab Lawyers Union, 71
Arab-Muslim world: and anti-
Semitism, 62; and Holocaust, 63
Arabs, 51, 52, 53; and anti-Arab
racism, 100; and blacks,
superiority over, 95; and
intellectual elites, 86, 100; and
nationalism, 86; and racism, 99,
100; and unity, 133n. 36
Arafat, Yasser, xiii, 27, 85; and bin
Laden, 181n. 110; corruption of,
180n. 104; Israel, denouncement
of, 72; Palestinians, right of
return, 84

Arendt, Hannah, 8
Arkoun, Mohammed, 79, 173n.
54, 178n. 87
Armed Islamic Group (GIA), 59,
92, 159n. 59, 184n. 7; and
massacres, 181–182n. 112,
201n. 83
Arnaldez, Roger, 173–174n. 54
Arnett, Peter, 139n. 67
Aruri, Naseer, 180n. 102
Asia, 29, 65
Assad-al, Bashar, 66
Atheism, 54
Auschwitz, xix
Austria, xiii
Aziz, Abu Abdel: savagery of,
179–180n. 100
Azouz, Ben, 23
Azzam, Abdallah, 179–180n. 100

Bakunin, 77
Banna-al, Hassan, 14, 129–130nn.
19, 20; 141n. 80
Barak, Ehud, 51, 84
Barber, Benjamin, 96
Bauer, Bruno, 133–134n. 38
Bauman, Zygmunt, 119
Begag, Azouz, 193–194n. 55
Beghal, Djamel, 170n. 39
Belhadj, Ali, 21, 22, 23, 137n. 49;
and democracy, as sin,
137–138n. 59; and GIA
Islamists, 201n. 83
Ben Abdalaziz al-Saud, Adbullah,
48
Ben Aknun University, 53
Ben-Ami, Shlomo, 51, 127n. 2
Bencheikh, Soheib, 117, 178n. 87
Bendaoui, Hocine, 186–187n. 19
Benot, Yves, 198n. 70
Bensaid, Daniel, 145n. 111, 198n.
70
Bergé, Marc, 173–174n. 54
Beurs, 94; in French housing
projects, 107; and Palestinians,
107
Bghioua, Safir, 186–187n. 19

Bidet, Jacques, 198n. 70
Bin Baz, Abd al-Aziz, 78
Bin Laden, Osama, 25, 26, 27, 48,
   60, 66, 79, 86, 92, 96, 104, 113,
   117, 139n. 67; and genocide, 69;
   and "good terror," 39; as hero,
   61; intellectuals, war on, 200n.
   77; and Israel, 55; jihad, call for,
   33, 34, 35, 57; jihad,
   justification for, 58; and
   megasects, 110; and 9/11
   attacks, 57; and religious war,
   36; solidarity with, 61; support
   of, 58, 92; and world, as two
   camps, 60
Bioterrorism, 27, 28
Bishara, Marwan, 47, 153–154n.
   26
Blachère, Régis, 173–174n. 54
Black September, 144n. 102, 189n.
   31
Bolshevik Revolution, 113
Boniface, Pascal, xi, xiii, xv,
   190–191n. 40
Bosnia, 198–199n. 71; and Bosnian
   Muslims, 83, 179n. 98
Bouguelane, Mouloud, 186–187n.
   19
Boutih, Malek, 95, 185n. 17
Bouyali, Moustapha, 137n. 49
Bouzar, Dounia, 182–183n. 2
Bové, José, 96
Brafmann, Jacob, 166n. 28
Breton, André, 121
Buffet, Marie-George: and France-
   Algeria soccer match, 193n. 50
Bush, George W., 35, 36, 60

Camp David, 10
Camus, Renaud, 102, 103
Cana, 99
Canto-Sperber, Monique, 16
Carlos, 86, 144n. 102; and
   Taliban, 181n. 110
Carpentras (France), 100
Carré, Olivier: and Islamic
   radicalism, 124n. 7

Catholic church, 126n. 13
Catholicism, 81
Céline, Louis-Ferdinand: and anti-
   Jewish propaganda, 173n. 48
Charfi, Mohamed, 80, 82, 178n.
   88; on Algeria, 181–182n. 112
Chebel, Malek, 178n. 87
Chechnya, 66, 198–199n. 71
Chemical weapons, 140n. 76
Chevènement, Jean-Pierre,
   105–106, 188n. 25, 197n. 67
Chirac, Jacques, xiv
Chomsky, Noam, 180n. 102
Christian Arabs, 127n. 4
Christianity, 10, 39, 48, 90; and
   charity, 68; demonization of,
   54; and Jesus, 50; Islam,
   converts to, 49; Islam, plots
   against, 56
Cohn-Bendit, Daniel, xi, 167n. 28
Cohn-Bendit, Jean-Gabriel,
   155–156n. 30, 167n. 28
Colonialism: and imperialism,
   151n. 18; and racism, 151n. 18
Communism, 8, 53, 112, 113, 118;
   and anti-Zionism, 18, 37; and
   terrorism, 37
Conspiracy theory: and American
   imperialism, 53; and communism,
   53; and freemasonry, 53; and
   Jews, 53; and Muslim world, 52,
   53. *See also* Zionism.

Damascus, 66, 98
Dar es Salaam (Tanzania), 27
Darwish, Mahmud, 50
Dayton accords, 83
De Gaulle, Charles: resignation of,
   xi
Deicide, 50
Deir Yassin (Palestine), 99; Nazi
   atrocities, comparisons to, 152n.
   20
Delcroix, Éric, 155–156n. 30,
   167n. 28; 171n. 43
Delorme, Christian, 89, 193–194n.
   55

206

Index

Delphy, Christine, 198n. 70
Democracy, 82; Islam, as enemy of,
  21, 22, 23, 75; and Muslim
  countries, 82
Democratic Front for the
  Liberation of Palestine, 152n. 20
Desert Storm, 77
Dessailly, Marcel, 95
De Ton, Delfeil, 200n. 77
De Vitray-Meyerovitch, Eva,
  173–174n. 54
De Wenden, Catherine Withol,
  149n. 14
Diouri, Moumen, 189–190n. 36
Dray, Julien, 150n. 15
Dreyfus Affair, 11, 120
Drumont, Édouard, 84
Dualism: between Jews and
  Palestinians, 53; and religious
  dichotomy, 53
Durban (South Africa), 67, 70, 72,
  110

Eastern Europe: anti-Semitism in,
  xiii
Egypt, 14, 76, 199n. 72
El Mounquid, 23
Enlightenment, 120; dark side of,
  203n. 95
Étienne, Bruno, 124–125n. 7,
  138n. 63
Europe, xix, xx, 7, 37, 82;
  demonstrations in, xi;
  immigrants in, 83
European Union: and Palestinian
  Authority, xii

Fanaticism: religious, 112, 120
Farrakhan, Louis, 11–12,
  170–171n. 42
Fascism: and Islam, xviii; new form
  of, 109
Faurisson, Robert, 63, 99; and
  Holocaust denial, 167n. 28; trial
  of, 155–156n. 30
Fedayeen, 97, 98
Finkelstein, Norman, 165–166n.
  28, 180n. 102

Finkielkraut, Alain, xiv
Fourest, Caroline, 71
France, 3, 23, 39, 58, 61, 103; of
  Algerian descent in, 148–149n.
  13; and Annemasse, 41; and anti-
  Americans, 118; and anti-Arab
  racism, xv; and anti-Israelis, 118;
  anti-Jewish cartoons in, xiii; and
  anti-Jewish hatred, 88, 120; anti-
  racism in, 44; anti-Semitism in,
  xv, xvii, 4, 40, 43, 45, 151n. 17;
  anti-Western militants in, 31;
  anti-Zionist rhetoric, spread of,
  17, 83; Arab population in, xv,
  xvi; crime in, 105; delinquency
  in, 88, 102; discrimination in,
  45; dual identities in, 193–194n.
  55; and Front National, 99, 100;
  Holocaust denial in, 167n. 28;
  and housing projects, 94–95; and
  immigration, 88; Islam of, 111;
  Jewish community in, xii, xiv, xv;
  Jewish population statistics, xv;
  Jews, attacks on, 40, 41, 42, 43,
  147n. 3, 147n. 5; Judeophobia
  in, 45, 101; and Lyons, 41; and
  mainstream media, xiii; and
  Marseilles, 42; and
  multicommunalism, 89; and
  multiculturalism, 89, 94;
  Muslims in, 104, 111, 192–193n.
  48; Muslim vote in, 100; and
  new radicalism, 37, 145n. 110;
  and North African immigrants,
  100; and organized crime,
  94–95; and Palestinian
  nationalism, 13; and political
  correctness, 100; and racism, 94;
  and Strausbourg, 41; and
  suburban youth, 88; and
  terrorism, 112; and Toulon, 41;
  and 2002 elections, xii–xiii;
  violence in, xv, xvi; violence,
  reaction to, xix; World War II,
  teaching of, 195n. 59; and youth
  crime, downplaying of, 106; and
  Zionism, 20; and Zionist

movement, 99. *See also* French suburbs.
France-Algeria soccer match, 193n. 50; violence at, 194–195n. 58
Francophobia, 91, 93
Frankel, Glenn, xix
Freemasonry: and Islam, as enemy of, 157n. 41
French Islam, 111
French suburbs, 88; anti-Christian discourse in, 90; and bin Laden, identification with, 93; and France, contempt for, 94; hate, culture of, 105; indulgence in, 102; and Islam, 89; social disintegration in, 93; spirituality in, 89; violence in, 89
Friedländer, Saul, 132n. 29
Front National, 99, 100; and anti-Arab racism, 190n. 39
Fundamentalism, 73, 82, 117

Gaillot, Monseigneur, 97
Gangster terrorism: and Roubaix gang, 186–187n. 19
Garaudy, Roger, 30, 31, 50, 97, 99, 114; in court, 171n. 43; and Holocaust, denial of, 63, 64; Israel, as illegitimate, 162n. 11; West, as criminal, 145–146n. 12
Gaza City, 59
Gaza Strip, 9
Geertz, Clifford, 135n. 41
Genet, Jean, 97; at Palestinian camps, 189n. 31
Genoa (Italy): mass demonstrations in, 145n. 110
Genocide: and Jewish nationalism, 68; and Israel, 70; and Muslims, 69
Germany, 12, 39; anti-Semitism in, xiv; and Holocaust, 63; and racism, 99; and terrorism, 112
Globalization, 34, 37, 84, 96, 108; French electorate, opposition to, xiii; and identity, 97; and McWorldization, 97

Goldhagen, Daniel Jonah, 131n. 28
Gothenburg (Sweden): mass demonstrations in, 145n. 110
Great Britain, 23, 70
Green parties, 96; and anti-Semitism, xiv
Gresh, Alain, 180n. 102
Guevara, Che, 16, 92
Guillaume, Pierre, 167n. 28; in court, 171n. 43
Gulf War, 18, 22, 57, 93

Hadash Front for Peace and Equality, 154n. 28
Haddad, Wadi, 144n. 102
Hamas, xi, 13, 34, 53, 65, 130–131n. 20
Heine, Heinrich, 43
Heisbourg, François, 110
Hezbollah, 53
History: and values, conflict of, 33–34
Hitler, Adolf, xx, 46; and Allah, 12; and Israel, 72; Holocaust revisionism, 167–168n. 28; and Palestine, 72; and redemptive anti-Semitism, 132n. 29; and Schopenhauer, 63
Hobeika, Elias, 152n. 21
Holocaust, xx; denial of, 63, 64, 67, 167n. 28; as myth, 64; and Palestinians, 72; revisionists, 155–156n. 30, 167–168n. 28
Holy war. *See* Jihad.
Huntington, Samuel, 36, 59, 79
Hussein, Saddam, 6, 114; and chemical weapons, 140n. 76; and Palestinian cause, 57
Husson, Michel, 198n. 70
Hyperterrorism: and mass destruction, 110; and messianic movements, 110. *See also* Terrorism.

If This Is a Man (Levi), 119
IMF, 37, 116
Immigrants: defense of, 83, 110; in France, 88; from North Africa,

Immigrants (*cont.*)
  88; as slave labor, 49; as
  victimized foreigners, 91; and
  xenophobia, 106
Immigration and Suburbs
  Movement (MIB), 188n. 25
Indonesia, 26, 49, 58
Inequality: categories of,
  142–143n. 92
Institute for International and
  Strategic Relations, xi–xii,
  190–191n. 40
Institute for Palestinian Studies
  (Beirut), 18
International Symposium of
  Zionism and Racism, 68
Intifada, 65, 91, 156–157n. 37;
  Islamization of, 53, 54; and
  martyrs, 65; militarization of, 54
Iran, 23, 76; as dangerous, 199n.
  72; and nuclear weapons, 199n.
  72
Iraq, 58; blockade of, 118; and
  chemical weapons, 140n. 76; as
  dangerous, 199n. 72; embargo,
  lifting of, 112, 114, 115; and
  Iraqis, deaths of, 116; and
  nuclear weapons, 199n. 72; war
  in, protesters of, xi
Islam, xvii, 10; and anti-colonial
  struggles, 52; anti-Jewish hatred,
  expansion of, 73; authentic form
  of, 74; and citizenship, 75; as
  civilization, 129–130n. 19; and
  colonization, 21; and
  community, 75; conspiracy
  against, 74; converts to, 49;
  criticism of, ban on, 110;
  crusade against, 60; and cultural
  identity, 73; and delinquency, as
  cure for, 182–183n. 2; diversity
  of, 25, 73, 86, 129–130n. 19;
  and education, 85; enemies of,
  21; fascination of, 73; and
  fascism, xviii; of France, 111;
  fundamentalism of, 73; and holy
  war, 23; and impiety, 78; and

intellectual terrorism, 159–160n.
  59; and intimidation, 74; and
  Islamism, 80, 117; jihad, forms
  of, 26; and Koran, as perfect, 75;
  and liberation theology, 30; and
  modern culture, 73; non-Muslim
  religions, co-existence with, 66;
  as perfect religion, 28, 75; and
  political correctness, 110; and
  political Islam, 76; power of, 73;
  and *Protocols of the Elders of
  Zion*, 22; pure form of, 74, 75;
  and radical Islam, 76; as religion,
  129–130n. 19; as religion, of
  underprivileged, 48, 49; and
  religious criteria, 76; and science,
  78; and secularization, 111; and
  slavery, 33; and spiritual needs,
  73; superiority of, 30; and unity,
  138n. 63; and universality,
  32–33; and West, 120; and
  Western civilization, 29, 30; and
  Westerners, attitude toward, 73;
  and Westernized Islam, 32
Islamabad, 66
Islamic Center (Geneva), 28, 69
Islamic Jamaa Mujahedeen, 26, 27,
  37
Islamic Jihad, 13, 53
Islamic Liberation Army, 34; and
  worldwide jihad, 116
Islamic Liberation Party (PLI),
  137–139n. 59
Islamic Resistance Movement, 65,
  130–131n. 20. *See also* Hamas.
Islamic Revolution, 155–156n. 30
Islamic Salvation Front (FIS), 20,
  21, 24, 53, 55; demonstrations
  by, 22, 23; and Ahmed Rami,
  190n. 37
Islamic studies: and Islamophobia,
  195–196n. 60
Islamism, 8; and active nihilism,
  79; as alternative to, 111; and
  anti-Americanism, 116; and anti-
  globalization movement, 134n.
  39; and anti-Jewish language, 55;

and authoritarianism, 24; and bioterrorism, 27, 28; in Britain, 70; and children, 77; and civilizations, clash of, 36; and Communism, 37; as communism, of twenty-first century, 114; and conspiracy theory, 52, 53, 65; and crime, 95; and cultural imperialism, 82; cultural pessimism of, 73; definition of, 74; and democracy, rejection of, 21, 22, 24, 115; and dogmatism, 75; and education, 77; and Egyptian Islamists, violence of, 139n. 68; enemies of, as subhuman, 28; and ethnocentrism, 195–196n. 60; fanaticism of, 78; features of, 77; freedom, concept of, 22; in French prisons, 90; in French suburbs, 89; and fundamentalist movement, xvii, 14; and holy war (jihad), 33, 48, 52, 55, 77, 116; and imperialism, 79, 195–196n. 60; and indoctrination, 77; and integrist dimension, 124n. 7; and Islam, as authentic form of, 74, 75; and Islam, as corruption of, 75; and Islam, difference between, 10, 80, 117; and Islam, enemies of, 157n. 41; and Islamic correctness, 109; and Islamic state, establishment of, 55; and Israeli-American imperialism, 53; and Jews, as enemies, 60; and jihadism, 124–125n. 7; and Judeophobia, 61, 106; and literalism, 78; in London, 70; martyrs, celebration of, 25; modernity, rejection of, 75; and Muslim fundamentalism, 124n. 6; and 9/11 attacks, 15; neoracism of, 36; and nihilism, 79; and pacifism, 74; and Palestinian cause, 57, 164n. 18; political uses of, 124n. 6; and

poor, as good, 48; and propaganda, 59, 75, 110; and radical Islamism, 109; as religion, of poor, 107; and religious authorities, 80; and rich, as evil, 48; and Salafism, 118, 137n. 49; and secularism, 21, 23, 24, 25; solidarity of, 58; stereotypes, of Jews, 20; stupidity, as organized form of, 78; and suicide bombers, 55; and technology, 75; and terrorism, 10, 15, 34, 36, 75; and terrorism, justification for, 59; and terrorist organizations, financing of, 52; and theocracy, 75; and third world war, provocation of, 78; threat of, 114; and tolerant Muslims, 80; totalitarianism of, 77, 114, 117; and transnational terrorism, 115, 120; and United States, 54; victims of, 116; violence of, 28, 78; and West, resentment toward, 52; and West, war against, 27, 30, 32; and women, inferior status of, 77; and Zionist imperialism, 55
Islamophilia, 74, 91
Islamophobia, 69, 70, 74; and Arabophobia, 169n. 34; denunciation of, 110, 135–136n. 44; and elites, 108; as intellectual terrorism, form of, 135–136n. 44; as Islamic correctness, 135–136n. 44
Israel, xii, xiii, xvi, xviii, xix, 4, 5, 7, 9, 19, 40, 59, 77, 79, 84, 85, 92, 93, 96, 98, 102, 117; and anti-Israeli propaganda, 64; and anti-Zionist rhetoric, 17; apartheid in, accusations of, 47, 70, 71; and army, 107–108; attacks against, 41; and bin Laden, 55; and binational state, in Palestine, 198–199n. 71; and conspiracy theory, 62; demonization of, 6, 8, 37, 39, 68,

Israel (*cont.*)
112; denouncing of, 109;
elimination of, call for, 85, 199n.
72; and evil, source of, 112; and
genocide, acts of, 70; and
genocide, against Palestinans,
152n. 20; as guilty, charges of,
48; and Hitler, 72; and
Holocaust, 63, 64; illegitimacy of,
162n. 11; and imperialism, 99; as
infidels, 57; jihad against, 35; and
Judeo-Christian conspiracy, 56; as
military regime, 46; as Nazi state,
100; and original sin, 48; and
Palestine, 18, 41, 58, 72; and
Palestinian state, recognition of,
112; policy of, 83; as racist, 47,
68, 70, 71, 172n. 47; and right to
exist, 51, 85; and self-defense, as
terrorism, 59; and Six Day War,
64; and South Africa,
comparisons to, 47; and suicide
bombers, 59; as terrorist state,
accusations of, 59; and war, 72;
and Zionism, 71
Israeli-Palestinian conflict, xvii, 9,
19, 40, 88; and Mitchell Report,
10; and Oslo peace process, 10;
Taba peace talks, 10
Israelis: and double standards, 51;
and new historians, 154n. 28;
and racism, 67; and Zionists, 72,
73, 96
Italy, xiii; anti-Semitism in, xiv;
and terrorism, 112

Jacquard, Albert, 188n. 25
Jambet, Christian, 173–174n. 54
Jelen, Christian, 150n. 16
Jerusalem, 9, 23, 35, 85
Jesus, 50, 66, 67
Jews, 8, 87; and animals, likened to,
56; and anti-Jewish attitudes,
levels of, 123n. 3; and anti-Jewish
hatred, 84, 88, 100; and anti-
Jewish mythology, 53, 125n. 8;
and anti-Jewish propaganda, 72;

and Ashkenazi Jews, 12; and
conspiracy theory, 52, 53, 118;
elimination of, call for, 85, 86; as
enemies, of Islam, 101; as evil,
54; in France, xii, xiv, xv, 41, 42;
and genocide, 68; and global
conspiracy theory, 56, 62; hatred
of, 4; and Holocaust, lie of, 63;
as intruders, 50; and Islam, as
enemies of, 60; and Israel, defense
of, xii; and Israel, historical links
to, 85; and Jesus, 66; jihad
against, 35, 56; as liars, 63; and
Mohammed, 66; and Muslims,
57; and Nation of Islam,
170–171n. 42; and nationalism,
51, 68; as Nazis, 71; and
Palestine, 116; and Palestinians,
persecution of, 50; and peace
accords, 51; and racism, 67, 99;
as scapegoat, xv; stereotypes of,
52; and transnational terrorist
network, 115; in United States, 7;
violence toward, 4, 100, 101,
103; and war, responsibility for,
72, 73; and World War II, 73;
and Zionists, 6, 72, 73, 96. *See
also* Anti-Semitism, Anti-Zionism,
Judeophobia, Zionism.
Jihad, 14, 15, 18, 34, 61; anti-
imperialist struggle, vanguard of,
86; condemnation of, 111; and
conspiracy theory, 68; and
defensive jihad, 26; definition of,
26; as global war, 35, 36;
globalization of, 97; and Islamic
Liberation Army, 116; Jews,
stigmatization of, 56; as
legitimate, 55; as liberation
struggle, 74; as martyrdom, 56,
60; as permissible, 35; and
offensive jihad, 26; as religious
war, 36; and sacrifice, 56;
technology, use of, 75; and
Zionism, 66
Jindi, Anwar-al, 138n. 61
John XXIII, 126n. 13

John Paul II, 126n. 13; in
Damascus, 66
Judaism, 10; as affliction, 43;
demonization of, 54; and Islam,
as enemy of, 157n. 41
Judeophobia, xvii, xix, xx, 3, 8,
64, 84, 96, 114, 118, 121; and
anti-North African xenophobia,
111; and anti-Semitism, 11; and
anti-racist propaganda, xviii; and
anti-Zionism, 87; denial of, 7;
features of, 67; forms of, 44; in
France, 93, 108; growth of, 101;
Holocaust, denial of, 67; and
intellectual elite, 103, 108; and
Islamism, 10, 12, 61, 106;
justification of, 103; and the left,
83; and the media, 103; and
Muslim radio, 101; and
politicians, 103, 108; and post-
Nazism, 11; propagation of, by
Jews, 133–134n. 38; and racism,
67; and redemptive anti-
Semitism, 132n. 29; and self-
hatred, 166n. 28; silence toward,
101, 103, 108; tolerance of, 103
Just wars, 33
Juvenile delinquency: and
consumerism, 105; excuses for,
89, 95; glorification of, 90, 91;
in France 88, 102; in housing
projects, 94–95; identity of, 94;
indulgent attitude toward, 89;
and narcissism, 105; and
organized crime, 94–95; as
outcast, 105; as outsider, 105;
and petty crime, 105, 106;
segregation of, 95; and
unemployment, 105; as victims,
95, 107; violence of, 106. *See
also* French suburbs.

Kaddoumi, Farouk, 72; and Israel,
as racist state, 172n. 47
Karnoouh, Claude, 155–156n. 30
Kashmir, 36; 198–199n. 71
Kassab, Mohammed Yacine, 55, 56

Kayyali, Abdul Wahhab, 131n. 26
Kelkal, Khaled, 92, 184nn. 7, 8
Kepel, Gilles, 26
Kergoat, Danièle, 198n. 70
Khomeini, Ayatollah, 155–156n.
30; and Salman Rushdie, 174n.
61
Kosovo, 83

La France juive (Drumont), 84
Lanzmann, Claude, 152n. 21,
200–201n. 77
Laoust, Henri, 173–174n. 54
Laqueur, Walter, 117
Lasfar, Amar, 75
Latouche, Serge, 134n. 39
LBC Television, 86
League of Anti-Semites, 127n. 6
League of Human Rights, 80
Lebanon, 31, 53, 58, 64, 103; and
Lebanese Christians, 46,
152–153n. 21; and Philangist
units, 65, 152–153n. 21
Left: and anti-Jewish hatred, 88;
and indulgence, 105
Lémann, Joseph, 166n. 28
Lenin, 15, 114; and Leninism, 114
Le Péché original d'Israël (Israel's
Original Sin), 48
Le Pen, Jean-Marie, xii–xiii, 83,
99, 100
Leroy-Beaulieu, 120
*Les Territoires perdus de la
Republique* (The Lost Territories
of the Republic) (Brenner), xvi
Levi, Primo, 119
Lévy-Valensi, Éliane Amado, 109,
152–153n. 21
Lewis, Bernard, 142–143n. 92
Libya, 103
Libyan Bar Association, 68
Lilienthal, Alfred M.: and Zionism,
denunciation of, 168n. 33
*L'Islam face au nouvel ordre
mondial* (Islam Facing the New
World Order) (Kassab), 55
London, 70; Islamists in, 170n. 39

Luttwak, Edward, 96
Luxor (Egypt): massacre in, 26
Lyons (France), 41, 89

Mafia: and chemical weapons, 140n. 76
Margalit, Avishai, 179n. 92
Marr, Wilhelm, 127n. 6
Martyrs, xviii, 121; and culture of death, 164n. 18
Marx, Karl, 133–134n. 38
Marxism, 8, 48, 52, 53; and Islam, as enemy of, 157n. 41; and social-economic determinism, 107
Marxist revolutionism, 109
Masri-al, Abu Hamza, 170n. 39
Mawdudi, Abul A'la, 141n. 82
Mecca, 23, 35
Media: and anti-Jewish hatred, 88
Medina, 23, 35
Mein Kampf (Hitler), 63
Meirieu, Philippe, 150–151n. 16
Meridor, Dan, 199n. 72
Messianic movements: and megasects, 110
Middle East, xv, xvi, 26, 72, 84
Minguettes (France), 89
Miquel, André, 173–174n. 54
Moderate radicalism, 77
Modernity: and family ties, 29; and Islamism, 30, 74, 75; and religion, revolt against, 29
Mohammed, 36, 66
Mohammed, Omar Bakri: and Al Mahajirun movement, 170n. 39
Monteil, Vincent "Mansour," 49, 155–156n. 30, 167n. 28
Moralism, xviii; and pacifism, 115
Moussaoui, Zacharias, 170n. 39
Movement Against Racism and for Friendship Among Nations (MRAP), 187–188n. 24
Multicommunalism (multiculturalism): in France, 70, 113, 89
Multinational society: and abstract utopianism, 113; and blind angelism, 113

Musharaf, Pervez, 66
Muslim Brotherhood, 14, 82, 141n. 80; holy war, definition of, 14–15
Muslim International Brigade, 154n. 27
Muslims, xv, xviii, xix, 73; and conservative neofundamentalism, 124–125n. 7; cultural tradition of, 173–174n. 54; and democracy, 81, 82; dualism of, 49–50; and fanatical Islamists, 80; in France, 100, 104; and fundamentalism, 82, 117; and genocide, 69; humiliation of, 107; as innocents, 49; and intellectual elites, 117; and Islamism, 75, 117; Islamist terrorists, as victims of, 116; and Jews, 57; and jihad, 59–60; malaise among, 74; and modernity, 74, 117; non-Muslims, cooperation with, 116; and Palestinian struggle, 87; as perfect, 75; persecution of, 49; and petroleum, 116; and political Islam, 124–125n. 7; as poor, 107; poverty of, 48; and racism, 99; and religion, privatization of, 81; and religious authorities, 80, 117; and secularization, 81, 82; and self-defense, 49; solidarity of, 58, 59, 86, 87, 102, 110; as superior race, 29; and Third World, affinity with, 49; victimization of, 89; and Western civilization, 29, 48, 74; in Western Europe, 111
Muslim Youth Congress, 175n. 68
Mythical Foundation of Israeli Policy, The (Garaudy), 63

Nablus (Palestine), 93
Nasser, Gamal Abdel, 64
Nation of Islam: and slavery, 170–171n. 42
Nation-states, 113

Nationalism: and Judeophobia, 121
Natour, Suheil, 152n. 20
Nazism, 11, 13, 17, 64, 71, 96, 109; and Israel, 100; and Zionism, 68, 69
Nechaev, 184–185n. 9; and militarist sect, 92
Neo-Christianity, 109
Neocommunism, 193n. 50
Neoleftism, 92, 96, 108, 113, 118
Neo-Nazis, xiv
Neo-Palestinism, 54
Neo-Third Worldists, 50, 116
Neowahhabism, 77
NGO Forum, 70
Nice (France): mass demonstrations in, 145n. 110
Nietzsche, Friedrich, 79, 121
Nihilism: and Islamism, 79
Nigeria: violence between Muslims and Christians, 175n. 68
9/11 attacks, xx, 15, 17, 27, 38, 39, 65, 70, 92, 93, 110, 119; justification of, 58; and Palestinian cause, 58; as self-defense, 170n. 39
North Africa, 83; immigrants of, 91, 94, 148–149n. 13, 149n. 14; and Palestine, 92
North Korea: and chemical weapons, 140n. 76
Novick, Peter, 162–163n. 12

Omar, Mullah, 26, 36; and 9/11 attacks, 118
Organized crime: and delinquents, 94–95; in France, 94–95; and Islamist terrorist networks, 95
Osman-Bey, 166n. 28
Othman, Omar Mahmud. *See* Imam Abu Qatada.
Our Struggle Against the Jews (Qutb), 74

Pacifism, xviii, 74; and angelism, 120; and moralism, form of, 115

Pailler, Aline, 198n. 70
Pakistan, 58, 60, 76
Palestine, 23, 30, 36, 56, 57, 60, 66, 119; as binational state, 198–199n. 71; and Hitler, 72; and Israel, 58; and Israel, existence of, refusal to accept, 85; and Israel, legitimacy of, 198–199n. 71; jihad in, legitimacy of, 55; massacres in, 53; and North African immigrants, 92; Palestinian state, creation of, 112, 113
Palestine/Israel: Peace or Apartheid (Bishara), 47
Palestinian Authority, 58, 72, 93; and European Union funds, xii
Palestinian Liberation Organization (PLO), 14, 72; and anti-Zionism, 19
Palestinians, xviii, 14, 98; and anti-racism, 96; and anti-Zionism, 18; and Beurs, 107; cause of, 5, 31, 54, 55, 56, 57, 58, 59, 83, 87, 115, 164n. 18; as Christ, symbols of, 50, 67; demonstrations for, 96; and double standards, 51; expectations of, 51; and Holocaust, 63, 72; and international community, reaction to, 51; and Intifada, 65; and Israel, historical links, denial of, 85; and Israeli euthanasia, 84; and Israeli policy, 72; and Jews, persecution by, 50; and Lebanese Phalangist units, 65; and martyrs, 65; and nationalism, 13, 51, 53, 68, 85; and 9/11, reaction to, 93; pampering of, 51–52; peace, obstacles to, 52, 85; poetry of, 50; and proletarian cause, 198n. 70; and right of return, 84, 153–154n. 26; support of, xi, 108, 109; and terrorism, 55, 59; as victims, 45, 49, 51, 52, 54, 68, 70, 97; and Zionism, xviii, 71

Palestinophilia, 50
Pappé, Ilan, 154n. 28, 180n. 102
Paris, 70, 103; anti-Semitism in, xi,
    xvi; demonstrations in, 100;
    housing projects in, 107, 187n.
    23; riots in, xi; violence in, 101
Pelletier, Willy, 198n. 70
Pierre, Abbé, 68, 97, 98, 99
Pluralism, 82; and religious, 70;
    and tolerance, 169n. 34
Poliakov, Léon, 83
Politics: and geopolitics, 115; and
    plurality, 120; and unity, 120
Poulat, Émile, 124n. 7
Prior, Michael, 180n. 102
Pro-Choice NGO, 71
Proletariat: reinvention of, 90
Protocols of the Elders of Zion,
    22, 55, 64, 65, 72, 86, 202n. 85;
    and Israel, as source of evil, 112;
    and Middle East, introduced to,
    125–126, n. 10; serialization of,
    137–138n. 59

Qutb, Muhammad, 174n. 56
Qutb, Sayyid, 74, 174n. 56

Rabin, Yitzhak, 99
Racism, 53, 84, 99, 109; anti-Arab,
    111; anti-immigrant, 111; and
    Judeophobia, 121; and Zionism,
    67, 70
Radical Islam, 124–125n. 7; and
    anti-modernism, 76; and
    equality, rejection of, 76; and
    jihadism, 76; and literalism, 76;
    origin of, in France, 175–176n.
    71; purity, quest for, 76; and
    sanctified terrorism, 77;
    secularism, rejection of, 76; and
    wahhabism, 77. *See also*
    Terrorism.
Radio Islam: and racism, 99,
    189–190n. 36; and Ahmed
    Rami, 190n. 37
Raffarin, Jean Pierre, xix
Ramadan, Hani, 28, 65, 69, 141n.
    80

Ramadan, Sa'id, 141n. 80
Ramadan, Tariq, 69–70, 89, 141n.
    80
Rami, Ahmed, 99, 189–190n. 36
Rassinier, Paul, 73, 167n. 28
Re-Islamization, 79, 143n. 97; of
    young people, 89–90, 103
Religion: political use of, xvii, 10;
    and violence, 28
Revel, Jean-François, xiii
Rodinson, Maxime, 124n. 6
Roha, Pilar, xix, xx
Romania: anti-Jewish circles in,
    163n. 13
Rosenfeld, Alvin, xiv, xvi
Roty, Yakoub, 28
Roubaix gang, 186–187n. 19
Roy, Bruno, 118
Roy, Olivier, 58
Rushdie, Salman, 74; and fatwa
    against, 174n. 61
Russia: and chemical weapons,
    140n. 76

Sabra (Palestine), 46, 65, 99; and
    Nazi atrocities, comparisons to,
    152n. 20
Said, Edward, 7, 68; Zionism, as
    European imperialism, 168n. 31
Saint-Fond (France), 90
Salafism, 118, 137n. 49
Sanbar, Elias, 198n. 70
Sanchez, Vladimir Illich Ramirez,
    35
Sarkozy, Nicolas, xix
Satanic Verses, The (Rushdie),
    174n. 61
Saudi Arabia, 23, 26, 35, 54, 76,
    115, 177n. 76; and United
    States, 158n. 42; and women,
    status of, 77
Sayegh, Fayez A.: and PLO
    Research Center, 153n. 22; and
    United Nations resolution, 153n.
    22
Schools: anti-Semitism in, xvi, xvii;
    and anti-Semitic attacks,

response to, xix; and Holocaust, teaching of, xvi, 195n. 59
Seattle: mass demonstrations in, 145n. 110
Secularism, 54, 80, 81, 138n. 61, 178–179n. 90; in France, 111; of Islam, 111; Islam, as enemy of, 157n. 41; jihad, condemnation of, 111
Senegal, 49
Serbs, 83
Sharafuddin, Abdullah, 68; and Zionism, 168n. 33
Sharon, Ariel, 46, 71; demonization of, 152n. 20
Shatila (Palestine), 46, 65, 99; and Nazi atrocities, comparisons to, 152n. 20
Shuaibi-al, Hamud, 35
Sivan, Emmanuel, 82
Six Day War, 50; and anti-Israeli propaganda, 64; and anti-Semitism, 62
Slavery: and Nation of Islam, 170–171n. 42; in Sudan, 129n. 17
Socialist party: in France, xii, xiii, xvi; and French Muslims, xii, xvi; and Middle East conflict, attitude toward, xii; and the poor, 48
SOS Racisme, 44; youth violence, in suburbs, 150n. 15
South Africa, 30; and Israel, 47
Sperling, Daniel, 147–148n. 6
Strauss, Leo, 151n. 19
Suburban youth, 88; humiliation of, 88; integration, lack of, 88; and violence, 150n. 15. *See also* French suburbs.
Sudan, 76, 198–199n. 71; Islamist dictatorship in, 129n. 17
Sufyani-al, Khalid, 171n. 43
Syria, 199n. 72

Taliban, 36, 48, 54, 60, 78, 112, 118, 181n. 110; support of, 58

Tanzania, 27
Technology: and Islamism, 75
Terrorism, xvii, xviii, 39, 112, 117; and anti-Americanism, 38; and Arab-Islamophile intellectual terrorism, 109; binational state, creation of, 113; and bioterrorism, 27, 28; and Christians, 13; financing of, 52; as global, 115; glorification of, 91; good v. bad, 39; and hyperterrorism, 110; intellectual form of, 108; and Iran, 199n. 72; and Iraq, 199n. 72; and Islamic solidarity, 58; and Islamist, 75, 114; Jewish state, existence of, right to, 113; and jihad, 14; justification of, 16, 17, 55; and martyrs, 14; means of, 16; and 9/11 attacks, 33; and Palestinian cause, 55; and Palestinian state, creation of, 113; as resistance fighters, 13; struggle against, 115; and suicide attacks, 13, 15, 17; and Tibetans, 13; as transnational, 97, 115
Texier, Jacques, 198n. 70
Theocracy: and Islamism, 75
Third World, 7, 91; and anti-Zionism, 18; and Muslims, affinity with, 49; and Re-Islamization, 79
Third Worldism, 5, 6, 48, 99; and neo-Third Worldists, 50
Thuram, Lilian, 95
Tito, Marshall, 113
Tlass, Mustapha, 86, 181–182nn. 111, 112
Tlilani, Fayçal, 136n. 45
Totalitarianism, xviii; and intellectuals, 119; and Islamism, 77, 114
Trabelsi, Nazir, 170n. 39
Tribalat, Michèle, 66, 148–149n. 13
Tripoli, 68

Tristani, Jean-Louis, 155n. 30
Trotsky, 15–16; and Trotskyism, 114; and Trotskyists, 96, 112, 113
Tsahal, 41
Tunisia, xv, 80, 137–138n. 59
Turbo capitalism, 96

Union of Muslim Youth (UJM), 89
United Nations, 36; and double standards, 51; and genocide, 69; and Resolution 3379, 67, 70, 71, 153n. 22, 155–156n. 30; and Resolution 3379, rescinding of, 165n. 27; and Zionism, 71
United States, xiii, xviii, xx, 23, 26, 77, 87, 92; arrogance of, accusations of, 58; and "bad terror," 39; and bin Laden, 57, 58; and chemical weapons, 140n. 76; crimes of, accusations of, 58; demonization of, 5, 6, 37; enemies of, 49; as evil, 54; foreign policy of, 54; Holocaust denial in, 167n. 28; and Islamist movements, 54; and Israel, 58; Jews in, 7; jihad against, 35; and Saudi Arabia, 54, 58, 158n. 42; Taliban, negotiations with, 54; as terrorist state, 118; and universal legal ideas, 54; and Zionist movement, 98, 99
Unleavened Bread of Zion, The (Tlass), 86
USSR, 113

Vatican II, 111, 126n. 13
Vaulx-en-Velin (France), 92
Vénissieux (France), 90
Vergès, Jacques, 171n. 43
Vidal-Naquet, Pierre, 198n. 70
Vietnam, 118–119
Vigipirate Plan, 196–197n. 64

Wahhabism, 77, 78; and universal Islam, conception of, 79
Warraq, Ibn, 120

Weber, Max, 115
Weitsmann, Marc, 192n. 46
West Bank, 9
Western civilization, 117; defense of, 54; demonization of, 39; enemies of, 54; evil, embodiment of, 37, 71; humanity, crimes against, xviii; immigrant populations in, 83; and individualism, 74; and Islam, 73, 120; and Islamophobia, 74; Jews, in control of, 56; and the left, 83; and modernism, 29; and Muslims, 48; and polarization, 50; rejection of, 114; and repentance, 39; self-defense, as terrorism, 59
Western Europe: anti-Semitism in, xiii, xiv, xvii; Muslims in, 111
Women: inferior status of, 77; in Saudi Arabia, 77
World Bank, 37, 116
World Conference against Racism, 67, 70, 71
World Cup, 94
World Islamic Front for Jihad against Jews and Crusaders, 27
World Trade Center: Jews at, 118; and 9/11 attacks, 15, 26, 118; and 1993 attack, 110
World Trade Organization, 37
World War II, xvii, 3, 13, 64; and Jews, responsibility for, 73, 202n. 85

Xenophilia, 91, 105, 109
Xenophobia, 83, 100, 105, 111; against immigrants, 106; anti-North African, 111

Yahya, Muhammad, 138n. 61
Yana, Clément, 147–148n. 6
Youth: and chronic unemployment, 149n. 14; and dual identities, 193–194n. 55; in France, 88, 102, 149n. 14; identity, demand for, 150n. 15; as noble savages, 104; Palestinians, identify with,

102; and re-Islamization, 103,
150n. 16; responsibility, lack of,
194–195n. 58; social mobility,
inequality of, 95; as victims, 102,
104, 193–194n. 55; violence of,
150n. 15. *See also* French
suburbs; Juvenile delinquency.
Yugoslavia, 113

Zakariya, Fouad, 24, 25, 178n. 89
Zawahiri-al, Ayman, 27, 56
Zemmiri, Omar, 186–187n. 19
Zidane, Zinedine: and France-
Algeria soccer match, 94, 95
Zimmeray, François, xii
Zionism, 35, 83, 151n. 18;
demonization of, 112; as enemy,
49, 66; and European
imperialism, 168n. 31; and
Israel, 71; as new Nazism, 69;
and racism, as form of, 67, 70,
153n. 22; as racist, 99, 153n.
22, 153–154n. 26; and United
Nations, 71; and United States,
98, 99; as world threat, 69,
168n. 33; and Zionist
movement, as imperialist, 99;
and Zionist plot, 68, 100–101,
202n. 85. *See also* Anti-
Zionism.
Zionists, 6, 72, 73, 96; and
American Zionist aggression, 49;
and Zionist-American
imperialism, 90

A NOTE ON THE AUTHOR

Pierre-André Taguieff, a philosopher, political scientist, and historian of ideas, is a director of research at France's National Center for Scientific Research (CNRS) and teaches at the Political Studies Institute in Paris. His other books include *La Force due préjugé, Théories du nationalisme, Sur la Nouvelle droite, Les Fins de l'antiracisme, La République menacée, Le Racisme, La Couleur et le Sang, Du progrès,* and *Résister au bougisme.*